JACQUES FAITLOVITCH AND THE JEWS OF ETHIOPIA

JACQUES FAITLOVITCH AND THE JEWS OF ETHIOPIA

EMANUELA TREVISAN SEMI
Ca' Foscari University, Venice

Translated from Italian by Sally Bennet

Foreword by
Tudor Parfitt

VALLENTINE MITCHELL
LONDON • PORTLAND, OR

First published in 2007 in Great Britain by
VALLENTINE MITCHELL
Suite 314, Premier House, 112-114 Station Road
Edgware, Middlesex HA8 7BJ

and in the United States of America by
VALLENTINE MITCHELL
c/o ISBS, 920 NE 58th Street, Suite 300
Portland, OR 97213 3786

www.vmbooks.com

British Library Cataloguing in Publication Data

An entry is available on request

ISBN 978 0 85303 654 8 (cloth)
ISBN 978 0 85303 655 5 (paper)

Library of Congress Cataloging-in-Publication Data

An entry is available on request

Printed by Biddles Ltd., King's Lynn, Norfolk

In memory of
Ottavia Schmidt
di Friedberg

Contents

List of Maps and Plates

Acknowledgements

It would be impossible to thank adequately all the people who helped me during my research. I am grateful to some of the leading figures in the Beta Israel community: Tadesse Jacob, who agreed to talk with me in his house in Addis Ababa even though he was extremely frail; Beniamin Meckurie, who translated and explained to me many Amharic words; and Shelomo Akale, who translated for me parts of the manuscript written by his father Wube Akale. I am indebted to Anbessa Teferra, who showed me his translations of the *tomare* written by Faitlovitch. I would particularly wish to thank Faith's family, Faitlovitch's descendants in London, and Viterbo's family. This book would not have been possible without the help of many librarians and archivists: Simha Zaharur (Sourasky Library, Tel Aviv University), Daniela Yoel (Hebrew University of Jerusalem), Renato Spiegel (Central Archives for the History of the Jewish People), Brad Sabin Hill (Yarnton Manor, Oxford), and Seth Jerchower (Jewish Theological Seminary, New York). Marcella Simoni and Michela Gribinsky read a previous version of the manuscript, offering significant suggestions. I am extremely grateful to Elena Cassin-Vernant, who first introduced me to the story of the conversion in San Nicandro and showed me a manuscript in her possession written by the founder of the group. A special thank you goes to Maria Grazia Masetti-Rouault, who offered to accompany me during my trip to Ethiopia and discussed with me on my research projects. Haim Admor offered me special assistance with the new arrangement of the Faitlovitch archive he had recently finished at Tel Aviv University. I am profoundly grateful to Tudor Parfitt, who showed great interest in many parts of this work and was always supportive of my research. I would also like to thank Michela Andreatta, Elisa Bianchi, Micael Corinaldi, Daniel Friedmann, Steve Kaplan, Julien Klener, Giovanni Levi, Monica Miniati, Ottavia Schmidt, Sigrid Sohn, Joseph Tubiana, and Shalva Weil. I would also like to collectively thank my friends in SOSTEJE (Society for the Study of Ethiopian Jewry).

I would also like to thank Robin Holding, who offered special assistance in editing the English version, and Davide Mano for his editorial support. My last thanks to my husband, Antonio Alberto Semi, and to my children Giovanni and Maria, who listened patiently to this strange story.

Emanuela Trevisan Semi
2007

Foreword

From early mediaeval times the Jews have attempted to define their identity and peoplehood both in an abstract, more or less theological way, and in a geographical way. Among other things they were anxious to determine their outer limits. Who belonged to this people? Where did they live? How different were remote groups of this nation? What were their histories? The fascination the writings of Eldad ha-Dani, the ninth century Jewish traveller and romancer, the twelfth century traveller Benjamin of Tudelah and many others held for Jews in mediaeval and later times arose largely from the glimpses they gave or purported to give of the life of marginal members of the Jewish people in remote parts of the world. Groups that claimed Jewish status through conversion such as the Khazars (Koestler 1976) in the ninth century or the Himyarites five centuries earlier fared badly in early Jewish historiography: they were almost totally ignored. But equally, remote groups with an imagined blood-line to the Jewish people were of great interest.

The outer edge, if you like, of this imagined blood-community always included the Lost Tribes of Israel shimmering faintly over the horizon of the known world whose ongoing reality was taken to be axiomatic by the majority of Jews until fairly recent times. The periodic sightings of representatives of the Lost Tribes in various other parts of the world caused great, even messianic excitement as the conventional geography of the Jewish people was challenged or asserted. Over the last century or so the further away a given group of exotic claimants to membership of the Jewish people were, the greater the interest other Jews had in them. Currently one of the most studied Jewish groups is the minuscule handful in Kaifeng in China about whom a colossal amount has been written as two recent bibliographies indicate. The two recent and substantial bibliographies on the Falashas of Ethiopia mostly containing works written by Jews similarly denote a fierce interest by Jews in the Jewish periphery which may be perceived as the frontier of the Jewish people – that is the ultimate line which divides them from others. Until his death in 1955 Jacques Faitlovitch was perhaps the foremost figure of his age to be involved in the definition of this frontier. His main preoccupation was with the Beta Israel community of Ethiopia, but his interests extended to most of the groups in the world who were in one way or another part of the margins of the people of Israel. And as historians now recognise there is much of immense value in the study of the margins. Professor Trevisan-Semi has devoted a great deal of her academic life to the study of Jewish margins. She has done valuable scholarly work on the Karaites, the Beta Israel and a number of other groups including some of the Black Israelite groups of the United States. This eagerly awaited volume casts new light on the fascinating life of Faitlovitch – scholar, adventurer and public figure – and is likely to remain the definitive work for some time to come.

Tudor Parfitt
School of Oriental and African Studies
University of London

Introduction

Jacques Faitlovitch was the architect of the ingathering of one of the most problematic groups of the Jewish Diaspora. This adventurer, traveller, missionary, and scholar was a Jewish traditionalist, a Zionist close to the Mizrahi movement, an *ish ma'aseh*, and in some ways a *schnorrer*. The life of this Polish-born Jew, who lived in Paris, Palestine, Ethiopia, and the United States, was marked by his devotion to the cause of the Beta Israel, the Jews of Ethiopia, the Falashas.[1]

The term 'Falasha' is used in this book in order to be consistent with the sources, which refer to the period in question. This term began to take on negative connotations after the mass migrations to Israel in 1984–85 (Operation Moses) and 1991 (Operation Solomon). However, the term was not derogatory in Faitlovitch's time, and he used it to refer to the young people who went to Europe to study.

Faitlovitch was an Ashkenazi Jew of the neo-Orthodox school, the son of an ultra-Orthodox family, who became Joseph Halévy's favourite student at the School of Oriental Languages in Paris. He took up the task that Halévy had begun earlier, assisting the Falashas, particularly in their struggle against the Protestant missionaries. Despite the havoc caused by two world wars, he remained devoted to the Beta Israel cause for the rest of his life, and his work on behalf of the Beta Israel constituted the primary source of income for himself and his family. He successfully played the *schnorrer* among the Jews of America. In his tireless efforts to interest the Jewish world in the plight of the Falashas, he met most of the great Jewish leaders of his day. He had close links with the leading Jewish institutions – particularly the Alliance Israélite Universelle, the Hilfsverein, and the Joint – and with prominent Ethiopists and Ethiopian leaders, notably Emperor Haile Selassie. He was comfortable in diplomatic circles and was well connected to the powerful legations of his time. His correspondence with many people, perhaps most engagingly with his student Taamrat Emmanuel, reflects many of the great issues of the time – not least the Italian occupation of Ethiopia – and illustrates the gradual integration of the Falasha community into the mainstream Jewish world.

Faitlovitch's impact on the Beta Israel culture was immense, despite the fact that his education programme did not involve large numbers of people, as pointed out by D. Summerfield.[2] The reason for this was that those few young people invited to study abroad became the first Falasha élite in Ethiopia after their return, and after the Negus had been restored to power. These young people held important positions in the country, which was moving toward modernization.

Faitlovitch also had a considerable impact in terms of the changes in religious practices that he managed to implement. In fact, the introduction of Talmudic-Rabbinical Judaism into a population that had not known the Talmud initiated changes that would subsequently spread, ultimately affecting all of the traditional Falasha religious practices by the time of the mass migrations in the 1980s and 1990s. This included the gradual abandonment of the ritual of sacrifice and of monasticism, the inauguration of the tradition of keeping lights burning at sunset on Fridays, the waning of practices linked to codes of ritual purity, and the introduction of the previously unknown Hebrew language. For the first time, Jewish ritual objects such as *tefillin*, *mezuzot*, *kippot*, and *siddurim* began to circulate among Faitlovitch's students, along with shirts, European-style hats, and ties. There was also increased protection for the Falasha population, as Faitlovitch was successful in obtaining a decree from *ras* Tafari ordering that all craftsmen be paid for their work, thus ending the deportation of Falasha craftsmen as slaves, and denouncing those who would accuse the Falashas of witchcraft, or of being *Buda*, sorcerers who could turn into hyenas during the night.

When the State of Israel was founded, Faitlovitch felt that the time had arrived for the Zionization of the Beta Israel, and he began to organize the *aliyyah* of the Falashas to Israel. The first group of boys that arrived in 1955 to study in Kefar Batya were able to do so thanks to the involvement of the Mizrahi movement, which had always worked closely with Faitlovitch. However, Faitlovitch's activity was not limited to the regeneration of the Falashas. His work to find the *nidhei Yisrael*, the lost tribes dispersed among other nations, led to his presence among the Italian converts of San Nicandro and the Black Jews of Harlem, and to the creation of many committees for converts in the Eretz Yisrael of the 1940s and 1950s. Some of these were intended to be purely missionary in nature, following the model of the Christian missions, whose activity he intended to counter with his own work at the beginning of the twentieth century. Faitlovitch saw the Beta Israel as part of the *nidhei Israel*, but his perception of them was distorted by the lens of Orientalism. He was rather embarrassed about them, and saw them as superstitious, ignorant, and primitive. Yet somehow he idealized them and thought they might revive the religious spirit among Western Jews, who in his view had become corrupted by the secular West and its spirit of modernity. Faitlovitch was unconcerned with the loss of ancient and accepted Falasha customs. He expected the Falashas – the 'other' Jews – to abandon their 'backward' culture and tradition and transform themselves into Western religious Jews.[3]

The documentation for this volume was found primarily in the Faitlovitch collection in Tel Aviv, but also in archives in Israel, France, England, Italy, and the United States.

The diaries in French that Faitlovitch kept scrupulously over the years were also of valuable assistance in the writing of this book.[4]

NOTES

1. For the vast amount of literature regarding the Beta Israel see S. Kaplan and Sh. Ben Dor, *Ethiopian Jewry: An Annotated Bibliography* (Jerusalem, 1988); H. Salomon and S. Kaplan, *Ethiopian Jewry: An Annotated Bibliography 1988–1997* (Jerusalem: Ben Zvi Institute, 1998); Sh. Weil, *Bibliography on Ethiopian Jewry (1998–2001)* (Paris: Sosteje, 2001). For a general view see J. Quirin, *The Evolution of the Ethiopian Jews: A History of the Beta Israel (Falasha) to 1920* (Philadelphia: University of Pennsylvania Press, 1991) and S. Kaplan, *The Beta Israel (Falasha) in Ethiopia: From Earliest Times to the Twentieth Century* (New York and London: New York University Press, 1992).
2. D. P. Summerfield, *From Falashas to Ethiopian Jews. The External Influences for Change c. 1860–1960* (London and New York, 2003).
3. Summerfield (*From Falashas*, p. 88) wrote that some of the people he interviewed declared that Faitlovitch 'instead of criticing these practices … professed that they were not necessary but none the less accepted them as part of their culture' but this was part of Faitlovitch's devices for obtaining the change of those practices without hurting people's feelings.
4. The diaries cover the years 1904–05, 1908–09, 1911, 1913–15, 1920–39, 1948–50.

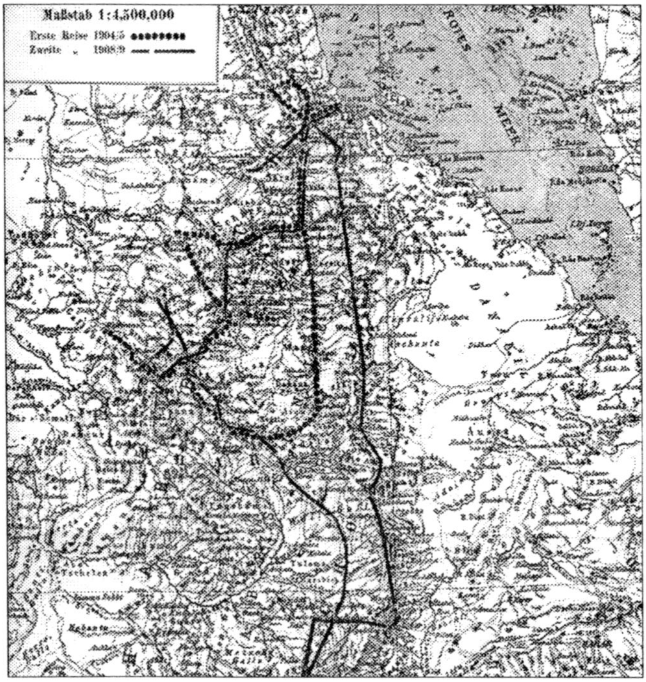

1. First and Second Mission

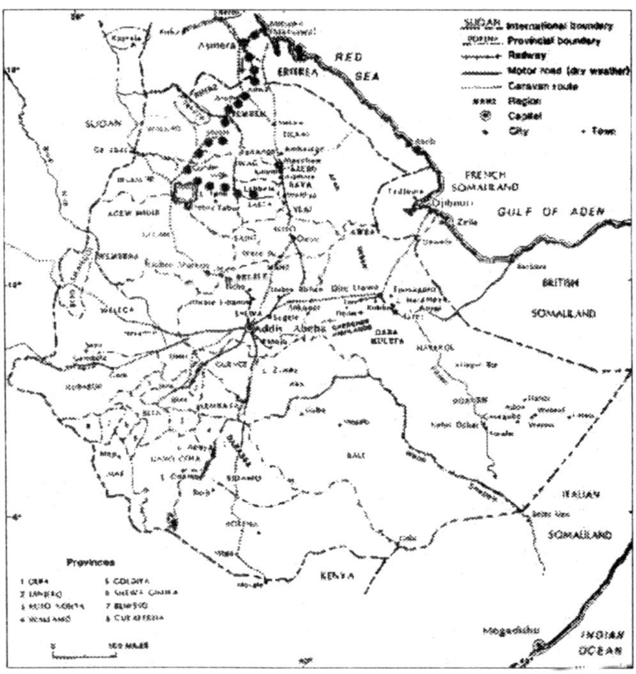

2. Third Mission

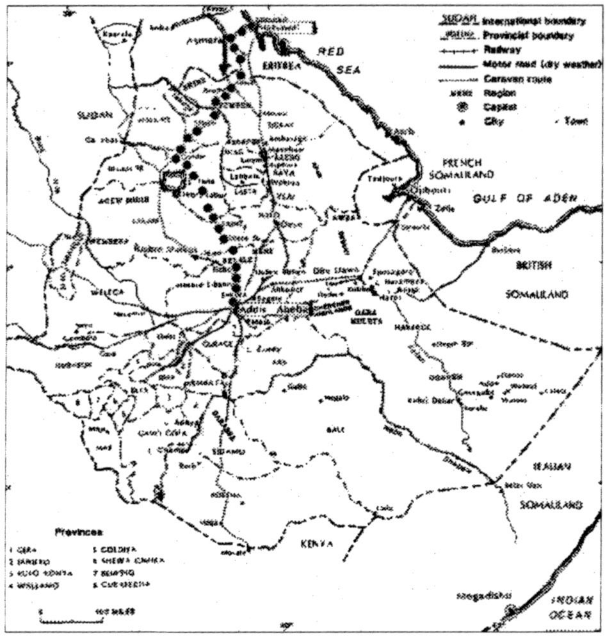

3. Fourth Mission

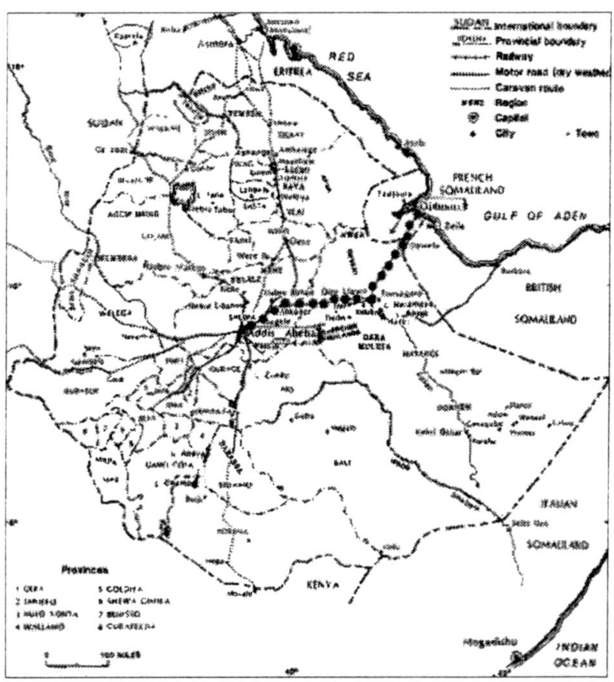

4. Fifth Mission

1

Jacques Faitlovitch, the 'Discoverer of the Falashas', and the Fulfilment of the Prophets' Dream

SLOUSCHZ'S ORATION AT FAITLOVITCH'S FUNERAL: LOOKING BACK AT HIS LIFE

Faitlovitch died in Tel Aviv on 15 October 1955 (29 *Tishri* 5716) and his funeral commemoration speech was delivered two days after by Nahum Slouschz, who was eight years his senior. Both Ashkenazi Jews from Eastern Europe, they had met in Paris through their participation in the Jewish and Oriental studies world of the late nineteenth and the early twentieth century. They were both students of Joseph Halévy,[1] and were influenced by the dream of a Jewish renaissance that would be linguistic as well as cultural, religious, and national. In addition to Slouschz (portrayed in more detail below), another person who made a speech at his commemoration service was Rabbi Berman, the second husband of Faitlovitch's sister Leah.[2] In her youth, Leah shared Jacques' experiences with Ethiopian Jews and is still remembered by the students to whom she taught English at the school her brother founded for the Falashas at Addis in July 1923.[3] A few words were also spoken by M. Nurock, a Mizrahi Zionist leader who represented the *Knesset*, while Israel Ben Zeev (Wolfenson/Abu Zuaib), a witness to and important protagonist in Faitlovitch's activities, spoke on behalf of the *Chevrat nidhei Yisrael* (Association of the Dispersed of Israel), and a neighbour from the street where the Orientalist had lived for ten years, spoke on behalf of those living in the area, proud that the house at 10 Vitkin Street was also a cultural centre.[4]

It might seem unusual to begin a discussion of Faitlovitch's intellectual and working life with his funeral commemorations. In fact they ably summarize his world and each of them reveals part of the activities in which Faitlovitch was involved during his life.

Also present at the funeral were many Italian *olim*, another segment of Faitlovitch's world, and a reminder of Zvi Margulies' period as rabbi (1858–1922) in Florence at the end of the nineteenth and the beginning of the twentieth century. It was at that time that the first Pro-Falasha Committee (1907) had been formed, and some young Ethiopian Jews were brought to Europe to study. However, the presence of the Italians also recalled Faitlovitch's actions among the converts of San Nicandro (Apulia) in the 1930s and his relationship with Carlo Alberto Viterbo, the Italian lawyer who, in July 1936, shortly after the Italian conquest of Ethiopia, presented himself at Faitlovitch's school in Addis Ababa and visited the Falashas' settlements with Taamrat Emmanuel, Faitlovitch's favorite Falasha student.[5] Viterbo had expressed his disapproval of Faitlovitch's educational policies, accusing him of promoting the construction of the Falashas' school in Addis near the emperor's court when it would have been more appropriate for it to be located in the areas of the Falashas settlements, a few days' journey from Addis.[6]

The commemoration of the *sheloshim* took place at the residence of the President of Israel, Y. Ben Zvi, as part of a series of monthly meetings dedicated to the 'tribes of Israel' (*nidhei Yisrael*), the term used at that time to define Jewish communities that were not part of the two large Jewish sub-cultures (Ashkenazi and Sephardi) and that included the Oriental communities as well as the Beta Israel and the Italian Jews. Ben Zvi, the second President of Israel, shared Faitlovitch's interest in these communities – which he did not hesitate to define as 'exotic' – and in the mythical search for the 'lost tribes'.[7] Also present on that occasion were young Falashas, who at the beginning of 1955, had arrived in Israel to receive instruction on the institutions of the young state. They were the first sizeable group (ten boys and two girls)[8] to arrive from Ethiopia and the crowning achievement of the efforts made by Faitlovitch, who intended to involve Israel in the work of educating the Beta Israel. The project for educating Ethiopian Jews had started back in 1904, on the occasion of Faitlovitch's first journey to what was then Abyssinia, a term used to refer to Eritrea as well as Ethiopia. Faitlovitch believed in the 'regeneration' of the black Jews of Ethiopia and the possibility of expanding to Africa the educational programs that the Alliance Israélite Universelle was then implementing in the Jewish communities of the East. This arrival of the young people from Kefar Batya coincided with the fiftieth anniversary of the journey, made in 1904 and prefigured the two great migratory waves at the end of the twentieth century, Operation Moses in 1984–85, and Operation Solomon in 1991. But the possibility of an Ethiopian *aliyyah* in Eretz Yisrael had entered Faitlovitch's head only during his final years. Before that, he had always maintained that the young people educated in the West should return to Ethiopia to take charge of educating the rest of the community.

Other people who spoke at the commemoration were H J. Polozky, an Egyptologist and Orientalist and the dean of the Faculty of Arts, members of the executive board of the Jewish Agency who had taken an active part in the education project in Eritrea and Ethiopia, and Taamrat Emmanuel. Taamrat was the principal of the school founded by Faitlovitch in Addis Ababa from 1923 until 1937, the year he was forced to leave Ethiopia to escape capture by the Italian regime for being an anti-Fascist activist and a supposed danger to the Italian empire of Ethiopia. When Faitlovitch died, Taamrat was in Jerusalem, officially as a member of Haile Sellassie's diplomatic-cultural staff, but in reality having been exiled by the *Negus*, who considered him an undesirable element in Ethiopia because he was too frank, too intransigent and too well-educated and did not hesitate to express his opinions, even in public. While in Israel he stopped visiting the home of Faitlovitch, who had brought him over from Ethiopia as a young boy and had taken him to study in Europe. Feelings of bitterness and frustration, combined with deep-rooted differences of opinion, forced him to take issue with Faitlovitch, although he still called him 'sir'. One of their biggest differences involved Taamrat's opposition to the mass emigration of Ethiopian Jews to Israel after the creation of the State of Israel, which Taamrat, unlike Faitlovitch, considered premature.[9]

The next day, another evening of commemoration was organized in the large library at Faitlovitch's house, this time in the presence of the mayor of Tel Aviv. In addition to his widow, Mara Halevi Davidov,[10] and other members of the family, there were Martin Wurmbrandt and dr Garfunkel, and various students and assistants who had participated in Faitlovitch's final projects, particularly the programs for converting the populations of Africa, Asia, and America to Judaism. Alexander Rosenfeld, director of *Brit Ivrit Olamit*, who had recently launched the Falashas' Hebrew literacy programme in Ethiopia, also attended. Telegrams were received from the *Negus*, who knew Faitlovitch very well, and only thirteen years earlier had appointed him Inspector General of the Ministry of Education in Ethiopia (1942–43) and advisor to the Ethiopian Embassy in Egypt (1944–46). Two senior Ethiopian civil servants, Jona Bogale and Tadesse Jacob, once young Falasha students brought by Faitlovitch to study in Europe and Egypt, sent messages. A *qinah* was composed by the *balambaras* Ezra Shatta.[11] Many of the great scholars of Ethiopian matters with whom Faitlovitch kept in contact, such as Ignazio Guidi and Carlo Conti Rossini, had already died. Even A. Z. Aeskoly (Weintraub), also from Lodz, with whom he frequently argued about the existence of traditions and customs among the

Falashas as outlined by Aeskoly,[12] was no longer alive, having died at an early age. Wolf Leslau, a Polish Jew who had followed the same path as Faitlovitch, going to Paris and becoming a teacher of Amharic at the École Pratique des Hautes Études and the École des Langues Orientales, sent a telegram. After taking refuge in the United States in 1942, Leslau started field research in Ethiopia in order to conduct ethnographic investigations in Ethiopia amongst the Beta Israel, assisted by Taamrat Emmanuel.

At the time, the Israeli press proclaimed that Israel had lost above all an *ish ma'aseh*. Yet at the turn of the century Faitlovitch was considered a promising scholar and a leading light in the world of Ethiopian studies, although today he is not remembered for his writings on Ethiopia. In fact, despite Conti Rossini's great insistence that Faitlovitch continue the work begun by him, which he defined as giving 'flesh' and life 'to the skeleton of the history of Ethiopia',[13] Faitlovitch never found the time or the interest required to devote himself to studying the mass of documents he had collected on his many expeditions in Ethiopia. He donated his home and library in 10 Vitkin Street to be as a centre for study and religious research so that others could continue the work he had begun.[14]

The presence of all these people during the days of commemoration makes it possible to reconstruct not only the story of a multi-faceted, complex, and contradictory person, but also the various contexts in which his work must be viewed.

These people lead us into the intricate networks formed by Jacques over a lifetime spent crossing real and metaphorical borders; they show us items grouped by subject matter, as though we were looking at a card index. We are therefore tracing the story of an individual who influenced not only the history of the Ethiopian Jews, but also that of many Jewish communities in Europe, Asia and America, in years that were crucial to Judaism around the world, setting in motion irreversible processes – from the conversion movements among the *gerim* of San Nicandro in Italy to those among the blacks of Harlem – and participating in the history of Zionism and *yishuv* from within revisionist and religious Zionist circles.

FAITLOVITCH'S EARLY YEARS

On 15 February 1881, in the city of Lodz (then in Russia), Moshe Faitlovitch[15] and Rosalie Nussel had a son, Yaacov Noah. Yaacov was born into a traditional Jewish family that would have liked to give Yaacov a religious education. As often happened among young people of that generation, he found secular studies more attractive. Yaacov, while he was no different from many other young Jews of the period, secretly studied the *haskalah* and learned languages. At the age of eighteen, he enlisted in the Polish army, but soon left it[16] and went to Berlin to pursue an education, a first step along the path that would lead him to the Jewish studies milieu in Paris,[17] where he became known as Jacques.

Jacques Faitlovitch belongs in the category of individuals able to alter the course of events, thanks to their strong personalities, great determination, and conviction. On this sense he may be compared with Theodor Herzl, the 'father' of the Jewish State or Eliezer Ben Yehudah, the 'father' of modern Hebrew. Jacques himself is known as the 'father' of the Falashas, or *avi ha-falashim.*

This does not mean that these people were the only architects of the achievements that are so well known today. In fact, there was a profusion of initiatives and important collaborations that contributed to the establishment of the Jewish State and the modern Hebrew language. Nor does it mean that these people were the first to conceive of what was subsequently achieved. It simply means that they had a special mechanism for activating processes and dynamics which, over time, proved to be irreversible and became fact due to favourable external conditions. Faitlovitch participated in these events, but he was also carrying out a personal plan in which there was room for romantic, universalist, and redeeming pan-Jewish dreams. The prophets had said that the Jewish people would become the light among the people and *am gadol*, and Faitlovitch tried to make that happen. In a report celebrating the twenty-fifth anniversary of Faitlovitch's activities among American Jewish communities, his story is described as one of 'the most romantic tales in the annals of Jewish history'.[18]

During the first half of the twentieth century, Faitlovitch was described in the leading Jewish encyclopedias as an explorer, Orientalist, activist, and founder of the Falasha movement,[19] and by Jewish journals at the beginning of the twentieth century as a *goel*,[20] an 'apostle', and a researcher.[21] Protestant missionaries hastened to announce the arrival of the 'French Jew' in Ethiopia in their newsletters, visibly annoyed by his presence. He was known as the 'missionary' of the Jewish counter mission, created to oppose the Protestants' conversion campaign. In Ethiopia, Faitlovitch still enjoys legendary status. The letters he wrote in Amharic and distributed among the

Falashas are still held in veneration, kept respectfully by the descendants of those who saw him cross the most impenetrable areas of Ethiopia on a mule.[22] His young Falasha students called him 'sir'; others said he was like the 'sun shining'.[23] In celebration of the fiftieth anniversary of his first expedition to Ethiopia, a year before his death, Wurmbrand wrote that Faitlovitch had devoted his whole life to the Falashas.[24] After his death he would be remembered as an 'expert on the Falashas',[25] and an 'Orientalist, devoted to Falasha research and relief work'.[26] So the definitions of Faitlovitch are consistent: researcher and man of action.

But what was Jacques Faitlovitch like? He was often berated for having a strong, authoritarian personality and a difficult nature. His correspondence with his students and with other protagonists of Jewish history, indicates that he was meticulous to the point of obsession, particularly in his diaries. His relationships with most members of his family, apart from his sister Leah (at least until she married), were conflicted. Jacques married late in life, when he was 55 years old. He wrote of himself that he was 'proud inside but modest in appearance',[27] but in the many photographs taken of him, especially with the Falasha students, he is always in the middle of the picture and usually sitting while the others stand. He was certainly a contradictory character. He introduced himself to the Parisian circle as an *explorateur* at the very beginning of his career, and he remained attached to this quite romantic image of himself for the rest of his life. But he was also a skilled fundraiser and a bit of a *schnorrer*, well known among Jewish communities in Europe and the United States for his conference tours in aid of the Falashas' cause, a cause which, in the end, became his own. He was a traditional, observant Jew with an ambivalent eye on modernity – a Zionist with close ties to the Zionist Mizrahi party and the revisionist movement, who nevertheless dreamed of becoming a professor of Semitics in America.

THE PARIS INCUBATOR AT THE TURN OF THE CENTURY: HALÉVY, SLOUSCHZ, AND FAITLOVITCH

Nahum Slouschz's funeral oration, which reveals the history of the search for the lost tribes as the basis of Faitlovitch's scientific development, provides the story that serves as a backdrop for Faitlovitch's many activities. It is a story that began in the Parisian circle at the beginning of the twentieth century, which served as an incubator of ideas for many Jews who had come from the East, full of dreams of personal and national redemption.

Slouschz's letters accompanied Faitlovitch on his journey in 1904 (and on his return from Ethiopia to Cairo in 1905), just as his funeral speech accompanied him at his death. Curiously, while the relationship between the two during the Paris period (particularly during Faitlovitch's first journey) and during the final years in Israel is well documented, there is little documentation of their relationship during the most important part of their lives. We may assume that they were linked by a common thread even when their paths diverged. Slouschz, who had explored the area of the Atlas Mountains as a member of General Lyautey's staff at the time of the conquest of Morocco (in the First World War), emigrated to Palestine in 1919 just as Faitlovitch was about to undertake his fourth mission to Ethiopia.

The letters Slouschz wrote in Hebrew in 1904 take us back to the exciting climate of Paris in those years. It was the post-Dreyfus period, when the values of freedom and tolerance seemed to have been established once and for all, and the French Jewish community was trying to spread modernization, which had begun in the previous century, to the most backward areas, a process described at the time as 'regeneration'. In the same year, while Faitlovitch was in Ethiopia, Slouschz obtained a post at the Sorbonne teaching Hebrew language and literature. He wrote to Faitlovitch to tell him about Herzl's death, and to give him the news of his teaching post and his emotional involvement in the mission among the 'lost brothers of Cush'.[28]

Slouschz was born in 1873 in a small town near Vilna but grew up in Odessa. He was the son of a rabbi who was a member of the central committee of the *Chovevei Tziyyon*. A Zionist himself, he had visited Palestine at various times (in 1891 and 1896) on behalf of the Odessa Committee. He was an assistant at *Ha-melitz* and *Sefirah* and a Hebrew translator. While in Paris from 1909 to 1912, he was also an editor of the *Revue du monde musulman*. After studying classical French literature at the University of Geneva, he moved to Paris to study at the Sorbonne, where he later taught. In 1899 Alfred Dreyfus had finally been exonerated and Paris was once again attracting Jews from the East. France could once again see itself as 'the home of world progress',[29] to use the expression coined by Slouschz, who defined French civilization as 'the only one that has freed itself of the religious chains of the Middle Ages to the extent that every individual Jew feels free in spirit'.[30] The speech, made during the celebration of the tenth anniversary of the teaching of Hebrew language and literature at the

Sorbonne, attended by the elderly Joseph Halévy as well as by Slouschz's students, mentioned the importance of modern Hebrew. In the other courses of Hebrew (at the École des Hautes Études and the Faculté des Arts), according to Slouschz, Hebrew was studied ' in the same way as Sanskrit and Egyptology, on gravestones or the ruins of Palestinian monuments'.[31] Only at the Sorbonne Hebrew was taught as an everyday language by Jewish poets, novelists, and philosophers. Slouschz was among those who had always spoken Hebrew, having learned it from his father at a very early age, even outside the Palestinian environment. This link with Hebrew was no doubt shared by all of Joseph Halévy's students. Halévy, also a *chovev Tziyyon*, was the first to use the direct method of teaching Hebrew,[32] as he was convinced of the pre-eminence of the language question within the context of a national renaissance, and he had a strong influence on the Parisian circle of Jews studying Semitic languages.

Slouschz preceded Faitlovitch in his studies in Paris by several years. He attended the École Pratique des Hautes Études from 1899 to 1900, while Faitlovitch started taking courses in Semitic languages in Paris in 1902. That same year, Faitlovitch obtained various certificates, one from Jules Julius Oppert declaring that he had attended his course in Assyrian philology and archaeology for two semesters at the College de France, one from Hartwig Derenbourg certifying that he had taken his Arabic course at the École Spéciale des Langues Orientales Vivantes, and one from Halévy indicating that he had started Ethiopian courses at the École Pratique des Hautes Études.[33] At that time, the teaching of Semitic languages was undertaken primarily by Jewish scholars, most of whom were of Ashkenazi origin.

In 1904, Faitlovitch was ready to undertake his first mission to Ethiopia. In 1905 he had already become a member of the Societé asiatique thanks to recommendations from Halévy and Casimir Mondon-Vidailhet. In 1906, Faitlovitch was awarded a diploma in the Abyssinian language, with the distinction *très bien*, from the École Spéciale des Langues Orientales Vivantes.[34] It was a brilliant start to an academic career. But then things changed.

Faitlovitch too was struck by Halévy's teaching, which was not limited to academic learning but extended to a commitment to the Jewish cause, in this case the ideology of the education and regeneration of the Asian and African communities. After only two years of learning Ethiopian languages, Faitlovitch was ready to undertake his first mission to Ethiopia, following the trail aready blazed by Halévy

SLOUSCHZ AND FAITLOVITCH: PAN-HEBREW AND PAN-CANAANITE IDEOLOGY

Slouschz may have become particularly influenced by Halévy's teachings in the area of Jewish studies and pan-Hebrew ideology because he was very committed to the Zionist camp; or he became interested in Zionism because he was already very involved in Hebrew studies.

Slouschz was part of the Jewish Territorial Organization in 1907 and a member of the Zionist Federation of France.[35] He was also a great friend of Max Nordau, and he moved closer to Zangwill's position when he realized that a refuge for the Jews needed to be found quickly,[36] as they were under the constant threat of pogroms. He agreed with Nordau's idea that it was necessary to find a *nachtasyl* (night shelter)[37] for the Jews. This was the start of his commitment to finding real ways to enable European Jews to settle in Tripolitania, at a time when a return to Palestine still seemed out of the question. During World War I, when the United States became increasingly important, Slouschz went to New York in order to put pressure on France to accept the Balfour Declaration.[38]

Slouschz's interest in Jewish-Phoenician history was due to the fact that he considered it the starting point of Jewish history. The Sorbonne lecturer felt that only a knowledge of the past could provide the lifeblood for the new chapter in Jewish history that was opening with Zionism. It was his interest in the future of the Jews that led him to travel to other countries in search of the Jewish past, intending

> to retrace the steps of the lost brothers and the extent of the spread of the Hebrew language. From these archaeological excavations and ... the special interest that it brings to the remains of the *anusim* of Portugal ... and these works in Hebrew on Hebrew literature.[39]

Slouschz thought he could rediscover 'the great Semite empire on the shores of the Mediterranean'[40] whose language had been Hebrew or Aramaic, and that this knowledge would benefit the political cause of the time. His vision of the world was largely determined by a romantic pan-Hebrew or pan-Canaanite idea. Slouschz, and in a sense, Faitlovitch too, may be considered architects of what was later to be known as the Canaanite movement,[41] which was especially important in literature. The future Israeli culture and society that Slouschz and Faitlovitch had in mind was not to be restricted to the borders of the new country but enlarged to the ancient Semite-Canaanite world, through the links and traces recovered. Slouschz envisioned the creation of 'a Hebrew and Jewish cultural empire, spreading from the Middle East to North Africa and some European countries on the Mediterranean'.[42] At a conference on Jewish and Canaanite culture held in Carthage in 1911, he maintained that there was no great difference between classical Hebrew and Canaanite and that the biblical expression 'Canaanite language' was none other than a synonym for 'Hebrew language'.[43] This was the source of his fame as a pan-Hebraist or pan-Canaanite. It is within this pan-Hebrew and pan-Jewish school of thought that the search for the lost tribes (especially in northern Africa) acquired particular importance. The traces that those populations must have left behind, while moving through the regions of Asia and Africa had to be found and the remnants of past Jewish culture recovered.

Faitlovitch shared Slouschz's ideas on this pan-Hebrew issue from his very first steps in the direction of Ethiopia up to his creation of conversion committees in the new State of Israel in the 1940s and 1950s with Slouschz at his side. The need to introduce new lifeblood into a Jewish people corrupted by the spirit of the West, and the search for the spirit of the East led Faitlovitch to seek out the Falashas of East Africa, while Slouschz headed for North Africa. Though the routes they took were different, what Slouschz and Faitlovitch had in common was a spirit of adventure and the search for a new breath of life, linked through common ideals to the winds that prevailed in ancient times.

Slouschz, consistent with his Zionist beliefs, immigrated to Eretz Yisrael in 1919. In those years, the French spirit and French culture, considered synonymous with a libertarian and secular culture, had begun to decline in *Eretz Yisrael* because of the British occupation.[44] French and German culture, which until then had been considered essential to the middle classes of the Middle Eastern region, came to be seen as no longer necessary. Paris, as a centre of attraction for Eastern European Jews involved in the study of Semitic languages and the revival of Hebrew language and literature, was losing the central role it had enjoyed in previous decades.

Faitlovitch didn't share the same Zionist commitments of Slouschz.

We do not know the exact date of Faitlovitch's *aliyyah.* He began having property registered in his name in Palestine in 1927,[45] and we know that he spent several months in 1933, 1934, 1935, 1936, and 1937 (the year he married),[46] and the years 1939 to 1942, in the house at 26 Mea Shearim Street (now *rehov* Ha-Kovshim) in Tel Aviv. His family left Lodz for *Eretz Yisrael* towards the end of the 1920s, and thus were saved from the *shoah*. There is a beautiful photograph of Jacques, his mother, his father – his face framed by a thick beard – and his brothers on the balcony of the house in Mea Shearim. After his mother's death, Faitlovitch left that house to move to 10 Vitkin Street in 1946. He has just returned from two years spent in the service of the emperor Haile Sellassie in Ethiopia and Egypt. The centre of Faitlovitch's activity was not in fact Palestine but Ethiopia and America. Later he turned his attention from Africa towards communities in Asia, always in search of the *nidhe Yisrael*.

Faitlovitch tried to create links between Jewish communities in Afghanistan,[47] India,[48] China,[49] and Japan. He was so interested in Japan as a potential country for missionary work that he was invited there in 1954 (with Rabbi Herzog) for the purpose of establishing a centre for Jewish studies with a missionary bent.[50]

He spent the last few years of his life fulfilling his aspiration to make the Jewish people a 'people of light' and *am gadol*. He worked on conversion and on establishing missionary centres, convinced that

> the time has come to raise the banner of Judaism, not only before the Gentiles but also within Judaism itself, as the prophet said: 'I will also give thee for a light to the Gentiles, that thou mayest be my salvation unto the end of the earth' (Isaiah 49–6).[51]

NOTES

1. On Halévy see M. Andreatta, 'Outlines of a First Bibliographical Survey of Joseph Halévy's Works', in D. Friedmann (ed.), *Les Juifs éthiopiens: de Joseph Halévy à nos jours, un siècle de rencontres et vingt-cinq années d'emigration massive* (Paris, 2007) and M. Miniati, 'Joseph Halévy: un outsider dans la ville', in D. Friedmann (ed.), *Les Juifs éthiopiens*.
2. Her first husband Halévy Gulak died in 1940.
3. Interview with Tadesse Jacov, Addis Ababa, 5 May 2000.
4. See commemorative article written by Leo Levi, *Israel*, 15 December 1955.
5. On Taamrat see E. Trevisan Semi, *L'epistolario di Taamrat Emmanuel. Un intellettuale ebreo d'Etiopia nella prima metà del XX secolo/La correspondance de Taamrat Emmanuel. Intellectuel juif d'Ethiopie dans la première moitié du XXème siècle* (Turin, 2000).
6. E. Trevisan Semi, 'The Dainelli and Viterbo Missions among the Falashas (1936–37)', in S. Kaplan, T. Parfitt,and E. Trevisan Semi (eds), *Between Africa and Zion. Proceedings of the First International Congress of the Society for the Study of Ethiopian Jewry* (Jerusalem, 1995), pp. 77–9.
7. On Ben Zvi and the Falashas see also M. Waldman, 'Letters of Yitzhak ben Zvi on the Jews of Ethiopia', *Peamim*, 22 (1985), pp. 75–88 (Hebrew).
8. Faitlovitch's visit to Kefar Batya and meeting with young people is reported in *Mizrahi woman*, 27 March 1955.
9. Y. Etan, 'The first Falasha', *Ha-aretz*, 23 January 1956 (Hebrew).
10. Mara Halevi Davidov came from a family of merchants from Riga. They married on 11 April

1937 at Tel Aviv, Faitlovich Collection (hereafter *Fait. Coll.*), f. 199.

11. Sh. Weil, 'An Elegy in Amharic on Dr. Jacques Faitlovitch', *Peamim*, 33 (1987), pp. 125–7 (Hebrew).
12. J. Faitlovitch, 'The Presumed Traditions of the Falashas', *Tarbitz*, 7, 3–4 (1936), pp. 373–9 (Hebrew).
13. Conti Rossini's letter of 18 November 1913, *Fait. Coll.*, f. 116. Here Conti Rossini expressed his regret at being a victim of the academic prejudice then prevalent in Europe, which consisted of attributing interest only to written sources which, in his opinion, could provide only the external skeleton of history, while traditions and spoken legends could flesh it out and give it life. For Conti Rossini's activity with regard to the Falashas at the time of the Italian conquest see E. Trevisan Semi, *Allo specchio dei Falascia: Ebrei ed etnologi all'epoca del colonialismo italiano* (Florence, 1987), pp. 80–3.
14. The house was purchased in 1946, *Fait. Coll.*, f. 125, see H. Admor, 'Le testament de Jacques Faitlovitch', in Friedmann, *Les Juifs éthiopiens*.
15. Moshe Faitlovitch and Rosalie Nussel had four sons (Yaacov, Jehoshua, Haim, Eliezer) and three daughters (Haya, Hana, Leah).
16. Private communication.
17. M. Elon, 'Dr. Y. N. Faitlovitch, father of the Falashas, a week after his death', Fait. Coll., f. 2 (Hebrew).
18. *Fait. Coll.*, f. 142.
19. Faitlovitch was defined in the Jewish Encyclopedias of the first half of the twentieth century as essentially an explorer, Orientalist and activist: *Juedisches Lexicon, Ein enzyklopaedisches Handbuch des juedischen Wissens* (Berlin, 1928): 'Er gruendete zur Foerderung der Auklaerungsarbeit unter den Abessienischen Juden in verschiedenen Laendern'; *Encyclopaedia Judaica* (Berlin, 1930): 'Orientalist und Forschungsreisender, Begruender der sogennanten Falaschabewegung'; *Philo-Lexicon, Handbuch der Judischen Wissens* (Berlin, 1937): 'Erforscher und Foerderer der Falaschas'; *The Universal Jewish Encyclopedia* (New York, 1948): 'Explorer and Originator of the Work among the Falashas'; *Enciclopedia Judaica Castellana* (Mexico, 1949): 'Orientalista y explorador'.
20. *Ha-mitzpeh*, 4 April 1913, in *Kressel* (Hebrew).
21. *Ha-shahar*, 13 March 1911, in *Kressel* (Hebrew).
22. D. Summerfield, *From Falashas*, p. 78, seems to overestimate the importance of illiteracy and to forget the power of the symbolic impact of the possession of printed matter among the Falashas when he writes that 'the booklets which were distributed among the Falashas had little impact owing to the high level of illiteracy among the Falashas'. Even if he recognizes that the possession of a book was a symbol of prestige he didn't consider it enough relevant: 'During the course of of my fieldwork, I also came across many Falashas who were very proud to show me their copy of one of Faitlovitch's publications. However, in the majority of cases, they were unable to read.' (Ibid., p. 183, n 133) The fact to possess a printed booklet addressed to the Falashas in a context in which there was no printed matter circulating was important as a matter of fact, even if the family couldn't read it and this is proved by the fact of keeping those books as precious items at the point that when they left Ethiopia for Israel they took them with them.
23. Private communication by Shelomo Akale referring to the expression used by his father Wube Akale.
24. M. Wurmbrand,'The Falashi Folklore and its Collector', *Yeda Am*, 2, 2–3 (1954), p. 107 (Hebrew).
25. *The Standard Jewish Encyclopedia* (London, 1966).
26. M. Wurmbrand, 'Faitlovitch', *Encyclopaedia Judaica* (Jerusalem, 1972), vol. 6, coll. 1137–8.
27. Diary, 17 December 1909.
28. Letter of 10 October 1904, *Fait. Coll.*, f. 116.
29. *Genazim*, 109–46621.
30. Ibid.
31. *Genazim*, 109–46622.
32. See Sh. Haramati, *Three Who Preceded Ben Yehudah: Sephardi-Oriental Forerunners in the National Revival* (Jerusalem, 1978) (Hebrew).
33. *Fait. Coll.*, f. 139/140.
34. Ibid.
35. *Genazim*, 109/46622/M.

36. I. Cohen, 'Nahum Sluschz', *Aspaklariot*, 1968, p. 153 (Hebrew).
37. On territorialism and Nordau, see L. Stein, *The Hope Fulfilled: The Rise of Modern Israel* (Westport, CT, 2003), pp. 75–83.
38. 'Slouschz', *Encyclopaedia Judaica* (Jerusalem 1972), vol. 14, col. 1677; *Ha-boqer*, 14 November 1947.
39. *Genazim*, 109/46622/K.
40. I. Cohen, *Aspaklariot*, p. 154.
41. On Canaanite movement see J. Shavit, *The New Hebrew Nation: A Study in Israel Eresy and Fantasy* (London, 1987).
42. *Ha-Boker*, 14 November 1947 (Hebrew).
43. A. Elmaliah, 'To Professor Nahum Slouschz arrived at Manhood', *Am sofer* (July 1953), p. 13 (Hebrew).
44. Y. Shavit, '"French Spirit" and "French Culture" in the Jewish Yishuv in Eretz Israel (1882–1914)', *Katedra* 62 (1991), pp. 37–53 (Hebrew).
45. *Fait. Coll.*, f. 132.
46.. Ibid.
47. Letter to Khan Fhuja-Ud-Daula, 2 February 1928, *Fait. Coll.*, f. 117.
48. Letter from A. B. Salem, 31 October 1939, *Fait. Coll.*, f. 117.
49. Faitlovitch wrote to Lieutenant Shih of Formosa to obtain information 'in the descendants of the Jews scattered all over the world in ancient times ... and create contacts with these groups'. Ibid.
50. *Fait. Coll.*, f. 82. See Trevisan Semi, 'Universalisme juif et prosélitisme. L'action de Jacques Faitlovitch, "père" des Beta Israel (Falashas)', *Revue de l'Histoire des religions*, 216, 2 (1999), pp. 193–211.
51. *Fait. Coll.*, f. 114 (undated document).

2

Faitlovitch's First Mission among the Falashas in Ethiopia (1904–05): from 'Regeneration' to 'Tradition', from Alliance to Hilfsverein

At the beginning of the twentieth century, the ideology of regeneration, which played such an important role in the founding of the Alliance Israélite Universelle in Paris and the network of Alliance schools, was invoked in connection with the outreach toward the Beta Israel in Ethiopia. The term 'regeneration', first introduced into the vocabulary of the Jewish movement by Henry Grégoire in 1785,[1] was intended to reshape Jewish attitudes and behaviour in order to create modern Jews for a modern French society. The history of this term and of the *mouvement régénerateur* in nineteenth-century French Jewish society has already been well documented,[2] but its relevance to the movement created by Halévy and Faitlovitch in favour of the Beta Israel has not yet been examined.

It was the idea of regeneration, of the urgent need for a rebirth of the Jewish communities in the East and in North Africa that was behind the network of Alliance schools. Faith in the importance of education was typical of secular French society in the mid-nineteenth century. A sort of socialization of education was taking place as the Church became more and more separate from the state,[3] and a similar attitude could be found in the French Jewish community.[4]

The Alliance was deeply committed to the project for the regeneration of eastern Judaism and its network of schools and teachers was an essential instrument of that policy. This project entailed exporting a more secular model of western Judaism to various geographical areas, some of which were under French colonial rule,[5] including those of eastern Africa.

The term 'regeneration' encompassed various views on education and on Judaism, and all of the actors coming on to the stage to perform in the Beta Israel drama of the twentieth century would have to confront the ambivalent ideas underlying this term.

The first Beta Israel boy brought to Europe by Joseph Halévy, in order to be regenerated by Western Judaism, was named Daniel.

Halévy brought Daniel, who belonged to the Beta Israel community, back with him on his return from his journey to Abyssinia in 1868. In his memoir,[6] Halévy wrote that on leaving Matamma (near the Sudan border) he had bought some gourds 'to carry water for my Falasha, who refused to drink from skins which he considered impure'. But these vessels had been broken due to the camel's movement and the boy could no longer drink.

Then, Halévy writes:

> overcome by an unendurable thirst, [he] eventually became so irritable that my patience was put to a very severe test. It was only on the verge of death that he decided to break with the rigorous custom of his sect, and to use the most indispensable food items although prepared by Muslims.

This was what everybody had expected from the boy. Although in this case he had to do it in order to physically survive, he would later be forced to behave similarly with every step he took in the new environment. The path he was expected to follow was that of full assimilation to western Judaism and acceptance of the ideology of emancipation espoused by French Jews through the Alliance Israélite Universelle in Paris.

The word 'regeneration' was used by Halévy when he decided that the town of Matamma should be the centre of activity for the Alliance 'whenever this Association shall deem it fit to undertake the regeneration of our Abyssinian brethren'.[7] Halévy expected the AIU to open a school in Ethiopia where the Beta Israel could learn the Hebrew language. But this did not happen because the members of the Alliance were not convinced that the Falashas were Jews and because they didn't think that an African tribe with a 'primitive mentality' could benefit from the education provided by their organization.

Faitlovitch was aware of the opportunities that only the Alliance could offer in the area of education, but he was also aware of the French institution's ambiguous attitude. He initially tried to exploit the situation, while attempting to keep control of the undertaking firmly in his own hands.

THE FIRST MISSION TO ETHIOPIA IN 1904–05

Faitlovitch's first mission to Ethiopia was financed by Baron Edmond de Rothschild (through the good offices of the Chief Rabbi Zadoc Kahn), and not by the Alliance.

The mission was conducted under the direct supervision of Halévy, who sent precise instructions from Paris regarding the routes to be followed and the information to be collected. The suggested ways for making initial contact with the Falashas were typical of the culture of the time, and involved enticing them with small gifts and rewards. Halévy hoped that there were Falashas in Massawa too, although he did not know for sure.

Halévy recommended that Faitlovitch leave immediately for Asmara if there were no Falashas in Massawa, and that he 'try to attract one or two Falashas with financial incentives'.[8] If he did not find any Falashas in Asmara, he was to leave immediately for the Walqayt border and then head inland. Halévy thought Faitlovitch should act discreetly, limiting his correspondence with Wormser while keeping Halévy himself informed in detail.

Faitlovitch set off from Naples on 29 January 1904 and arrived in Massawa on 13 February 1904, scrupulously obeying Halévy's orders. After a few days in Massawa, where he met several Jews from Aden but no Falashas, he moved on to Asmara. There he met various official delegations of the Italian colony. He also paid several visits to the Swedish mission where he is known to have met Taamrat, the brilliant young student and son of Fanta Dawit, a Falasha convert. Faitlovitch probably noticed the young man on his very first visit to the Swedish mission, but in his diary he made no note of the meeting, which marked the beginning of a fundamental stage in both their lives. In April, he received new instructions from Halévy, who was anxious to know if Faitlovitch had personally met any Falasha workmen in Asmara: 'you must try to attract them gently with small gifts, with the pretext of learning their language. If you keep to this plan we are assured of success ...'[9] Faitlovitch's diary recounts his initial contacts with the Falashas and his expeditions to the surrounding areas, which took place during his first four months in Asmara.

He left the town for the first time on 8 June to conduct the first of two important expeditions inland. He went to Addi Ugri on the Eritrean border, and continued on from there as far as Adua and Axum. He was so struck by Addi Ugri that he wanted to build the first Falasha school there. This plan never came to fruition due to the opposition of the Italian authorities, but Faitlovitch pursued it for decades. During this journey he met many Falashas, including several *debtera* and priests. At Adenkato (in the province of Shiré) he met *debtera* Barok,[10] who asked Faitlovitch to teach him Hebrew. He spent the Sabbath in prayer, starting at three o'clock in the morning in the *mesguid* with *debtera* Baruch, and he noted that the Falashas prayed in the same way as the Aden Jews. He also wrote in his diary that everyone called the Falashas *yehudi*, Jews.

By October, Faitlovitch was back in Asmara, where he stayed only a short time, just long enough to receive new instructions from Halévy on how to proceed with the mission and to cash the francs forwarded to him by Halévy on behalf of Baron Edmond de Rothschild.[11] After that, he set off on his second important expedition inland. The route suggested by Halévy began in the region of Lasta, continued via Lake Tana, Godjiam, Kwara, Dembea, etc., and returned through Walqayt. It was a route that Halévy considered original, which would not only bring him honour, but would allow him to 'do Judaism a precious service'.[12]

In the second part of the mission, Faitlovitch met several groups of converts, and while in Debra Tabor he received a delegation of converts, whom he described as Christian Falashas. He wrote that Tedda, which had once been a Falasha village, had become Christian.

From the reactions of the Protestant missionaries of the Church Mission among the Jews,[13] we learn that Faitlovitch was not simply contacting Christian Falashas but was determinedly trying to get them to convert back to Judaism. He did this by offering them money and education, and by refuting the arguments spread by the missionaries, including one that had led them to believe that all the Jews in Europe had already converted to Christianity, and another that raised doubts about the possibility of being reunited with deceased relatives in heaven after death. The Walqayt missionaries' reports[14] read:

> the same French Jew ... scolded them for having become Christians, tempting them to come back to the Falashas. To the Falashas he gave plenty of money to rebuild their Mesgid (synagogue) (in the village of Abora). Our converts were surprised to hear that there are in Europe unconverted Jews

while in Belesa a Falasha was reported to have said:

> We have heard you now, but we were told that a French Jew at

> Gondar said to our people, 'Remain what you are, don't believe the teaching of Mr. Flad's children [an expression used to describe native missionaries] ... for they are apostates.' If our fathers, who died as Falashas, are in heaven, we shall meet them, if not, we wish to meet wherever they may be. You had better leave us and don't return again. The French Jew promised us teachers and plenty of money.[15]

All of Faitlovitch's missions were marked by his battles against conversion. His trips were announced in advance in missionary circles, as they were considered troublesome and interfered with the work done by the missionaries.

It is worth noting that the original purpose of the Church Missionary Society (founded in 1799) was to regenerate the Eastern Orthodox churches (Armenian, Nestorian, Coptic, and Ethiopian) and to convince their members to serve as missionaries among their Muslim or pagan neighbours.[16] The ideology of regeneration was shared by western Judaism, western Christianity, the Church Missionary Society, and the Alliance. The idea that Middle Easterners or Africans could convert groups of people among whom Jews were living also became one of the main purposes of Faitlovitch's activities.

During his first journey Faitlovitch also met the Qemant (and their priest Negussié), a group regarded as Jewish-Pagan that was of particular interest to the missionaries, who considered them ripe for conversion.[17] He visited Fendja, went on to meet Taamrat's mother at Genda,[18] and ventured as far as Semien to meet the Falashas there. Faitlovitch was accompanied on this expedition by Gete Yirmiahu, the young man he later took with him to Paris, referred to in his diary as Gerémie.

CHANGING NAMES

The practice of giving someone a Hebrew last name to replace his father's name started during the first mission in Ethiopia. Ethiopians, who do not have permanent family names, customarily add their father's names to their personal names. Among Orthodox Christians, according to Bahru Zewde, a child could be given a Christian name of his own and this would become his children's last name:[19] 'Instead of a secular name, the Church name that a child was given at baptism in the Orthodox Christian Church may be retained as a personal name.' Gete was called Gete but became known to Faitlovitch as Gerémie. From a letter that Faitlovitch wrote in Amharic, we see that Taamrat Emmanuel's first name was Taamrat. In this letter, Faitlovitch referred to Taamrat Emmanuel as Taamrat Dawit.[20] His second name, Dawit, was his father's name before conversion. Faitlovitch used to change the father's names of the young boys he took with him to be educated in Europe or Palestine, where their Hebrew names became the first names by which they were known in Jewish communities. So Taamrat Dawit became Taamrat Emmanuel, or Emmanuel in the Jewish world, and Gete became Gete Yirmiahu, or Gerémie.[21] The Ethiopian tradition was therefore quite different from Faitlovitch's habit of calling young people by their last names, names which were not connected to the paternal line of descent, but reflected a new Jewish line of descent, a Jewish genealogy. The practice of changing names was continued by the Jewish State when the large waves of Beta Israel immigrants arrived in Israel. The imposition of more Jewish-sounding names also became a common practice for the *mizrahim* but was later rejected as being typically eurocentric and indicative of the Orientalism introduced by Ashkenazi Jews. In the case of the Falashas, Faitlovitch, by trying to impose a new Jewish identity, destroyed the Ethiopian one, cutting young people off from their Ethiopian genealogy. The Jewish Agency did the same thing when the Beta Israel arrived in the country, obscuring the line of descent of many large Ethiopian families.

THE END OF THE MISSION

Faitlovitch spent his last few months in Asmara with Gete and Taamrat, waiting to receive money from Europe for the journey home. After receiving a small sum of money,[22] he and the two young men set sail for Suez from Massawa on 4 July. On the way, they stopped for a few days in Cairo to visit the Karaite synagogue, the Alliance school and the Pyramids. Faitlovitch arrived in Marseilles on 2 August; by the eleventh he was in Paris, and on the twelfth he was at Halévy's house, reporting on the expedition.

That was the conclusion of the second expedition among the Ethiopian Falashas organized by European Jews, and the first of Faitlovitch's twelve expeditions.

The journey, which had gone according to Halévy's instructions, ended at the famous maestro's house with a detailed account of the mission.

Faitlovitch also followed Halévy's instructions regarding the attitude to adopt with the Alliance.[23] He had only just arrived in Africa when Halévy told him not to inform the Alliance that he had reached Massawa as 'he had been dismissed by the secretary', but simply to inform the French organization once the mission had been successful.[24] The Alliance did not know about the two young Falashas who were going to study in Paris. When Halévy told Faitlovitch that his exploratory mission should be considered complete and that it was time for him to return to Europe 'to undertake action in favor of the Falashas', he added that it would now be up to 'the Alliance and the Chief Rabbi to decide whether or not they wanted to accept the honor of receiving the Falasha delegates'.[25] Halévy loved surprise moves and *faits accomplis*, strategies he may have passed on to Faitlovitch, who also made use of them in the ensuing years.

Halévy was worried that during the journey Faitlovitch might stray from the mission's main objective and engage in other research on his own. The research on the Falashas 'had to be the *only* purpose of his mission', and Halévy made it clear to Faitlovitch that he was not to get involved in other projects. Until '*the current state* of the Falashas has been completely clarified', Halévy told him, he was not to think about anything else.[26] Halévy wanted Faitlovitch to return to Europe with handwritten responses from priests, in various dialects, rather than information trusted to memory, and he asked him to buy or copy Falasha manuscripts. In fact, he purchased a lot of them: 'the religious leaders have for the first time agreed to sell me the manuscripts of their religious writings.'[27] Some of the Falasha manuscripts in the Faitlovitch Collection at the University of Tel Aviv may date back to the 1904–05 mission.

FROM ALLIANCE TO HILFSVEREIN: TOWARDS THE SECOND ETHIOPIAN MISSION

The Alliance was unenthusiastic about the unexpected arrival of the two young Ethiopians who were to study at their school in Auteuil, and Faitlovitch was disappointed by their lacklustre cooperation and the level of instruction offered. Consequently, the following year Gete was transferred to Florence to study with Rabbi Margulies; Taamrat followed him in October 1907. The withdrawal of the two youths from the Alliance School, particularly that of Taamrat Emmanuel in 1907, caused a lot of trouble with the Alliance, as will be seen in the next chapter.

From the moment he became involved, Faitlovitch, partly in reaction to Halévy's problems with the Alliance, looked for other allies and sources of protection, which he found in Rabbi Margulies and the Hilfsverein.

Zvi Margulies,[28] like Jacques Faitlovitch, was an Ashkenazi Jew, referred to in many letters from Alliance representatives as 'German'. Margulies came from a traditional Orthodox family. He was born in Galicia, attended the Jewish seminary in Wroclaw, and later studied Semitic languages at Leipzig University. Margulies was an extremely active member of the solidarity fundraising campaigns that the Alliance often promoted. He was also a member of the Alliance Central Committee, although he disagreed with the AIU on many issues because of his more traditional religious views.[29]

When Margulies became Chief Rabbi of Florence, he showed enthusiasm and interest in the success of Faitlovitch's Falasha project, and he had the advantage of being in Italy, the country that had colonized Eritrea. The Hilfsverein des Deutschen Juden, the Charitable Society of German Jews, created to assist Jews in Eastern European and Middle Eastern countries, was also involved in education but put more emphasis on strictly religious observance than the Alliance.[30] The Alliance was under attack from the Orthodox Jewish press, which criticized the low priority given by Alliance schools to teaching Hebrew and providing religious instruction, and the Hilfsverein was in competition with the French organization.

Margulies had more traditional views than Faitlovitch, although they were not strict enough to meet the standards of the Hilfsverein des Deutschen Juden. Therefore it was necessary to reassure the German organization of Faitlovitch's orthodoxy,[31] and Margulies tried to present himself as the guarantor of the orthodox education to be given in the schools in Abyssinia. In reality, Faitlovitch aimed to give the Falashas both a Jewish and a secular education and to transform them into modern Jews who would be respectful of tradition. He intended to train people to become teachers, rabbis, or professionals. His views were too traditional for the Alliance but not traditional enough for the Hilfsverein. However, in keeping with Halévy's example, when it came to the importance of teaching Hebrew, his way of thinking was similar to that of the Hilfsverein; he believed that Hebrew should be one of the priorities in the Falashas' training. He complained about the instruction that Taamrat and Gete had received in Paris, precisely because of the poor Hebrew they had learned. The argument that the Hebrew instruction offered by the Alliance was of poor quality, and not up to the desired standards, was also used as a tactic for convincing the Hilfsverein. When Taamrat Emmanuel was moved to Florence, Margulies had to explain the reason for this change to Franz Philippson, the vice-president of the JCA and a supporter of the Pro-Falasha Committee. Margulies asserted that the education of the two youths in Paris

> had been irresponsibly neglected … one of them has been in Florence for several months and … during his stay in Paris he has learned almost nothing about Hebrew teachings and Jewish life. My colleague Dr. Chajes has confirmed likewise with regard to the second Falasha, whom he has seen and talked to recently in Paris.

He added that they had both complained that Mr Bigart had 'treated them with disdain'.[32] Bigart was the secretary of the Alliance and the target of sarcastic remarks by Faitlovitch, who often accused him of having a bureaucratic attitude and of being a conspirator. In a letter to Claude Montefiore,[33] Margulies referred to the controversy over the education received by the two youths. First of all, he explained, 'Mr Faitlovitch … although not strictly religious, feels largely responsible for the education of the two youths entrusted to him.' He went on to state that in good conscience, Faitlovitch felt he could no longer accept responsibility for leaving the second youth at the École normale, 'as the religious teaching in that school was not suitable for preparing the youth well enough for his future profession as teacher in Abyssinia'.[34] The Florentine rabbi added that it had been impossible to allow the Falasha boy to remain at the École normale, 'where he would not have had the opportunity to get to know and love traditional Judaism'.[35] The comments to be found in some of the letters sent by Margulies[36] to Montefiore and Philippson – and particularly in the correspondence between Narcisse Leven and Raffaele Ottolenghi, the treasurer of the Italian Pro-Falasha Committee – emphasize the type of education given by the Alliance and the importance that the matter had acquired.

The lawyer Ottolenghi was indignant at the situation. He defended Faitlovitch's work and explained that there were real reasons, of a purely educational nature, that had led Faitlovitch to take the two boys away from the school. According to the Italian treasurer, 'Faitlovitch … maintains that the education given by your [the Alliance's] schools is too western and the young Gete complained that he was not learning Hebrew.'[37] When Faitlovitch came back from his second trip to Abyssinia (1908), he thanked the Florentine rabbi for his commitment to Taamrat's education and remarked that Margulies had turned the boy into a good Israelite after 'he had become anti-Semitic due to the spirit of the École normale of the Alliance'.[38] Faitlovitch did not care which second language the Beta Israel were to be taught; it could be French (the language of the Alliance), German (the language of the Hilfsverein), or Italian (the language of the Pro-Falasha Committee). But he fought for the teaching of Hebrew, which was exactly what the Hilfsverein wanted. Those Falasha students who stayed in Ethiopia were taught some English by Leah in 1926 and 1928–29.

Faitlovitch knew how to exploit the rivalry between the two organizations, insisting on the position that the education offered by the Alliance was not sufficiently traditional and initiating an intense press campaign against it, particularly when he was about to organize his second mission.

The Alliance's ambivalence increased during the preparations for the second Ethiopian mission, during which Faitlovitch hoped to find his first school. The Alliance tried to dampen Faitlovitch's enthusiasm when he attempted to involve the organization in a more extensive operation. The Alliance's aim was simply to investigate the feasibility of an educational programme in Africa, not to create a school. In 1907, when the mission was being organized, there was a frantic exchange of letters between the president of the Alliance (Narcisse Leven) and Margulies, and between Margulies and Faitlovitch. The Alliance mentioned that it merely wished to gather information on where to establish a school, how to recruit staff, how to find a sufficient number of boys, which languages to teach, and whether to open the school to girls. They did not want to become too involved in educational programmes in Africa. Faitlovitch, meanwhile, continued to look for a way to achieve his goal, which was the immediate foundation of a school.

Faitlovitch, realizing that he would not be able to get real support from the Alliance, accused it of being uninterested in the traditional teaching of Judaism and turned to its rival, the Hilfsverein. He asked its president, Paul Nathan, to commit to the establishment of schools in Abyssinia and to the possibility of housing youths in the Hilfsverein schools in Palestine. Thanks to his quarrel with the AIU, he managed to win Nathan's trust, obtaining funding and accommodations for the young Falashas in the Hilfsverein's schools in Palestine.[39]

The closer Faitlovitch became to the Hilfsverein, the more worried the AIU became. In a rough draft of a letter, Leven mentioned the campaign conducted by Faitlovitch among the Jews in Italy and Germany[40] in an irritated tone.[41]

Faitlovitch was therefore skilled enough to get the Hilfsverein involved by exploiting the strong antagonism between the two organizations, thus obtaining the schooling he had in mind for the Falashas, which was both modern and traditional. He had embarked along a road that was to lead to modernization through the regeneration of the Eastern and African populations, but when faced with scepticism from the organization fighting for these ideals, he tempered his plan to suit the Orthodox tradition supported by the German Jews in the Hilfsverein. The rebirth of Hebrew and the ideology of pan-Judaism helped make it possible to meet this challenge. Moreover, the Alliance's ideology was too secular to allow him to stay on his chosen path of developing traditional, conservative movements and practices furthering the Zionist cause, neither of which were on the AIU's agenda.

NOTES

1. J. R. Berkovitz, *The Shaping of Jewish Identity in Nineteenth-Century France* (Detroit, 1989), p. 128.
2. Ibid., pp. 128–49.
3. F. Dubet, 'La laicité dans les mutations de l'école', in M. Wieworka (ed.), *Une Société fragmentée: le multiculturalisme in débat* (Paris, 1996), pp. 85–112.
4. On the founding of the Alliance Israélite Universelle, its ideology and the French Jewish community, see Ph. Cohen Albert, 'Ethnicité et solidarité chez les Juifs de France au XIX siècle', *Pardes*, 3 (1986), pp. 29–53.
5. A. Rodrigue, *De l'instruction à l'emancipation. Les Enseignants de l'Alliance israélite universelle et les Juifs d'Orient 1860–1939* (Paris, 1989) and A. Rodrigue, *Images of Sephardi and Eastern Jewries. The Teachers of the Alliance Israélite Universelle, 1860–1939* (Seattle- and London, 1993).
6. J. Halévy, 'Travels in Abyssinia,' in A. L. Loewy (ed.), *Miscellany of Hebrew Literature* (London, 1877), vol. 2, ser. 2, p. 252.
7. Ibid., p. 235.
8. Letter of 7 March 1904, *Fait. Coll.*, f. 116.
9. Letter of 3 April 1904, *Fait. Coll.*, f. 116.
10. J. Faitlovitch, *Quer durch Abessinien* (Berlin, 1910), p. 44 shows a photograph of *debtera* Barok.
11. He received 2500 francs, letter from Halévy of 6 October 1904, *Fait. Coll.*, f. 116.
12. Letter of 7 October 1904, *Fait. Coll.*, f. 116.
13. For the beginnings of a mission to the Falashas see Summerfield, *From Falashas*, pp. 17–38.
14. *London Society Reports* (1906–08), p. 109.
15. Ibid.
16. See Summerfield, *From Falashas*, p. 19.
17. Diary, 13 March 1905.
18. Diary, 23 March 1905.
19. Bahru Zweide, *The History of Modern Ethiopia 1855–1974* (London, Athens and Addis Ababa, 1991), p. 235.
20. The letter is *Tomara ebiwna.* I am indebted to Ambessa Teferra for the translation of the letters from Amharic.
21. Another boy, Makonnen, son of Gobiaw, become Makonnen Levi. J. Toubiana ('Noms Falacha', *Nouvelles de l'ARESAE*, January–March 1995) wrote that unlike the Amhara name system, in which the child's name precedes the father's, among the Agau (the Falashas are considered of Agau origins) the father's name is put before the child's. Toubiana quotes the case of Taamrat's father (Fanta Dawit) whose own name was Dawit and whose father's name was Fanta. When he entered the service of the future Emperor Theodorus, he stopped calling himself Dawit and took on the Christian name of Gabra Maryam (Servant of Mary) in an attempt to pass unnoticed. Toubiana concluded that further research was necessary to deter-

mine the origins of Taamrat Emmanuel's two names, as neither is his father's name. According to the cases just mentioned, it seems that the Falashas adopted the Amhara name system and that Faitlovitch changed their father's names.

22. 500 francs.
23. Letter of 7 March 1904, *Fait. Coll.*, f. 116.
24. Ibid.
25. Letter of 5 April 1905, *Fait. Coll.*, f. 116.
26. Letter of 6 October 1904, *Fait. Coll.*, f. 116. The underlining is in the original.
27. Letter of 22 November 1905, *Fait. Coll.*, f. 116.
28. For a description of Margulies, the rabbi of Florence, and of the Florentine environment see L. Viterbo, 'La nomina del rabbino Margulies: un excursus nella Firenze ebraica di fine Ottocento', *La Rassegna mensile di Israel*, 60, 3 (1993), pp. 67–89; and L. Viterbo, 'Cronache dal passato fiorentino: la difficile successione del Rabbino Margulies (1920–1926)', *La Rassegna mensile di Israel*, 60, 3 (1994), pp. 148–68.
29. In addition to the dispute that is the subject of this chapter, see also the letter in which Leven contested the reasons put forward by Margulies for opposing S. Reinach's candidature. Leven explained: 'Non dobbiamo preoccuparci della scelta di filosofia religiosa che può professare l'uno o l'altro dei membri del Comitato centrale: è un affare privato che non impegna che lui e per la quale i suoi colleghi non son tenuti ad essere solidali ... Pensereste che sarebbe giusto privarci di un collega di tal valore perchè ha delle idee diverse dalle nostre sulla religione?' Letter of 5 May 1911, *Arch.* AIU, Italy, ID4, 9832.
30. For the conflicts and differences of opinion in the Jewish Associations of those years, see Z. Szajkowski, 'Conflicts in the *Alliance Israélite Universelle* and the founding of the Anglo-Jewish Association, The Vienna Allianz, and the *Hilfsverein*', *Jewish Social Studies*, 19 (1957), pp. 29–50.
31. Letter from Margulies to Faitlovitch of 30 January 1908, *Fait. Coll.*, f. 120. Hilfsverein wanted to know 'if the proposed school will be directed with an orthodox spirit'.
32. Letter of 10 November 1907, *Fait. Coll.*, f. 120.
33. Letter of 12 November 1907, *Fait. Coll.*, f. 120.
34. Ibid.
35. Letter to Philippson of 12 November 1907, *Fait. Coll.*, f. 120.
36. Margulies even publicized the dispute in the press, see Z. Margulies, 'Per la storia del movimento Pro-Falasha', *Rivista Israelitica*, 6 (1909), pp. 152–9.
37. Letter to Leven of 21 January 1907, *Arch. AIU*, Italie, ID4, 9820/2.
38. Letter of 15 December 1908, *Fait. Coll.*, f. 120.
39. Letter of 8 January 1907, *Fait. Coll.*, f. 94.
40. For the campaign among the Jews in Italy, see Trevisan Semi, *Allo specchio*, pp. 44–7.
41. Letter of 21 November 1907, *Arch. AIU*, Italie, ID4, 9778/9789. One of the crossed out sentences said that Faitlovitch: 'dopo una campagna fatta presso i nostri correligionari d'Italia e di Germania ... si è fatto una réclame personale ...'

3

The Alliance Israélite Universelle and the Dispute with Faitlovitch: Towards the Second Mission to Ethiopia

The first signs of conflict with the Alliance were noticeable at the time of Faitlovitch's first expedition among the Jews of Ethiopia (1904) and became fully apparent in 1907 during the preparations for his second mission (1908–09). The quarrel led to the absurd situation of two Jewish missions, with conflicting ideological views, setting out at almost the same time – one financed by the AIU and the other by the Italian Pro-Falasha Committee and the Hilfsverein.

Various explanations of the cause of the disagreement have been put forward.

The ideology underlying the Alliance's education policy was one of emancipation and humanism, as shown by G. Weill's analysis.[1]

The conflict over traditional teaching from the Talmudic schools, and the rabbis who were placed in charge of this teaching, originated with the AIU directors. The latter became involved in various campaigns against the European, and above all German, orthodox Jewish groups, and the Hilfsverein der Deutschen Juden, the association that represented them.[2] At the same time, the type of instruction given by the AIU schools was also under attack from the Orthodox Jewish press, which criticized the low priority given to the teaching of Hebrew and to religious instruction, to such an extent that the Alliance's Central Committee was obliged (in 1909) to send an investigative mission to the Orient to clarify the situation.[3]

A variety of reasons have been put forward to explain the Alliance's sometimes sceptical and detached, sometimes openly hostile attitude towards the possibility of an education project for the Ethiopian Jews and the establishment of schools in Eritrea and Ethiopia. The fight against prejudice and backwardness was considered by the members of the Alliance to be a moral and religious duty. But while the Alliance had a strong sense of solidarity with Jews experiencing great suffering, it also had a sense of 'embarrassment and distaste', as Aron Rodrigue has pointed out,[4] when encountering oriental Jews, whom it perceived as rough, superstitious and ignorant. The oriental Jew was a sort of mirror in which the enlightened and modern Jew confronted the stigma of 'otherness', which was exactly what he was trying to conceal. Given this ambivalent attitude towards the oriental Jews, no wonder the members of the Alliance were so reluctant to act, in this case not even for oriental Jews but for a strange, puzzling group of African people claming to be Jews.

As David Kessler recalls, 'it has been suggested that a touch of colour prejudice may perhaps have played a part'.[5] James Quirin[6] considered the suspicion surrounding Faitlovitch to be a contentious remnant of the conflicts that arose within the AIU at the time of the mission among the Beta Israel led by Josef Halévy (1867–8), whom the Alliance leaders did not trust. They even doubted that he had actually gone to Ethiopia and that the youth he had brought back with him to Paris was truly a Beta Israel. M. Waldman,[7] who examined most of the documentation of that time, explained that the rather frosty and evasive attitude of the Alliance leaders (and their emissary Nahum) was a corollary of the bureaucratic code they had adopted because they lacked any initiative or enthusiasm for the undertaking. This was also the opinion expressed on several occasions by Faitlovitch, who referred to the 'intrigues of Bigart and his clerks'[8] within the Alliance.

The explanations given to date are all pertinent and illustrate certain aspects of the matter, the premonitory signs of which actually date back to Halévy's controversial mission and the ambivalence shown by the Alliance even then. The Alliance's wait-and-see attitude was already in evidence when Faitlovitch had to leave for Ethiopia in 1904 without any financial help on their part.[9] This attitude became increasingly hostile when Faitlovitch, without asking prior permission, brought two young Beta Israel, Taamrat and Gete, back with him to be educated in the Alliance teachers' school. It is obvious that with this act, Faitlovitch and Halévy were trying to force the situation. However, it was the subsequent withdrawal of the youths from the École normale d'Auteuil that most inflamed the Alliance leaders.

However, the question of whether or not the Falashas actually belonged to Judaism played a definite role in the French organization's lack of commitment. The Alliance was doubtful about the Falashas' Jewishness.

Were they Jews? This question arose during many debates within the Alliance. What is intriguing is that since Alliance members considered Judaism to be more of a religion than an ethnic movement, this question would appear to have had little reason to be raised. As a matter of fact, a more open-minded view concerning this group could be found in Orthodox rabbinical circles, and most of the supporters of the Pro-Falasha committees were rabbis. In 1924, the Alliance journal *Paix et droit* published an article[10] in which different opinions were expressed on the subject; in it, Rabbi Chajes of Vienna (a close friend of Margulies, the rabbi of Florence) strongly opposed the racist views of Professor Schefletowitz of Cologne.[11] The latter, after listing the Falashas' habits and traditions to show that 'many of their customs were similar to those of the Negroes', had concluded categorically that the Jewish religion could not have been influenced by what he termed 'Negro tribes' nor even have been attractive to such 'primitive mentalities'. He even went so far as to disassociate himself from practices that were also present to a certain extent in Judaism, stating that 'the laws governing their eating habits are close to those of the Moslems and the ones regarding purity are more similar to those of primitive peoples than the Jews'. Chajes replied that while it was certain that no ancient Jewish blood flowed in Falasha veins, it was also certain that the Falashas were penetrated by the spirit of Judaism. It is possible that in the eyes of the emancipated Jews of the AIU, who had fought for the dignity they deserved and for their rightful place in the new society, the so-called 'primitiveness' of this group was too embarrassing and obtrusive. If these people, too, were Jews, the emancipated Jews would have to reshape their identity and consider ancient traditions and obsolete habits, like the laws of purity, to be an integral part of their ancient religion.

In any case, the thinly veiled references to skin colour and race found in AIU documents related to the young Falashas in Paris, and to Falashas in general, can still be found in Jewish discourse today, particularly since the immigration of the Beta Israel to Israel.[12]

THE QUARREL

The first relevant signs of disagreement could already be seen in early 1907, when Margulies and Leven exchanged frequent correspondence over a long period. The correspondence was about the second expedition to Ethiopia, which Margulies and Faitlovitch intended to be the start of an educational programme in Eritrea, while the Alliance's intention was simply to investigate the feasibility of such a program. The Alliance was already reluctant to entrust this mission to

Faitlovitch, the 'German' Jew who was an exponent of neo-Orthodoxy and bound to the Hilfsverein, and after having equivocated and played for time, they tried to foist on him one of their own teachers from the schools in Cairo, S. Somekh.[13] Just when everything appeared to have been settled and Somekh had agreed to pass through Florence to receive instructions and letters of recommendation from Margulies (for the purpose of obtaining help from the Italian colonial authorities), there came the unexpected news that Somekh was not available.[14] The Alliance had become increasingly worried about the future of the project and had therefore substituted its own former student from the Séminaire israélite de France, H. Nahum, a protégé of Alliance secretary J. Bigart, in order to guarantee greater dependence and sharing of viewpoints.[15] Faitlovitch may have already met Nahum and decided that it would be difficult to cooperate with him. In any case, when he acted to take Taamrat away from Paris, sending him to Florence, events came to a head and the duplicate mission was initiated.

As has been seen, the conflict between Faitlovitch and the Alliance was an old one and had already been hinted at in the letters Halévy had sent to his student just after his arrival in Massawa at the time of the first journey to Ethiopia. Despite his age, Halévy had lost none of his fighting spirit and told his young student to keep his distance from the organization that had rejected him. The problem of the Beta Israel youths, as we have seen, would subsequently take on considerable importance in relations between Faitlovitch and the Alliance. Halévy simply wanted to present the AIU with a *fait accompli*.[16]

The AIU,[17] in informing its readers of the arrival of the two youths, let it be known that their arrival was a source of perturbation:

> The two young men are about twenty, they speak only Ethiopian and Amharic; we didn't know what to do with them when they arrived in Paris. Although they have dark skin they don't have the flat face that is typical of the African Negro ... The Alliance committee thought that a period at the École préparatoire, with young people of their own age, would quickly knock the rough edges off them. And this is what has happened.

Just four years later, when the case blew up, a less diplomatic version appeared in an edition of the regular *Bulletin de l'AIU*:

> To everyone's great surprise [Faitlovitch] brought back with him two Falashas who wandered round the streets of Paris for a few

> weeks. The Alliance was forced, in some way, to accept them at the École normale d'Auteuil. These young men had barely begun to lose some of their ignorant ways when Faitlovitch sent them away from the École normale – without informing the Alliance – to Florence, where a Pro-Falasha Committee had been formed.[18]

Gete was transferred to Florence near the end of 1906. Margulies explained to Leven, the president of the AIU,[19] that since the Alliance had financed neither the first mission nor the education of the youths in Paris (their expenses were paid by Baron Rothschild), it had no reason to protest nor should it consider itself responsible for the fate of the youths. Consequently, the rabbi of Florence firmly repeated,

> I therefore had no reason to consult the Alliance when Mr Faitlovitch asked me to take in one of the two Falashas for training since he told me that Baron de Rothschild had agreed and I had no reason to suppose that the Alliance could somehow be opposed.[20]

Faitlovitch – as shown in the previous chapter – operated quite pragmatically on various fronts in order to obtain financial support, and the difficulties with the Alliance induced him to consider the Hilfsverein as a source of financing. He turned to Paul Nathan to secure his organization's support for the establishment of the school and the boarding school in Dembea (near Gondar), and above all to ask him to take the initiative in pushing through the proposed programme.[21] He expressed the conviction that the best political support would come from the United States:

> For political reasons the school and its staff must be protected by the United States government. America, thanks to its neutral position in Ethiopian affairs, is the only power able to guarantee this protection without arousing the suspicions of His Majesty the Negus and the other European nations.[22]

He felt that political support could be obtained from the nations that had interests in the area, such as Italy, France, and England, and from the neutral America.

On this and other occasions, Faitlovitch's attitude was characterized by the utmost pragmatism and realism. Whether it had to do with which type of education should be given to the young Falashas, based on the Alliance or the Hilfsverein model, or which foreign power should be approached for political support, what determined Faitlovitch's decisions was simply the advantage of one solution over another in achieving his objectives. At the beginning of the twentieth century, he regarded the various European colonial powers present in the region as potential supporters of his work. Later, after the First World War, he appealed to the United States, and after Italy's conquest of Ethiopia, he tried to appeal to Italy, going so far as to threaten Taamrat when he rebelled against the colonial yoke because Faitlovitch was interested only in his own 'holy work'.

THE LEADERSHIP OF THE SECOND MISSION: SOMEKH, NAHUM OR FAITLOVITCH?

While Faitlovitch was knocking on the doors of the Hilfsverein, Margulies was trying to enlist the support of the JCA. Following a suggestion by Franz Philippson, then vice-president of the JCA, he sent several letters to Leven, asking in particular that the president of the Alliance exert 'his great influence on the Alliance and the JCA so that they would give a yearly grant to the Pro-Falasha organization founded here, which aims to set up a school in Eritrea'.[23] Leven replied, offering an assurance of subsidies from the Alliance and the JCA, but he also made it clear that he did not yet have all the information required to organize a realistic programme.[24] Margulies gave details about the organization of the school and suggested that the language of instruction should be Hebrew.[25] In a subsequent letter,[26] Margulies, reassured by the guarantee of funds offered by the JCA (10,000 francs) and by the Italian Committee (an approximate figure of 3,000 to 4,000 francs), added that he considered Faitlovitch to be the right person to send: 'I had Faitlovitch with me in Florence for a long time and deem him to be a well-bred person who loves Judaism and has taken the question of saving the Falasha to heart.'[27] The silence that followed his having named Faitlovitch, and his suspicion that this had been unpopular, induced Margulies to insist, 'I cannot believe that a man like you, particularly over such an important matter, is influenced by personal likes and dislikes,' and ask explicitly, 'Would you kindly tell me the motives which, it would seem, lead you to completely discard the possibility of Mr Faitlovitch.'[28] Again, Margulies, after having asked if Faitlovitch was under reproach, from a moral point of view, for something he had done,[29] insisted in nominating him: 'he not only seems to me to be the most suitable but the only suitable person. In fact you, honored

President, have not suggested or named anyone else.'[30] Faced with Margulies' insistence, the AIU president reiterated that they needed someone who was of 'stable character and judgment, intellectually capable and had professional experience', making it clear that in his opinion Faitlovitch did not have these qualities, but suggesting that perhaps he could accompany another person to be chosen by mutual consent.[31] Margulies accepted Leven's suggestion that Faitlovitch participate as an escort or interpreter and asked him for the name of the person chosen by the Alliance.[32] It seemed from Leven's reply[33] that an agreement had been reached, and that Somekh was to be a member of the mission, serving as a teacher in the Alliance schools. The chief rabbi of Florence told Faitlovitch that he was

> happy to be able to say that Mr Leven, according to his letters, was not prejudiced against him. It was simply his opinion, in itself not entirely incomprehensible, that a person who was also an expert in *school matters* was needed for the mission. For this reason he has made the following suggestion: the Alliance will send Mr Somekh from Cairo, headmaster of the Alliance schools, as their trusted man, and our Committee will send *you* in the same capacity in Eritrea and Abyssinia. You must naturally travel together and cooperate with each other.[34]

Margulies had therefore decided to agree, and to convince Faitlovitch to do likewise for 'the good of the cause', as he wrote in the same letter. The mission was to depart in November from Florence, in order to allow Somekh to receive instructions from Margulies. The Rabbi had accepted the conditions laid down by the Alliance and intended to put a certain pressure on Faitlovitch to accept the agreement.

In early August, Margulies raised another problem of great concern to Faitlovitch. In a letter to Bigart, he asked for Baron Rothschild to finance the departure of young Gete, so that he could accompany Faitlovitch and Somekh. According to the chief rabbi, it was necessary for the youth to go in order 'not to lose the trust of the Falasha'.[35] Of the two youths in Europe, wrote Margulies, the one in Italy had been chosen to go because his parents were still alive and he was homesick. In fact, Faitlovitch (along with Margulies) was firmly convinced that in order for him to be able to show his face again in the Falasha villages after three years, he would need to return with at least one of the two youths, who would later return to Europe to complete his studies. The reports of Faitlovitch's second journey confirm the importance of

Gete's role in the success of the expedition. By that time Gete's relatives thought he was dead.

At the end of August, Margulies, with a certain circumspection due to the Alliance's decidedly negative attitude toward allowing Gete to depart,[36] wrote to say that the Hilfsverein would be making a contribution[37] and concluded by saying, 'Now that we can hope for a considerable increase in funds, you too, Mr President, should put aside your objections, passed on to me by Mr Bigart, with regard to taking young Jeremy to Abyssinia.'[38] The criteria chosen by the Alliance, however, always seemed to be dictated more by decisions of a bureaucratic nature than by humanitarian goals, and the Hilfsverein's involvement was regarded with great suspicion.

One month later, Leven wrote that Somekh was unable to leave and would be replaced by Nahum. It is from this moment on that the opposing positions seemed to become entrenched. The differing aims of those participating in the undertaking were confirmed, the Pro-Falasha Committee's aim being to establish the school and that of the Alliance being a simple reconnaissance mission. It was at that time that Taamrat was invited to join his companion in Florence in order to receive the same training, to the great annoyance of the Alliance. The embarrassment of the AIU leaders at the possibility that financial help might be obtained from the Hilfsverein only increased the climate of suspicion towards Faitlovitch.

Margulies, who initially agreed to the replacement of Somekh, nevertheless wanted to insist that the journey would not be one of simple reconnaissance but that the two envoys should 'immediately put into action the necessary steps for establishing the planned school, in Abyssinia itself or in Eritrea'. In the same letter, the rabbi of Florence asked that Taamrat be sent to Florence:

> in the meantime it would be well for the two young Falashas who are presently in Europe to have the possibility of becoming elementary school teachers of Hebrew and religion as soon as possible in their own country. To this end I would ask you to consider whether it would not also be better for Emmanuel to come to Florence to be trained like Gete Yirmiahu.[39]

The same day, Margulies wrote to Faitlovitch to ask about Nahum: 'Do you know this gentleman? What do you think of him?' He reassured Faitlovitch that whatever the case, Nathan had agreed 'that you will go to Abyssinia as *our* trusted man'.[40] In the same letter, Margulies asked

Faitlovitch to be patient regarding the matter of Taamrat so that everything could be resolved in a friendly way, and not to make any hasty decisions.

These two letters – one to Leven and the other to Faitlovitch — written by Margulies on the same day, show not only the Rabbi's diplomatic skill but also his resoluteness and his faith in the justness of the cause. With Leven, he proved his flexibility by allowing Nahum to replace Somekh, while re-emphasizing the aims of the mission and trying to arrange for Taamrat to be sent to Florence without its becoming a bone of contention. Likewise, knowing Faitlovitch's impulsive nature, he encouraged the latter not to make any hasty decisions and to wait, trusting in his diplomatic ability.

Faitlovitch, however, did not wait for the results of Margulies' diplomacy, and Leven, for his part, was strongly opposed to Taamrat's departure.[41] Margulies 'continued his mediation for as long as possible, but became resolute once he determined that the fate of the entire educational programme among the Ethiopian Jews to be at stake'.[42] Faitlovitch, disinclined to accept compromise and mediation, had quite a different attitude. He had decided to take Taamrat away,[43] and he had already reached an agreement with the Hilfsverein about the education to be given the young people he would be taking with him on his next expedition.[44] At that point, Leven no longer wanted Faitlovitch to be part of the mission in any way whatsoever. It was then that Margulies threatened to resign from the Alliance Central Committee.[45]

The dispute continued with the departure of the two missions. Faitlovitch did not succeed in opening his school during that mission, but he returned from it with a clear programme for further action. Nahum, on the other hand, returned having made a clear decision that it was not worth taking action in that region. Two different reports were published, one by Nahum,[46] and another that would become the only book published by Faitlovitch on his own expedition.[47] Nahum wrote that these people did not deserve the Alliance's support, and that it could actually be harmful to create false hope among people whose intellectual capacity was not very well developed. At most, he said, the Falashas could be trained as skilled workers. These are the words Nahum used:

> We should not for a moment think of creating any educational programme in Abyssinia or Eritrea … At best it would bring about a category of 'downgraded' people … we should not create dangerous illusions: we are dealing with a people whose intellectual capacity is not generally very highly developed … Any different

> behaviour would mean destroying the mental equilibrium of the Falasha race ... thanks to the mediation of one of our co-religionists from Asmara, we could every year take a certain number of young men in Asmara and teach them a trade.[48]

We can imagine how this might have been music to Alliance ears. Twenty years later, when the Alliance's vocational school in Jerusalem had accepted four Beta Israel boys, an Alliance publication[49] reported that the boys had difficulty learning a skill. The argument put forward by the Alliance had not changed. Although they began to accept some pupils in their school, they did not expect any possible change from the Beta Israel, whose mentality was still considered 'too primitive' for the highly sophisticated Alliance. Taamrat Emmanuel was making his first steps as a scholar; in the ensuing years, he would publish important works, but he would still be too 'primitive' for the Alliance.

It was not until his third trip (in 1913) that Faitlovitch opened the school in Dembea and appointed as one of its teachers Gete Yirmiahu, the boy trained by Margulies in Florence and by the Hilfsverein school in Palestine.[50]

The education policy that Faitlovitch intended to put into practice met with a certain French scepticism, arising partly from a realistic view of the impossibility of working in a territory in which the Falasha communities were widely scattered (as a history of the Jewish schools in that area would demonstrate), and partly from its commitment to a different educational model involving a type of teaching considered 'too secular' by 'German' Jews like Faitlovitch and Margulies. However, it was primarily his evaluation of the various organizations' willingness to participate in educational projects that forced Faitlovitch, while not exactly in total agreement with the Hilfsverein's orthodoxy, to seek the support of the German organization rather than the French one. He skillfully used the controversy regarding the overly secular education of the French to obtain the maximum possible European support for his project. In any case, he would not tolerate having to share his 'holy work' with anyone else. He seemed to tolerate Somekh (especially in order to win the support of Margulies, who had asked him to be cooperative), but when the AIU replaced his trusted man with Nahum, he made clear that the second mission for the Falashas would have to be the Faitlovitch mission and nothing else. There was no place for a rival 'father of the Falashas': at best, Nahum could be a stepfather.

NOTES

1. 'Le Discours idéologique de l'*Alliance Israélite Universelle*. Emancipation et humanisme au XIXe siècle', *Les Nouveaux Cahiers*, 52 (1978), pp. 1-20.
2. See E. Benbassa, 'Alliance Israélite Universelle et l'élection de Haim Nahum au grand rabbinat del'Empire Ottoman (1908–1909)', *Ninth World Congress of Jewish Studies* (Jerusalem, 1986), vol. 3, pp. 83–90; and E. Benbassa, *Un grand rabbin sepharade en politique 1892–1923* (Paris, 1990).
3. *Bulletin de l'AIU*, 37 (1909), pp. 66–7.
4. Rodrigue, *Images*, p. 9.
5. D. Kessler, *The Falashas: The Forgotten Jews of Ethiopia* (London, 1982), p. 13.
6. J. Quirin, *The Evolution*, p. 193.
7. M. Waldman, *Beyond the Rivers of Ethiopia: The Jews of Ethiopia and the Jewish People* (Israel, 1989), p. 197 and *passim* (Hebrew).
8. In a letter to Margulies (from Addis Ababa) of 1 December 1908, Faitlovitch used these words: 'Oh, if I were in Europe now I could show the Jewish world the intrigues of Bigart and his clerks, these gentlemen in Paris could really be hit and the interests of Judaism saved', *Fait. Coll.*, f. 120.
9. Z. Khan in a letter to Faitlovitch of 6 April 1905 confirmed that only Edmond de Rothschild was really interested in the expedition, *Fait. Coll.*, f. 120.
10. 'Les Falachas sont–ils juifs?', *Paix et droit*, 5 (1924), pp. 5–7.
11. Previously published in *Monatsschrift für Geschichte und Wissensshaft des Judentums* (Breslau, October–December 1923).
12. S. Kaplan, 'Can the Ethiopian change his Skin? The Beta Israel (Ethiopian Jews) and Racial Discourse', *African Affairs*, 98 (1999), pp. 535–50; S. Kaplan, 'Black and White, Blue and White and Beyond the Pale: Ethiopian Jews and the Discourse of Colour in Israel', *Jewish Culture and History*, 5, 1 (2002), pp. 51–68.
13. Leven mentioned Somekh in a letter of 18 July 1907 and Margulies accepted him: 'Since you recommend him so warmly I have no problem in agreeing with the choice you have made. I hope I can succeed in persuading Mr Faitlovitch to accept the position you suggest', Arch. AIU, Italie, 1D4, 9185/3. See Rodrigue, *Images*, pp. 162–4.
14. Leven told Margulies in a letter of 27 September 1907 that Somekh, due to family reasons, would not depart and that Nahum would replace him: 'We are thinking of replacing him with Nahum, an old pupil of the rabbi's seminary in Paris. He has the chief rabbi's diploma as well as the *hautes études et langues orientales* diploma', *Fait. Coll.*, f. 120.
15. For the relations between Bigart and Nahum, see Benbassa, *Un grand rabbin*, p. 25.
16. Ibid.
17. *Bulletin de l'AIU*, 33 (1905), pp. 206–7.
18. *Bulletin de l'AIU*, 37 (1909), p. 65.
19. Letter of 23 January 1907, *Arch. AIU*, Italie, 1D4, 8131. Margulies was replying to a letter from Bigart dated 13 January 1907.
20. Ibid.
21. Letter of 3 April 1907, *Fait. Coll.*, f. 94.
22. Ibid.
23. Letter of 4 April 1907, *Arch. AIU*, Italy, ID4, 8567.
24. Letter of 10 April 1907, *Arch. AIU*, Italy, ID4, 8567.
25. Letter of 24 April 1907, *Arch. AIU*, Italy, ID4, 8567.
26. Letter of 23 April 1907, *Arch. AIU*, Italy, ID4, 8567. The education of girls was part of the *AIU* educational programs.
27. Letter of 3 May 1907, *Arch. AIU*, Italy, ID4, 3458.
28. Letter of 17 May 1907, *Arch. AIU*, Italy, ID4, 8974.
29. Leven had replied in a letter of 23 May 1907 that the mission required 'Attitudes and preparation that Faitlovitch does not have', *Fait. Coll.*, f. 120.
30. Letter of 24 June 1907, *Arch AIU*, Italy, ID4, 9185/3.
31. Letter of 4 July 1907, *Fait. Coll.*, f. 120.
32. Letter of 17 July 1907, *Arch. AIU*, Italy, ID4, 2209.
33. Letter of 21 July 1907, *Arch. AIU*, Italy, ID4, 8323.
34. *Fait. Coll.*, f. 120.
35. Letter of 5 August 1907, *Arch. AIU*, Italy, ID4, 9233.

36. Leven had replied negatively to the suggestion of sending Gete in a letter of 20 August 1907: 'the young Jeremiah, with his poor culture, would be of no use. We don't need him to gain the Abyssinians' trust', *Fait. Coll.*, f. 120.
37. Margulies wrote to Leven in a letter of 16 August 1907: 'The Hilfsverein, at my request, has stated that it is willing not only to be associated with our undertaking but also to encourage other Jewish organizations to take part', *Arch. AIU*, Italie, ID4, 9293.
38. Ibid.
39. Letter of 2.10.1907, *Arch. AIU*, Italy, ID4, 9537.
40. *Fait. Coll.*, f. 120.
41. In a letter of 8 October 1907 Leven replied: 'it is best to leave the young Emmanuel in Paris. He is making good progress, starting to become familiar with French, and he can translate from Hebrew to French, so it would perhaps be risky to compromise these excellent results. It would also cause confusion in the young man to uproot him to another country before he has really assimilated the knowledge he has acquired here. But now we learn that, before we have even discussed the question, Faitlovitch has decided to send this young man to Florence, without our consent', *Fait. Coll.*, f. 120.
42. Letter of 11 October 1907, *Arch. AIU*, Italy, ID4, 9596/2. Margulies wrote to Leven, 'I repeatedly and *very clearly* stated *months ago* to Mr Faitlovitch that I could only welcome Emmanuel *with the consent of the Alliance.* Mr Faitlovitch wrote to me a few days ago that if I refuse to welcome the youth to Florence, he is determined to take him to Germany or Austria. To avoid this and because I truly believe that it would be better to educate the two young Falashas in the same way for their future as teachers, I have written to you on the matter. It obviously remains understood that I will *not* receive Emmanuel without your consent and, as I mentioned, Mr Faitlovitch knows this full well. On the other hand, Mr President, allow me to express my conviction openly, in all fairness to you and to myself, that Mr Faitlovitch does not deserve any reproach for wanting to have his opinions recognized regarding the education of the two youths for whom he feels responsible. These opinions may be wrong, but we have no right either to doubt the honesty of his convictions or to condemn him if he believes he is acting in accordance with the same.
43. Margulies hoped that Baron Rothschild would provide economically for the maintenance of Emmanuel, and in a letter to Faitlovitch, when relations with the Alliance were finally broken off, stated that he wished to speak to the Baron personally. If he were to be refused, he said, he would send the boy to Berlin, *Fait. Coll.*, f. 120.
44. According to the agreements between Margulies and the Hilfsverein, on his return from his journey Faitlovitch was to bring back with him three or four youths to be educated in Jerusalem in the Hilfsverein schools. Letter from Margulies to Faitlovitch of 10 October 1907, *Fait. Coll.*, f. 120.
45. In a letter to Leven of 20 October 1907, Margulies wrote, 'Apart from the damage that it would cause, it would also be an outright injustice to exclude from the mission at this point the person who brought about the entire movement by the Falashas. I must frankly say that in that event I would find myself in the embarrassing situation of having to abstain in any case from participating in the action of the Alliance', *Arch. AIU*, Italy, ID4, 9676. His actual resignation was only announced in a subsequent letter: 'The Italian Pro-Falasha Committee agrees with me that we cannot forgo the cooperation of Mr Faitlovitch; it is therefore our firm decision to send him to Abyssinia, if need be at our expense and possibly with the help of other Jewish organizations. Should the Central Committee stand firm in its refusal, with deep regret I will find myself obliged to resign as a member in order to have full freedom to act.' Letter of 14 November 1907, *Arch. AIU*, Italy, ID4, 9765.
46. Nahum sent his greatly delayed 'Rapport sur les Falashas' in the midst of numerous disputes, see *Bulletin de l'AIU*, 37 (1909), pp. 5–35. For a critical review of the report see T. Parfitt, 'The Rabbi Nahoum's Anthropological Mission to Ethiopia' in T. Parfitt and E. Trevisan Semi (eds), *The Beta Israel in Ethiopia and Israel* (London, 1999) pp. 11–15.
47. *Quer*.
48. *Bulletin mensuel de l'Alliance Israélite Universelle*, 37 (1909), p. 34.
49. *Paix et droit*, 6, 9 (1926), p. 5.
50. See also E. Trevisan Semi, 'Continuity in the Educational Projects of Faitlovitch in the Light of his Correspondence', *Peamim*, 58 (1994), pp. 86–97 (Hebrew).

4

Early Dreams of Education Under Italian Colonialism: The Location of the School

Faitlovitch's primary interest was to promote and implement educational projects among the Beta Israel. From the beginning of his activity in Ethiopia until he died, he worked to pursue this goal. Over the years, he would make a few changes in his programmes as he changed his mind, for instance on the locations of the schools or the origins of the teachers. At the beginning, he preferred that the schools be established in border areas close to European colonies, and he succeeded in creating one in Dembea. Later, he thought that it would be better to create a school in the capital of Ethiopia, near the Court; and in the end he tried to build schools in the Gondar area near the Beta Israel villages. At first he thought that the school's teaching of traditional Judaism, secular subjects, and 'traditional religious patrimony' should be done by Yemeni Jews or oriental Jews (who were 'used to the climate and primitive life in Abyssinia'), but later he accepted the idea of European Jews and local teachers (*debtera*). In the end, only his sister Leah succeeded in teaching at the Addis Ababa school. Neither his brother Haim, nor any of the German, American, or Palestinian teachers he tried to engage, taught the Falashas until the 1950s. Up to that time, the teaching was done by the young Falashas trained either in Europe or in the Ethiopian Jewish schools (Dembea, Addis Ababa), and by local *debtera*. When Deborah Lifshitz visited the Addis Ababa school on the 22 April 1932, she observed that 40 students were studying six hours a day, reading the Bible, and learning prayers, mathematics, history, and geography.[1] Forty was one of the largest numbers of students that ever attended the school. Although at the beginning Faitlovitch dreamed of the school's being opened to 'unlimited numbers of boys and girls', this never happened due to scant financial resources. Girls studied in the Faitlovitch school for only a few months in 1926, while Leah was teaching there, and they never went abroad to study to become future Falasha teachers.

Faitlovitch's decision to accept Falashas who had been converted to Christianity by the Protestants into his schools never wavered. From his first mission to his last, he hoped that the conversion made possible through education in Protestant schools could be undone, and that the people he called the Christian Falashas could return to Judaism.

THE LOCATION OF THE SCHOOL

He first tried to establish a school in Dembea, Ethiopia, but immediately afterwards he thought of founding one in the Italian colony of Eritrea. Initially he considered Tekul, a village located on the Abyssinian–Eritrean border, and later Asmara and Addi-Ugri. However, despite the tenacity shown by Faitlovitch in presenting these various plans to the representatives of Italian institutions (the Pro-Falasha Italian Committee, the Italian Embassy in Paris, the governors of Eritrea, the ministers of the colonies), no school was ever founded in the areas under Italian rule. He finally succeeded in establishing the school in Dembea in 1913 and the Faitlovitch school in Addis Ababa in 1923.

Immediately upon returning from his first journey to Eritrea and Ethiopia, Faitlovitch promoted the idea that the border areas, i.e., those areas bordering regions occupied by European powers, such as Sudan (an Anglo-Egyptian colony) or Eritrea (an Italian colony), were preferable. This was an interesting idea that offered the possibility of remaining close to the West, allowing Faitlovitch to have all the advantages and conveniences of being in proximity to a colonial power, while at the same time granting him full independence in his educational programmes.

In a letter to Paul Nathan, Faitlovitch announced his programme and asked for help in setting up schools, for grants to pay for the teachers and for the publication of materials in the local language.[2] Education was necessary, he wrote, in order to lift the group out of isolation and restore its contact with world Jewry 'with the aim of uniting this long-forgotten branch, preserving, regenerating and awakening it from its lethargy'.[3] The language used and the concepts involved were those in favor at that time. It was commonly believed that the Africans had entered a state of deep lethargy, that their history and culture were dormant, and that it was therefore up to the West to try and wake them up. It was a typically colonial attitude, but this time it was used to appeal to the forefront of paternalistic Jewish solidarity.

Faitlovitch chose the province of Dembea because it was a region on the Sudanese border:

> a lot of Falashas live there and their existence as Jews is threatened. Another important reason is that the province of Dembea is only a five-day journey from the border with Anglo-Egyptian Sudan, which means they have regular contact with the outside world.[4]

Faitlovitch estimated that he would need 50,000 marks to build the school and 15,000 to 20,000 marks for annual expenses. He suggested hiring Falasha workers on a daily basis and giving the headmaster a teaching staff consisting of both foreigners and natives. The school was to be open to unlimited numbers of both boys and girls, and was to provide boarding facilities so that children from remote areas could also attend (20 or 30 boarders during the first few years). It is interesting to note that in this letter (as in later ones), Faitlovitch made it quite clear that he intended to accept any converted Falashas who wished to be admitted to the school. He had already written punctiliously in his diary about his first meetings with Christian Falashas, making it clear that his educational programme was intended to counter the work done by the Protestants in Ethiopia.

BEFORE THE FIRST WORLD WAR

Aware of the complex political framework within which he would have to work, and caught between the aspirations of the various European nations meddling in the region, Faitlovitch from the start sought the backing of the United States, a country he considered more neutral and disinterested. Particularly after the First World War , he began to apply for help from the Jewish American philanthropic organizations, then better off than their counterparts in Europe, which were suffering from the economic crisis that followed the war. Faitlovitch's actions were thus characterized by the maintenance of intense diplomatic relations, particularly with the Ethiopian rulers, so much so that brokering an agreement between Ménelik II and the United States appears to have taken precedence over establishing the first school.

At the beginning, he thought that the teaching programme should be completely autonomous and controlled by the Italian Pro-Falasha Committee, chaired by Rabbi Margulies. When it came to appointing teachers, Faitlovitch thought of using Yemeni Jews, since 'being Oriental they will be able to get on well with the Falashas and will be used to the climate and primitive life in Abyssinia'.[5]

It was not only an agreement with the Negus that interested Faitlovitch. Upon returning to France from his first journey, he established negotiations with the Italian government for the colony of Eritrea, hoping to be able to open two schools within a short time. In 1890, Italy annexed all of the areas it had acquired on the Red Sea (beginning with the Assab Bay, purchased by the Rubattino Shipping Company in 1869) into one colony, called Eritrea. In 1906, while staying in Paris, Faitlovitch sent the Italian Embassy in Paris a request[6] to found a school in Eritrea and the adviser to the Italian Embassy in Paris, Paolucci di Calboli, asked him to present his concrete proposal on the matter.[7] During the conference tour that Faitlovitch organized among the leading Jewish community centres in Italy in 1906 in order to explain his plan for the establishment of a school in Asmara,[8] he did not neglect to illustrate the advantage that the arrival of the young Falashas, who were good craftsmen and serious workers, would create for the colonial government in Eritrea (most of them lived beyond the Eritrean borders). The project for the school in Eritrea was accepted by the Italian Pro-Falasha Committee, which wrote publicly that it had good reason 'to hope that the steps taken by Faitlovitch with Minister Tittoni and S. E. Martini have been fruitful'.[9] The president of the Alliance, who had received a sum of money from the Jewish Colonial Association for the founding of the school, wanted to make its use conditional on the result of the Nahum mission to Ethiopia.

There was some controversy behind the declarations of the governor of Eritrea, Salvago-Raggi, regarding the granting of land for the school. The *Corriere israelitico* (the mouthpiece for the position of the Jewish Community of Trieste) reported that Salvago-Raggi had granted the land for the school,[10] while Nahum denied this statement. Some years later, Raffaele Ottolenghi denied Nahum's statements regarding a meeting the latter had had with Salvago-Raggi (at the time of Nahum's mission in East Africa). During this meeting, the Italian governor had stated – or so Nahum maintained – that he wished to oppose the Pro-Falasha Committee initiatives. In a letter sent to The *Vessillo israelitico*,[11] Ottolenghi confirmed the allocation of the land in Eritrea.[12] The letter mentioned a sort of promise of land and stated that: 'the Governor of Eritrea … has no problem in granting to the International Committee represented by Dr Faitlovitch a plot of building land for the founding of a school'. The facts, however, proved Nahum right, since the promise was never kept.

Upon his return from his third journey, while passing through Florence to report on the work done among the Falashas,[13] Faitlovitch told the Florentine correspondent of the *Vessillo israelitico* that he had not founded the school in Tekul because the Italian government had feared that the school would create conflicts between the neighbouring populations and the Ethiopian government.[14]

Faitlovitch made it clear, however, that he had not lost the hope of being given a lot on which a school for training Falasha teachers could be built in Eritrea. He said he believed Asmara to be the most suitable town for the purpose, as it was 'near the center of the Falashas and ... not far from Europe'.[15] In the same interview, Faitlovitch announced that he had opened the first primary school in Dembea, near Gondar, and had entrusted the headmastership to Gete Yirmiahu. He provided some details about this school: it took in boarders and provided lodging, food, clothes, and books free of charge (expenses that were paid by the Pro-Falasha Committee) to students coming from remote regions. The education provided was a traditional one.

But Europe was on the verge of war.

AFTER THE FIRST WORLD WAR

At the beginning of 1915,[16] Faitlovitch made an appeal to American Jews to raise the necessary funds for maintaining the school in Dembea so that all of his efforts up to that point would not be in vain. In describing the educational activity at the school, Faitlovitch explained that he worked along two main lines – one aimed at transmitting the religious traditions of mainstream Judaism and the history of the Jewish people, and the other at preserving the traditional religious patrimony – although this second aim was not so clearly stated. Faitlovitch indicated the amount that had been spent on the school during 1913–14[17] and pointed out that this sum had been collected almost entirely in Germany, Italy, Austria, and, to a lesser extent, England. Faitlovitch therefore asked American Jews to raise a sum of $30,000 so that the plan for a teacher training school in Eritrea could also become a reality. This sum was to cover the purchase of the land, the construction of the building, and the appointment of European teachers. In 1920, after seven years away from the Falashas,[18] Faitlovitch, then preparing to leave Rome for Addis Ababa, communicated the details of his next expedition to Eritrea to the Minister of the Colonies (Giovanni Amendola). He asked for a re-evaluation of the application he had made years earlier for the establishment of Jewish schools in Eritrea, for the purpose of preserving the historical group constituted by the

Falashas, for Judaism and for civilization. Faitlovitch had not abandoned the plan[19] for a future teacher training school, to be established not in Asmara, but in Addi-Ugri, also in the Italian colony of Eritrea: 'I got a promise from the colonial authorities there to grant me the permission and the land for such a school.'[20] Addi-Ugri, a small town with an Italian garrison 60 kilometres south of Asmara and 50 kilometres from the Abyssinian border, enjoyed a good climate and was already inhabited by Jews from Arabia. Faitlovitch preferred it to Asmara, he said, because 'it has less contact than Asmara with the corruption of modern civilization'.[21] Faitlovitch had abandoned the plan for a school in Asmara, a town he deemed to be corrupt and unsuitable for providing young Falashas with a religious education. Also, from a practical point of view, it seemed to be easier to obtain land in a more remote area. Furthermore, Addi–Ugri would have the dual advantage of being both a quiet traditional centre and a town located near the Falasha settlements in Tigré, at that time a destination for large migratory waves of Falashas. The school in Eritrea could be the cultural bridge that Faitlovitch sought to build between the Falashas and world Jewry. His initial idea was to maintain his educational programme in virtual proximity to the West.

However, the Addi Ugri project never came to fruition.

The advent of Fascism in 1922 (a movement strongly hostile to Faitlovitch, who was considered a friend of the Negus and was accused of having Zionist sympathies),[22] and the death of Rabbi Margulies, Faitlovitch's great supporter in Italy, marked the end of the Faitlovitch's efforts in Italy and the beginning of a new era in his fund-raising.

Faitlovitch's last endeavour in Italy was precisely in 1923.

A few months before the Addis Ababa school was established,[23] in an exchange of letters with the chief rabbi of Rome, Angelo Sacerdoti, Faitlovitch once again raised the issue of a school in Eritrea. Mussolini had come to power in Italy the previous year, and representatives of Italian Jewry were trying to accommodate to the new Fascist regime, particularly in order to avoid any possible accusations of being not nationalistic enough, of being too cosmopolitan or pro-Zionist. In the beginning, Fascism had shown a tolerant face towards the Jewish religion, and the majority of Italian Jewry supported the regime. Angelo Sacerdoti, after having met Faitlovitch in Rome,[24] wrote to him[25] to say that he had obtained the support of the Ministry of Foreign Affairs for the establishment of a school in Asmara. In this letter, Sacerdoti also reported a conversation he had had with Luigi Federzoni (minister of the colonies), during which he was advised not to allow this school be built primarily as a school for the Falashas. Instead, was told, it should be a school 'not created especially for the Falashas but simply a 'Jewish school' to which Falashas could also be admitted' – in other words, the kind of school that the Union of Italian Jewish Communities and the Jews of Asmara might have asked for.[26] Moreover, Sacerdoti made it clear that the financing would have to be American. Federzoni's intent, completely in keeping with the earlier policies of Salvago-Raggi, was obvious. The minister of the colonies did not intend to support any initiative in favour of a local population unless the Italian Jewish communities, or better still the local organizations, were prepared to accept full responsibility. Faitlovitch encouraged Sacerdoti[27] to continue the work begun by Margulies and to cooperate in establishing a Jewish Centre in Eritrea, reminding him of the benefits and advantages. However, revealing his realism and his knowledge of Italian politics, he asked the chief rabbi of Rome to put every step taken at the ministry – and every promise obtained from the government – in writing. Faitlovitch proposed that the Union of Italian Jewish Communities be responsible for the management and administration of the school and maintain contact with the American Pro-Falasha Committee (established the previous year). He gave his assurance that, as far as he was concerned, Taamrat would be kept available for the school. Sacerdoti responded[28] by saying that he had interpreted Faitlovitch's previous letter as 'an evasive means of letting things drop'. The chief rabbi of Rome specified that neither he nor the Union of Jewish Communities had ever had any intention of establishing a school in Eritrea. They would consent to lend their names to the project, in order to give 'an Italian character to the school itself', but only and exclusively upon formal request by the American Pro-Falasha Committee, which would have to undertake to maintain the school. The Union would only merely assume political responsibility for the school, and would not be involved in its administration. This statement from the chief rabbi of Rome emphasized that the Union would not attempt to obtain the government's permission for the establishment of the school, since it would only benefit of the American Committee, while the Union would have to maintain educational and political control of the school and would be answerable to the Italian government. The school would have to be financed entirely by the American Committee, wrote Sacerdoti, but it should appear to be a school of the Union of Jewish Communities that was helping the Jews of Asmara, or a school of the Israelite community of Asmara. Sacerdoti and the Italian politicians were therefore asking the American Committee to accept all of the burdens and expenses of the operation while leaving the accolades to the Italian government and the Union of Italian Jewish Communities.

The outcome of the affair, which involved exponents of Italian Jewry as well as colonial officials, was that no school was ever built anywhere in the Italian colony – not in Tekul, or in Addi-Ugri, or in Asmara.

From 1923 onward, Faitlovitch preferred to embrace America, as Italy had become uncooperative and hostile, and Europe was becoming impotent.

Italian Jewry showed less and less interest in the Falashas until 1936; then, a few months after the conquest of Ethiopia and the proclamation of the Empire, Italian Jewry again came to the forefront of the Ethiopian scene, when it sent the Florentine lawyer Carlo Alberto Viterbo to Addis.[29]

NOTES

1. D. Lifschitz, 'A School for Jewish Children in Addis Ababa', *Ofaqim* (May 1932), p. 75 (Hebrew).
2. Letter of 3 April 1907, *Fait. Coll.*, f. 94.
3. Ibid.
4. Ibid.
5. Ibid.
6. Letter of 3 December 1906, *Fait. Coll.*, f. 117.
7. Letter of 28 November 1906?, *Fait. Coll.*, f. 117.
8. *Il corriere israelitico*, 45 (1906), pp. 334–5, and *Il vessillo israelitico*, 55 (1907), p. 89.
9. Ibid.
10. *Il corriere israelitico*, 31 January 1908, 31 March 1908, 1 August 1908, 31 September 1909.
11. *Il vessillo israelitico*, 60 (1912), pp. 108–9.
12. *La settimana israelitica*, 16 January 1913.
13. A few weeks before the Pro-Falasha International Committee decided to move from Florence to Frankfurt on 8 June 1914.
14. *Il vessillo israelitico*, 62 (1914), pp. 181–3.
15. Ibid.
16. Letter of 29 January 1915, *Fait. Coll.*, f. 100.
17. 40,000 marks, or $10,000.
18. Letter of 13 January 1920, *Fait. Coll.*, f. 100.
19. Letter to Harry Schneiderman (assistant secretary of the American Jewish Committee in New York) of 4 January 1921, *Fait. Coll.*, f. 100. This followed a letter addressed to Dr Adler, the future chairman of the American Pro-Falasha Committee, mentioned by I. Grinfeld, 'Jews in Addis Ababa: Beginning of the Jewish Community until Italian Occupation', *Sixth International Conference in Ethiopian Studies* (Tel Aviv, 14–17 April 1980), p. 227 and n. 27.
20. Letter of 18 February 1921, *Fait. Coll.*, f. 100.
21. Ibid.
22. See F. Del Canuto, 'Come si giunse alla missione in Etiopia presso i Falascia' in F. Del Canuto (ed.), *Israel: 'Un decennio 1974–1984. Saggi sull'ebraismo italiano* (Rome, 1984), p. 33.
23. The Addis Ababa school was built in 1923. See Chapter 7.
24. From Faitlovitch's diary. Faitlovitch met Sacerdoti in Rome on 18 January 1923.

25. Letter of 19 February 1923, *Fait. Coll.*, f. 100.
26. Ibid. 'on the request of a consortium of the Italian Israelite communities, if possible, in consequence of a demand of the Jews in Asmara, otherwise as a proper initiative'.
27. Letter of 15 June 1923, *Fait. Coll.*, f. 100.
28. Letter of 29 February 1924, *Fait. Coll.*, f. 100.
29. On Viterbo's visit to Ethiopia see Trevisan Semi, *Allo specchio*, pp. 107–23.

5

Faitlovitch's Second Mission (1908–09) and Faitlovitch the Scholar: Quer Durch Abessinien

As pointed out in Chapter 3, the second mission was financed mainly by the Hilfsverein. Faitlovitch spent the first few months of 1908 in Germany, going back and forth between the Hilfsverein and other leading representatives of German Judaism, as well as between scholars of Ethiopian matters such as Mittwoch and historians such as Elbogen. He also travelled back and forth between Germany, England, and Holland in the months preceding the journey to Ethiopia; the purpose of these comings and goings was to raise all of the necessary funds for the upcoming expedition, on which he would be accompanied by Gete. After returning to Paris to pack and to collect the last deliveries from Halévy, as he had done before his first mission, Faitlovitch left the capital on 9 March 1908 and set off for Italy to visit the headquarters of the Pro-Falasha Committee, the other backer of the expedition. He stopped along the way to meet Jewish representatives and Italian *éthiopisants* in Turin, Acqui, Genoa, San Remo, Florence, and Rome. There he picked up copies of the first pamphlet he had ordered printed in Amharic, *Tomare felasiyan* (Letter to the Falashas), to be distributed to the Falashas during his journey. Faitlovitch wanted to use this leaflet to inform the Falashas that in the years between his first and second missions he had become a promoter of the Falasha cause and had made many journeys in order to draw the attention of Jews the world over to their cause. The pamphlet also included the translation of a letter sent to Faitlovitch by European rabbis, promising to send books and support an educational programme for young Falashas. Some of the information in the *tomare* was intended to reassure the Falashas of the survival of the Jews in the East as well as in the West, specifically in order to refute the missionaries, who claimed that Judaism had died out and was now contained within Christianity.[1] The two young men who had been taken to Europe in 1904, referred to in the letter by their original names, Wondimagegnahu Gete and Taamrat (Fanta David's son), were reported to be well and immersed in the study of religion and wisdom. In any case, as we have seen, Faitlovitch succeeded in obtaining enough funds to take Gete with him, as proof of the young man's survival. They both set sail from Naples on 3 April. Their first stop was Cairo, where they spent the Feast of the Passover. This allowed Faitlovitch to form a local Pro-Falasha Committee, presided over by Dr Cohn, and to get the local community involved. They left Suez on 26 April and arrived in Massawa on 1 May. As we can read in *Quer*, Faitlovitch's goals for that journey were:

1. to convince the Falashas that they had not been wrong to base their hopes and expectations on my first stay in Abyssinia, to convince them to extend and deepen the relationships established at that time, to inspire their courage and strengthen their faith in Judaism.
2. to distribute a book I have written in the Amharic language,[2] in which I reassured the Falashas of the affection that the European Jews had for them and urged them to persist in the sincere faith of their fathers. Furthermore, I wish to deliver them a letter written in Hebrew and signed by many rabbis from different countries, which I have translated and printed in the book.
3. to pave the way for the organization of a school for the Falashas, consulting them about where to build it and the potential of such an institution.
4. to take some young Falashas from Abyssinia and offer them teacher training, as the *Hilfsverein* is willing to accept them at their institute in Jerusalem.[3]

After spending a few days in Massawa, which was just enough time to meet with the Italian authorities (Talamonti) and with two Falasha converts,[4] Faitlovitch and Gete continued on their journey, taking the same route that Faitlovitch had taken on his previous journey (Asmara, Addi Ugri, Axum) until they reached an area near Addi Shoa. Here Faitlovitch met up with Nahum and Eberlin (his travelling companion), who were coming from the opposite direction (Addis Ababa). Faitlovitch wanted to leave Gete in Ethiopia with his parents, but they insisted that he take their son back to Palestine and Europe so that he could complete his training.[5] It was during this trip that Faitlovitch took Gete's cousin, Salomon Isaac, who was being trained by the high priests of Guraba,[6] where he was to have become a *qes*, to study at the Hilfsverein's school in Jerusalem.

QUER DURCH ABESSINIEN AND *MASA EL-HA-FALASHIM*

This description of the journey is the only one in print that was written by Faitlovitch himself. The volume was published in German, in Berlin in 1910, and was written when his memories were still fresh and when he might still have had a future as a teacher of Ethiopian studies. It was dedicated to the lawyer Moise Finzi of Florence, a member of the Italian Pro-Falasha Committee. There is an abridged version of this book, accompanied by 60 photographs and a map showing the route followed, published in Hebrew in a translation by Martin Wurmbrand, with a preface by Yitzhak Ben Zvi and an introduction by Israel Ben Zeev.[7] However, the Hebrew translation also constitutes a rewrite of the book and is essentially a revised version of the journey, which Faitlovitch's friends took the opportunity to publish once the author had deceased. Some very important parts of the German text have been omitted from the Hebrew version. It is significant that these deleted parts referred to the disagreement between Faitlovitch and Nahum and their meetings during the journey. The intention was probably to promulgate a version that was purged of any account of the events of the early twentieth century, before the relationship between the two adversaries improved, leading to effective cooperation. The fact that Nahum, once he became chief rabbi of Cairo, had committed himself to finding solutions for the Falashas who had settled in Cairo (Tadesse Jacob[8] from 1931 to 1940 and Taamrat Emmanuel from 1937 to 1940) seemed to authorize the translator to create a different image of the Alliance's emissary, to supersede the one that had prevailed since 1908. The fact that Ben Zeev himself, under the name of Wolfenson, was the person responsible for Nahum and Faitlovitch's *rapprochement* in Cairo in the 1930s,[9] and the fact that he is one of the editors of the Hebrew version of the book, points to a work of censorship and historical revision.

The meeting between Faitlovitch and Nahum (with Eberlin) at Addi Shoa (in Sciré, not far from Adenkato) took place on Sunday 21 June 1908.[10] Faitlovitch was returning from a visit to Adenkato, during which the local Falashas had expressed their indignation at the fact that Nahum and Eberlin had passed through their village in the middle of the *shabbat*. They thought the two men must have been *frendji*, i.e. non-Jews, as it was unthinkable for a rabbi to travel on the *shabbat*.[11] Faitlovitch quoted the phrases used by two Falashas, who were absolutely furious about Nahum's non-observance of the Sabbath rules. Once they had ascertained that Faitlovitch knew the two *frendji* and that they were in fact Jews, the Falashas insulted Faitlovitch too:

> You're all imposters, not Jews! Our Rabbi says you want to teach our children! Are these two *frendji* supposed to be your brothers, are they supposed to be Jews? Why did they arrive here on the Sabbath? What do you want to teach our children? You want to teach them not to observe the Holy Sabbath and to become Christians![12]

Faitlovitch had to rely on the good offices of Gete in order to be recognized as a Jew!

This part of the story is completely missing from the Hebrew translation,[13] as are the quotations from Nahum, present in the German book, regarding the Falasha converts.[14] At the end of the German version, Faitlovitch strongly contested the conclusions that Nahum had drawn from his own journey, on the basis of which he had claimed that it was not worth pursuing any action in connection with the Falashas, particularly in view of their low population. (Nahum maintained that there were 700 families, while Faitlovitch said there were 50,000 people.)[15] Nahum also concluded that in any case, the Italian colonial authorities would not grant any land for the establishment of a Falasha school (in Eritrea) or cooperate in any way in educational projects. This observation, though contested by Faitlovitch, proved, in the ensuing years, to be correct. However, there is no trace of any of this in the Hebrew version. Even the controversy with the Alliance, which is described in detail in the introduction to the German volume, is summarized in just a few short sentences in the Hebrew version. Nothing remains, for example, of the derisory tone that enlivened the original version, particularly Faitlovitch's description of the Alliance's doubts about the accuracy of the research he had conducted on his first journey:

> They accused me of having met only a few Falasha families and of not having visited large Falasha settlements in the villages of a particular province. It is true that I was unable to make this visit, but for a not insignificant reason: these settlements did not exist.[16]

The other missing part concerns the leading characters in the history of the Italian colony in Eritrea, and the departure of the Italian colonial authorities from Eritrea,[17] apparently considered irrelevant in 1959 by the editors of this account of the second journey.[18] Also missing are many of the notes included in the German book, while others have been summarized and incorporated into the text.[19]

AT ADEN

From this second journey onwards, Faitlovitch adopted the habit of allowing himself a rest period at Aden before setting sail to go back to Europe. This period was also used for maintaining contact with the Jewish community in Aden, thereby keeping it involved in the project in support of the Falasha cause, and for acquiring the clothes his young students would need in Europe. In any case, the weeks spent in Aden became a habit during subsequent expeditions and were justified, in Faitlovitch's mind, by the fact that he was unable to tolerate the tropical climate of Ethiopia for long periods of time. The idea of his interrupting his mission in Ethiopia to spend some time in Aden at the expense of the American Pro-Falasha Committee would become a source of controversy between Faitlovitch and the American backers during the fifth mission. Stopping in Aden was also significant in his strategy of involving all of world Jewry. Through the Pro-Falasha Committees' embrace of his 'holy work', he worked to form a large network of Jewish philanthropists, extending from Florence and Frankfurt to Cairo and Aden, from Palestine to America and South Africa. He created an imagined community built up around the myth of the 'lost tribes' and the expansion of the ethnic boundaries of Judaism. When the boys accompanied him to Aden, for instance, he would take pictures of them, which he distributed to the committees or to the rabbis or families that might welcome the young Falashas in Europe, attempting to make concrete what had earlier seemed to be just an old myth. In a first step on the path that the boys were later to follow, Faitlovitch separated himself from the children while in Aden, leaving them in the care of local Jewish families. It is difficult to say whether this was part of a conscious strategy he had developed or simply a pragmatic way to take a breather after a long period spent in Ethiopia.

At the end of the second mission, which lasted a year, Faitlovitch started his return journey with the two boys on 11 May 1909. They arrived in Jerusalem on 28 May, after stopping to visit two settlements, Petah Tikva and Rehovot, which had been created in the previous century.[20]

FAITLOVITCH THE SCHOLAR[21]

The account of the second mission in Ethiopia is perhaps one of Faitlovitch's longest works. He published various pamphlets on the Falashas in different languages (French, Italian, German, English, and

Hebrew),[22] and five brochures in Amharic,[23] the second of which we know was proofread by Taamrat.[24] Faitlovitch had acquired many manuscripts during the three months of the second period that he had spent in Amba Gualit.[25] He had obtained various handwritten versions of the *Gadla Abraham* (Death and Will of Abraham),[26] and had patiently copied out other manuscripts, such as those containing the writings of Abba Zabra.[27] Faitlovitch took advantage of the long period that Taamrat spent in Ethiopia as principal of the Falasha school in Addis by having him buy more manuscripts. He also made him responsible for finding Ethiopian scholars who were experts in *ge'ez* and in the interpretation of biblical texts (according to the Ethiopian tradition) in order to have them transcribe and translate these texts. For example, the translation of the Psalms was entrusted to the *aleka* Estifanos,[28] an Ethiopian intellectual who was an expert in *ge'ez* literature, in traditional religious and civil codes, and, especially, in the different variations of the text of the Psalms.[29] Estifanos translated the Psalms from *ge'ez* into Amharic, and this work attracted the interest of the Negus, who sent a secretary to the Faitlovitch school[30] to copy the manuscript. Faitlovitch was also in touch with the Ethiopian monks of Jerusalem, whom he visited regularly during the periods he spent in Palestine. They helped him with the clarification, explanation, and interpretation of religious texts according to the Ethiopian tradition.[31] Faitlovitch's activities as a scholar of Ethiopian literature date back to the period between the first and second missions, particularly during the years 1906–10. He translated *Mota Muse* (The Death of Moses) (1907) into Hebrew and French,[32] and added versions in Arabic (in the French translation). He published his doctoral dissertation, which consisted of the editing and translation into French of *Proverbes Abyssins* (1907) (dedicated to his parents), followed by *Nouveaux proverbes abyssins* (1909). In 1910 he published *Versi abissini*, a collection of popular poems that he had translated from Tigrigna into Italian. This was an important collection that he had 'gathered from the voice of the people'.[33] While Faitlovitch was in Ethiopia in 1908, he copied out some manuscripts himself, with the idea of publishing them at some point in the future,[34] but never followed up on these youthful plans. In fact he wrote very few scientific papers, despite the fact that he was encouraged to publish more by Carlo Conti Rossini, the Italian *éthiopisant*, who never tired of reminding Faitlovitch that he had a duty to posterity, since he had so many manuscripts in his possession. Upon the premature death of A. Z. Aescoly, the scholars who had taught at the École nationale des langues vivantes in Paris and who could have taken Faitlovitch's place[35] as the expert in Falasha religious literature, Taamrat wrote some moving words in remembrance of him, adding that he was waiting to receive some photographs of a Falasha ritual taken by C. A. Viterbo, in order to compare them with the material collected by Aescoly, and concluding bitterly: 'What a pity that I can't do the same with the material in Mr Faitlovitch's possession!'[36]

From the time of his third mission onwards, Faitlovitch wrote mainly pamphlets or informative and propagandistic letters, in addition to the *tomare* distributed among the Falashas during his missions.

The last important work undertaken by Faitlovitch (with A. Kahana) was the translation from *ge'ez* into Hebrew of the book of *Enoch* in 1936.[37]

In the 1940s, Faitlovitch published a few articles in the journal *Ha-am ve ha-sefer*, the organ of Brit Ivrit Olamit, examining the 'revival' of Hebrew among the Ethiopian Jews, recounting the role played by Slouschz,[38] and proposing renewed action to support the school and the education of the Beta Israel.[39]

In the end, the only travel memoir that Faitlovitch published was *Quer durch Abessinien*, even though he had carefully completed the pages of his diary during every expedition. Perhaps his methodical way of noting even the most insignificant things was due to an obsessive nature rather than a real interest in a historical or ethnographical work. Faitlovitch was more interested in action, i.e. 'missionary' activity and wandering in search of the 'lost tribes': he wanted to be more of an *ish ma'aseh* than a scholar.

When he was old and weary, in the quiet of his house in Tel Aviv, he wanted to devote himself to the publication of the manuscripts and materials he had collected, but he had begun to suffer from failing eyesight. This prevented him from doing the things he had put off doing until the quiet time of his final years, but it would not have been easy in any event to undertake the scholarly work he had abandoned too many years before.

THE *TOMARE*

The first *tomare*, which Faitlovitch wrote in Italy (1908) and had printed in Rome at the Vatican Press,[40] was distributed during his second journey. This pamphlet was intended to re-establish contact and summarize the Falasha story that had begun in the previous century, from the arrival of the Protestant missionaries to Faitlovitch's first departure from Ethiopia.

In the second *tomare* (1912), written on his return from his second journey, Faitlovitch wrote about his meeting with Menelik II, which took place in the imperial residence of Entoto. This pamphlet summarizes the diplomatic speech Faitlovitch made before the emperor of Ethiopia. He praised the attitude of religious tolerance that Menelik II had demonstrated in allowing the Falashas to practise their faith. However, the letter ended with a condemnation of the difficult conditions in which the Falashas were forced to live in the regions inhabited by the Tigray and Amhara populations. The Falashas, wrote Faitlovitch, were being discriminated against because they were accused of being *buda*, or witch doctors, who, according to popular belief in Ethiopia, turned into hyenas at night and pillaged their neighbours' livestock. Many were enslaved and deported to other areas, where they were forced to build churches and palaces without receiving any kind of payment, leaving their wives and children reduced to starvation. On hearing this, according to Faitlovitch in this *tomare*, Menelik II promised to intervene with an appropriate decree to prevent it from happening again.

In the third *tomare* (1915), which he wrote after his third journey, Faitlovitch wrote that the outbreak of war had prevented him from getting back to Ethiopia as he had promised to do. He entreated the Falashas to remember that they belonged to the chosen people, to be proud of that fact, and to persevere in their faith.

The fourth *tomare* (1928), one of the pamphlets that were most widely distributed among the Falashas in the ensuing years,[41] was written in Aden in 1923, during the fifth mission. In this *tomare*, Faitlovitch expressed himself quite openly, criticizing the customs of the Falashas, maintaining that they had allowed themselves to be overly influenced by local society. He complained that during the time he had spent with the Falashas, he had observed a tendency among families to quarrel, and a high number of divorces, desertions, and new relationships that had led to the birth of children who, according to Jewish tradition, would be considered 'bastards' until after the tenth generation. The Falashas were encouraged to resist the temptation to abandon their religion, in order to avoid being foreigners among other populations without being illuminated by divine law. The suffering they endured in the name of Judaism, they were told, was a way of keeping their true religion uncorrupted.

The last *tomare* (1936), written in Addis in 1934, but, like its predecessors, printed in Rome, referred to the success of the negotiations initiated during the reign of Menelik II and continued by *ras* Tafari, the future Haile Sellassie, aimed at obtaining a decree to prohibit the deportation of Falasha craftsmen as slaves. Faitlovitch wrote that in 1928, *ras* Tafari had finally issued a decree ordering that all craftsmen must be paid for their work, that all work must be carried out under conditions of freedom, and that the work day must be limited to a maximum of eight hours. The decree also imposed financial sanctions on anyone who violated it. Another decree also prohibited the use of the insult *buda* (sorcery). This was clearly a personal success for Faitlovitch, who, taking advantage of his audiences at court and his good relationship with *ras* Tafari, had managed to direct the sovereign's attention to the most serious problems affecting the Falashas and to gain provisions for sanctions. Faitlovitch's pride in this great achievement can be felt in this letter.

The distribution of these letters in Amharic is further evidence of the influence of the Protestants' work on Faitlovitch's practices and on his code of intervention. In fact, the Christian missionaries were the first to translate the Gospel into Amharic and to distribute printed brochures among the Falashas. Thus they enabled families to possess printed texts – something very rare in Ethiopia – which, as demonstrated later, revealed itself to be a useful device in the conversion campaign. People had difficulty understanding *ge'ez*, the ancient holy language in which the Bible was written, and were enthusiastic about having something written in Amharic, their spoken language. It was common for Falasha young people to go to the mission school just in order to obtain a printed book. Faitlovitch used the same device, but transformed it into an instrument for creating an imagined community. With his *tomare* written in Amharic, he disseminated his ideas and an awareness of the fact that world Jewry really existed. His letters in Amharic are kept as precious relics among the families that still possess them, which is understandable given that these writings constitute evidence of the beginning of an imagined community, according to Anderson theory. The *tomare* demonstrate that Faitlovitch created bonds between Falashas and Jews throughout the world, the beginning of a process that continues today.

NOTES

1. I am indebted to Ambessa Teferra, who gave me his translations of the five letters written by Faitlovitch in Amharic.
2. This refers to *Tomare falasiyan*.
3. J. Faitlovitch, *Quer*, pp. 11–12.
4. See his journal, 6 May 1908.
5. Faitlovitch, *Quer*, p. 105.

6. Ibid. and see Weil, 'The life', p. 42.
7. *Masa el ha-falashim* (Tel Aviv, 1959).
8. Tadesse Jacob, 'The History of my Life', *Fait. Coll.*, f. 138 (Hebrew).
9. See Chapter 9.
10. Faitlovitch, *Quer*, p. 47.
11. Ibid., pp. 47–9.
12. Ibid., p. 47 and *Masa*, p. 55.
13. *Quer*, p. 94: 'as Nahum maintained'.
14. *Masa*, p. 83; here the text has been altered to 'as others wrote'.
15. *Quer*, pp. 172–4.
16. Ibid., p. 10.
17. *Quer*, pp. 162–5, *Masa*, p. 134.
18. *Quer*, p. 159–61, *Masa*, pp. 132–3.
19. The names of the people they met in Cairo (Mittwoch) or in Jerusalem, such as Ephraim Cohn and Goldschmidt (the principals of the Hilfsverein school in Jerusalem) have also been omitted.
20. *Quer*, p. 167, *Masa*, pp. 137–8.
21. For Faitlovitch as a scholar see Y. Grinfeld, 'Jacques Faitlovitch – "Father" of the Falashas' in Y. Avner, N. Berger and K. Kaufman Shelemay (eds), *The Jews of Ethiopia: A People in Transition* (Tel Aviv, 1986), pp. 28–32 (Hebrew).
22. *Notes d'un voyage chez les Falachas, Juifs d'Abyssinie* (Paris, 1905); *Les Falachas d'aprés les explorateurs* (Florence, 1907); *Gli ebrei d'Abissinia* (Acqui, 1907); *Falascha Briefe* (Berlin, 1913); *The Black Jews of Abyssinia* (New York, 1915); *Notice sur les Juifs d'Abyssinie* (Basle, 1916); *The Falashas* (Philadelphia, 1920); 'The Hypothetical Laws of the Falashas', *Tarbitz*, 7, 3–4 (1936) (Hebrew), in which he disagreed with A. Aeskoly, accusing him of having little knowledge of the subject; and *The Romance of the Falashas* (New York: The American Pro-Falasha Committee, 1939).
23. *Tomare felasyan* (Letter to the Falashas) (Rome, 1908), *Tomare ebiwna* (Letter of brotherhood) (Rome, 1912), *Tomare nazizo* (Letter of consolation) (Rome, 1915), *Tomare salam* (Letter of peace) (Rome, 1928), *Tomare absari* (Letter of the bearer of good news) (Rome, 1936).
24. See letter of 31 May 1927 in Trevisan Semi, *L'epistolario*, p. 133.
25. *Quer*, p. 103.
26. *Quer*, p. 95, n 2. In the Hebrew version this note omits the reference to the manuscripts in Faitlovitch's possession.
27. *Quer*, p. 89, n 1 (this note is omitted in the Hebrew version).
28. See letter of 10 December 1932 in Trevisan Semi, *L'epistolario*, p. 153.
29. Ibid. and letter. 29, p. 167.
30. See letter of 15 September 1933 in Trevisan Semi, *L'epistolario*, p. 177.
31. Ibid. and letter of 16 September 1933, p. 180.
32. This text (with *Proverbes abyssins*), which Faitlovitch gave to the 'Negus' Menelik II during his audience at Addis Ababa (30 November 1908), won great admiration from the sovereign, who congratulated Faitlovitch on his excellent knowledge of the Ethiopian language and expressed even more curiosity about the Hebrew language. After asking for confirmation that Hebrew was still used by the Jews, Menelik asked Faitlovitch to read some lines; see *Quer*, p. 133.
33. *Versi abissini* (Rome, 1910), p. 3.
34. *Quer*, p. 89, n 1.
35. A. Z. Aescoly, 'The Falashas: a Bibliography', *Qiriat sefer*, 12 (1935–36), pp. 254–65, 370–83, 498–505; 13 (1936–37), pp. 250–65, 383–93 (Hebrew); and *Recueil de textes falachas* (Paris, 1951), which was published posthumously.
36. See letter of 18 January 1949 in Trevisan Semi, *L'Epistolario*, p. 331.
37. *Fait. Coll.*, f. 139.
38. 'The Hebrew Language among the Jews of Abyssinia', *Ha-am ve-ha-sefer* (May 1941), pp. 24–5 (Hebrew).
39. 'The renewal of the action towards the Hebrew Schools in Abyssinia', *Ha-am ve-ha-sefer* (June 1942), pp. 32–3 (Hebrew).
40. The Vatican printing press had Ethiopian characters.
41. Taamrat reports that this pamphlet continued to be distributed during C. A. Viterbo's journey in 1936–37. See letter of 7 August 1936 in Trevisan Semi, *L'epistolario*, p. 225.

6

Faitlovitch's Third Mission (1913) and his Struggle Against the Protestant Missionaries: *A* Goel *in Ethiopia*

In a speech at the synagogue in Florence on the first day of *Pesach* 1907, Margulies reminded the congregants of their duty to show solidarity with the Falashas. He interpreted the precept regarding the dipping of a bunch of hyssop in blood as a paschal sacrifice (Exodus 12:22) in light of rabbinical tradition, reminding them that the brotherhood of a reunited Israel was held together by this spirit of sacrifice. They therefore had a commitment to their dispersed brothers, including 'a small branch of our race, hurled down there by one of the many storms that passed over our heads',[1] meaning, of course, the Falashas. During these months, Margulies used his full authority to support Faitlovitch's candidature for the Ethiopian mission. In Margulies' eyes, Faitlovitch was a modern version of the rabbis who had wandered for centuries from one community to another, reinforcing bonds, gathering information, discovering branches of the dispersed tribes, and bringing evidence of Western Jewish life to the remote regions of the East.

Their shared views on Judaism, despite a hint of secularism on Faitlovitch's part, were consolidated during the dispute with the Alliance. The trust Margulies had placed in Faitlovitch was the basis of a long friendship, which benefited the young members of Beta Israel who were brought to Europe by Faitlovitch to be educated in traditional Judaism. Just a few months before Margulies' death in 1922, Faitlovitch, returning from his fourth visit to Ethiopia, entreated him to take in Hizkiahu Finkas, one of the four young men he was bringing back to Europe.[2] Even their personalities complemented each other. Margulies, who was very diplomatic and not at all impulsive, exerted a certain influence and control over Faitlovitch, who was rather autocratic and self-assured.

In the correspondence between Margulies and Faitlovitch during the latter's third visit to Ethiopia, Faitlovitch emphasized the Beta

Israel's traditions. He revealed not only his interest and involvement, but also the contradictory feelings typical of the European Jew who is irritated because he doesn't understand the codes of a different culture. It made him uncomfortable when he was mistaken for the *goel* or asked to prove himself by revealing the exact year of the Messiah's coming or by interpreting the dreams (perhaps the hopes?) of the members of the group. When he wrote to Margulies, he gave free rein to his thoughts and expressed how he really felt, which he was obviously unable to do in his propaganda speeches and his official letters. The correspondence with Margulies provides a more well-rounded picture of Faitlovitch – including, for example, the longing to be alone that he often felt in the Beta Israel villages, which he confided only to his diary and to Margulies.

THE BEGINNING OF THE JEWISH COUNTER-MISSION SUPPORTED BY MARGULIES

During Faitlovitch's journey of 1908–09, Margulies, though convinced of the necessity for an immediate educational project, had to curb Faitlovitch's initiatives, as the funds from the Italian Pro-Falasha Committee and the Hilfsverein were barely sufficient to cover travel expenses for Faitlovitch and the young Gete. The rabbi was anxious to inform Faitlovitch (in Addis Adaba) that a sum[3] that had already been sent to him were the total funds available at that time. He gave a very explicit account of the financial conditions that would prevent the school from opening:

> Unfortunately, so far the International Committee has done nothing at all. We have not yet launched the appeal because the final Committee was not formed until July, when it would have been completely useless to launch the appeal[4] because everyone is on holiday. For this reason we have not received any money from abroad, but because I do not want you to have financial problems, I have asked Raffaele Ottolenghi to send you 2,000 (two thousand) lire, which I hope you received on your arrival in Addis Adaba. However, this leaves the Italian Committee's coffers *completely empty*. So you must use that money very *sparingly*, and for the moment you can take no more than *three* or *four* boys, who may possibly go on with you to Jerusalem. Because of this total lack of money, we cannot, unfortunately, even think about opening a school in Eritrea.[5]

In 1909, while Faitlovitch was still in Ethiopia, Margulies turned to the President of the Alliance, despite their past disagreements, to ask for a financial contribution on their part. The rabbi, disputing the figures in the Nahum report,[6] reminded Leven that there were substantial numbers of Falashas who had remained in the Jewish faith and who ardently wished to receive religious instruction, 'the only means of defence against the insidious dangers of the Christian mission'.[7] The following month, Margulies wrote another letter insisting that:

> 1) the Falashas are very anxious to have our assistance and they *urgently need it* if they are to remain Jews and not succumb in the struggle for their faith;
> 2) Dr Faitlovitch is the only person at present able to successfully carry out missionary work among the Falashas.[8]

Using the same type of language as the Christian missionaries, Margulies also requested that a small missionary post be established, to be run by Faitlovitch, assisted by a young rabbi.[9] 'At the same time,' he wrote, 'the missionaries would produce a Jewish calendar and the most essential basic books such as the catechism and history of the Bible in Amharic, which would be distributed among the Falashas.'[10] As pointed out in Chapter 5, the translation of the Gospel into Amharic was one of the successful tools employed by the Protestants, and Faitlovitch and Margulies wished to co-opt this initiative. The idea of the Jewish calendar, in particular, was considered a high priority by the Jewish mission; Viterbo, too, worked on this task during his trip to Ethiopia in 1936–37.

Margulies also pointed out that the Italian government 'not only does not oppose the founding of the school in Eritrea but has also decided to grant some special terms'.[11] In reality, as was to become clear during the third journey, Margulies was being rather optimistic about the special terms offered by the Italian government.

It is important to stress the extent to which the competition with the Protestant missionaries played a role over the years – from the beginning, when Halévy was sent to Ethiopia, through Margulies' time, all the way up to Faitlovitch's death. Pointing out what the Christian missionaries were doing was a good device for obtaining more financial help from western Jews, and Faitlovitch, in particular, emphasized the importance of the Jewish honour in the western world. The example of the Protestants' commitment, and the language and the programmes they used to convince people to convert, were taken as good models that could be used also by Jews.

THE THIRD JOURNEY

Faitlovitch arrived in Massara on 2 January 1913 and left Massara on 2 November 1913. The progress of the 'French Jew', as Faitlovitch was called, was promptly noted in the Protestant mission's reports, as were his previous journeys. The increased difficulties experienced by the Protestants as a result of the Jewish counter-mission were attributed to the money that Faitlovitch was distributing among the population:

> In some places the Falashas have become very difficult to be reached through the visits of Dr Faitlowitch [*sic*], who distributed much money amongst them. In some places the Falashas said 'We expect Dr Faitlowitch [*sic*] to come back and bring money. He will build us a synagogue and help us to strengthen the religion of the Falashas.'[12]

The money mentioned may have been the sum requested by the Falashas for the reconstruction of the ancient *mesgid* (synagogue) on Mount Hoharua, in the province of Djanfankera, which Faitlovitch had visited in 1908. The synagogue, dating back to the fifteenth century, had been destroyed by fire;[13] it was one of the rare buildings (two or three others still existed), as noted by Faitlovitch, to have been constructed along the model of the Temple of Jerusalem. Faitlovitch wrote to Margulies: 'The Falashas have asked me to intercede on their behalf to try and obtain some funds so that they can rebuild this important temple, which was always the intellectual centre of their religious figures.'[14]

The Protestants, with obvious satisfaction, also publicized the problems Faitlovitch had encountered in his programme for 'Judaizing' the Beta Israel. They wrote: 'Not all Falashas, however, are in favour of the French Jew and his teaching Talmudic doctrines in Abyssinia. Some monks in Wogera would not have nothing [*sic*]) to do with him and literally chased him away.'[15] This refers to the Falashas' opposition to the changes Faitlovitch had tried to make to the religion practiced by the Beta Israel, in particular the banning of monasticism and sacrifices.

But it is important to retrace the main steps of Faitlovitch's third journey.

As indicated above, during the period he spent in Asmara, Faitlovitch tried to lay the foundations of his educational programme and obtain from the Italian governor a small piece of land at Tekul, where most of the Falashas were living while waiting for the chance to settle in Asmara. The governor made it clear that the Italian government did not want any missionary work to be carried out in the colony, but that it had agreed to the building of a denominational school (that is, for the Jews of the colony) in Asmara. However, Faitlovitch harboured strong doubts about the appropriateness of opening a school in Asmara, a city that he considered corrupt, and he feared the negative influence of the resident Jewish community (made up of Turks, Adenis, and Yemenis). 'Asmara,' he wrote, 'is already a modern town with all the typical faults. There is also a Jewish community whose members surely cannot be models for the regeneration of the Falashas. The community here is made up of about fifteen Jewish families from Turkey and a similar number of Jews from the Yemen or Aden … Asmara will lead them to enjoy material advantage but suffer moral disadvantage.'[16] He feared that the Falashas might be corrupted by material advancement, and that it would no longer be possible for them to play a part in bringing the oriental spirit of the Bible to corrupted western Jewry.

The colonial government's attitude seemed to him to have changed since the days of F. Martini[17] (the Italian governor at the time of his first journey), which did not seem to augur well at all. The equivocation and lack of a firm decision led him to write:

> The government here is playing at politics with us and I cannot waste too much time now. I do not think we will get what we want from the colonial government … The colony has changed a lot since Governor Martini's days … but it could change again. Never mind! You know Italy better than I do and I hope that its people's spirit will gradually filter into its colony.[18]

Faitlovitch gained a more accurate perception of Italian hostility, and of the anti-Semitic feelings of some civil servants at Gondar, when he arrived there on 10 April 1913. After two months of tents and encampments, Gondar, with its concrete buildings and the presence of Europeans, seemed like 'a precious gift'.[19] However, the joy he felt at being once again in the company of Europeans soon changed to anger and bitterness when he realized that the Jewish military doctor, Vittorio Calò from Pisa (whose presence had been made known to Jewish circles), was 'first and foremost Italian'. He was concerned only about concealing his Jewish origins, and was not at all willing to get involved with the Falashas. Furthermore, Giuseppe Ostini (a former Member of Parliament), the head of the Italian trade office in Gondar where the Jewish doctor was based, was anti-Semitic; he was also a gossip who was 'not blessed with much intelligence',[20] and he was far more hostile to the pro-Falasha project than Faitlovitch had imagined. After his first meetings with Ostini in Asmara in 1909 (and later meetings in Rome), Faitlovitch had already observed 'that he has very little sympathy with our movement … the smell of modern anti-Semitism always emerged from his conversation'.[21] However, he had not realized that Ostini was actively putting spokes in the wheels of everything associated with the pro-Falasha project. Ostini's hostility is evident from the letters he sent to Raggi, the Governor of Eritrea, in which he declared that Jewish propaganda was contrary to the political and economic interests of Italy.[22] Faitlovitch's eyes were opened by Calò, who revealed to him in confidence that 'he [Ostini] and the director of Eritrean civil affairs, Mr Allori, are absolutely opposed to any Jewish establishment in the colony'. Faitlovitch added that Ostini had found in the Falashas 'a delicacy suited to his character', and was using them for his own ends, maintaining that Italian prestige would be diminished if the colony's authorities were to support the pro-Falasha project. Faitlovitch mistrusted both Ostini and Calò so much that he stopped sending his mail through their office.[23]

It was during Faitlovitch's stay in Abseghié (in Dembea, where Gete's parents came from) that the Falashas of the village and the surrounding area persuaded him to open a school in that region. 'Everyone applauded this proposal, urging me to hasten its establishment,' he wrote, 'and they all predicted that it would be a great success',[24] as long as *ras* Walda Giyorgis, under whose jurisdiction the area fell, promised to protect it. Faitlovitch therefore went to the *ras*'s residence at Debra Tabor and managed to gain the powerful Ethiopian leader's protection not only for the school, but also for its future principal (Gete). Faitlovitch immediately wrote to Margulies with the news that the school could actually open: 'After the success achieved here I do not want to waste any more time before responding to the Falashas' wishes, and I have decided to start implementing our plans for a small school in Abyssinia.'[25]

FAITLOVITCH AS A *GOEL* IN ABSEGHIÉ

Faitlovitch stayed in Abseghié for over a month, going on short reconnaissance expeditions to Amba Gualit and Debra Tabor, the provinces south of Dembea and west of Lake Tana, where he was overwhelmed by the comings and goings of people who considered him to be the *goel*, asking him all kinds of questions about the coming of the Messiah.

'They come up to me with sometimes bizarre questions to which they all want answers,' he wrote.

> They ask me to enlighten them about Israel's suffering and want to know when they will be liberated. They ask me the precise place where the Messiah is hiding and the precise day that he will come to Ethiopia to take them to their homeland in Palestine. 'Is it time for us to come back?' is their unanimous question and everyone asks me minute details about this. They all say they are ready for their exodus because they feel strongly that it is near. They are impatient for it to happen and they are now worried about their future voyage.[26]

The questions about the time of the Messiah's coming echoed those addressed in 1862 to the 'head of the Jews' in Jerusalem by a Beta Israel priest.[27] That was the period in which Abba Mahari was trying to convince the Falasha community, with promises of Bible miracles to be repeated, that it was possible to emigrate to Jerusalem. This was related by Halévy, an eyewitness to the desolation following the abandonment of the land.[28] In Faitlovitch's time, the Beta Israel were particularly concerned about the risk of the Sabbath not being observed[29] if they were to undertake a long voyage, so they bombarded the Orientalist, who was becoming less and less patient, with urgent questions. Faitlovitch explained that the Falashas were very worried about the prospect of a voyage and they asked him for his opinion about it, but remained convinced by his reasoning. 'I assure them that they will make the crossing in big ships and that they should not worry because these boats will go on their own,' he wrote,

> but all my arguments fail to reassure them and they ask if they can sail on nonautomotive boats so that the Sabbath may be observed. Some of them are more modest, not asking for these impossibilities, but are willing to walk to Palestine. However, they want to know if God will divide the Red Sea and create dry land so that they can cross it as the Israelites did when they left Egypt.

In the same letter, he wrote at length about the Falashas' beliefs about the Messiah, the creator of an 'empire of justice and happiness'. These beliefs were quite contradictory and confused, as S. Kaplan has shown.[30] In a letter to Margulies, after insisting on the traditional aspect of the liberator and restorer of peace, Faitlovitch added:

> The Falashas do not attribute the Messiah with any divine character or give him any particular competence. They call him *Tewodros* [Teodoros], gift from God, which ... is synonymous with the Hebrew word *Natanael* [Hebrew], perhaps used by the Ancient Jews of Egypt to indicate the liberator of the Israelites from the foreign yoke.

Faitlovitch emphasized the Falashas' completely human portrayal of the Messiah:

> His personality is of no particular importance to the Falashas ... He is as mortal as humans and, after fulfilling the destiny of Providence, he will give up his place to his successors who, like him, will reign over Israel in the promised land ... then Jerusalem will be the pivot of inspiration with all the eyes of the world on it for the supreme judge of all nations will reside there.

Faitlovitch was obsessed with the subject of the Messiah and he made no secret of this to Margulies:

> This is their favourite topic of conversation with me and they bombard me with strange, embarrassing questions. Although they no longer regard me as the actual Messiah, they would at least still like to consider me his messenger, who has come to Abyssinia to look for his brothers and prepare them to receive the elected one. They are trying very hard to persuade me of this mission of mine and they beg me to hasten my advent in the name of he who sent me to them. Oh! I no longer recognize myself, I no longer know how to answer them. How happy they would be if I gave them an answer that they are looking for.

Faitlovitch, who did not hesitate to present himself as a saviour, ended up getting into trouble when the role he was playing was taken too seriously by the people in the villages. Another thing that made him uncomfortable was being questioned on messianic subjects linked to science and modernity, such as the age and duration of the world. He added that his ignorance in these matters 'puts me in an irritating situation' in that his obvious annoyance was interpreted in the villages as though he had something to hide. He wrote, 'they are sure I am hiding the truth'. The Falashas of Abseghié even contested the date on the Jewish calendar (the year 5673):

> as they think they have too long to wait for the kingdom of Heaven, that is until the seventh or eighth millennium. This problem torments them and gives them a reason to torment me in their turn. Quite frankly I am really tired after a few days of conversing with these co-religionists and I often feel the need to be on my own for a few hours.

The *kahen* and *debtera*, in particular, wished to debate these subjects, and from the moment they saw Faitlovitch in the village they gave him no peace. Described by Faitlovitch as 'visionaries of the future', they told him their dreams and asked him to interpret them: 'They think I can do anything, even interpret dreams.' He got no rest from the discussion of these matters in any of the communities that he visited. He wrote that he had some respite only in Gondar, but that even there the Falashas who visited him, whether converted or living as Christians,[31] ended up questioning him on the same subjects he had been asked about in the villages.

Faitlovitch's role among the Falashas as a missionary rather than a scholar is quite clear from these sentences taken from his field notes. He was not interested in knowing more about native beliefs and habits, and he was very annoyed at being obliged to play the role that had evolved out of his own desires – he liked playing the missionary. In this ambiguous game, caught between his pleasure at being highly regarded by the natives, to the point of being proud to be seen as a modern Messiah, and his position as a 'French' scholar and a representative of modern European Jewry, he felt uncomfortable and nervous. But he played the game well, and his passion for action in the counter-mission took precedence over other tasks. He liked to increase his prestige by assuming the mantle of a powerful missionary, and when he got the chance he acted accordingly. So it happened with a young boy who had decided to become a Christian.

This event occurred while Faitlovitch was staying in Qouzela. A young Falasha man who had been living outside his community for a few years had recently decided to take the final step of baptism for himself and his family. On the eve of the baptism, no one was able to make him change his mind: 'Neither his family's begging nor the exhortations of the Kahens and Debteras in the region could make him change his mind.' Faitlovitch did what he could, despite the fact that the people around him thought that no one could 'save this renegade from the abyss'. He succeeded in persuading the young man to come to him:

> and to the Falashas' astonishment they saw that my exhortations softened this rebel and he started to change his mind. I managed to dissuade him from the course he had decided to take and to make him see reason … There was immense rejoicing among the people present, all the men and women, adults and children crying with joy when they saw the young man approach his elderly father and throw himself at his feet with a stone around his neck. This was a sign of humiliation and begging for forgiveness. The young man apologized for his shame and the unhappiness inflicted by his behaviour … after being forgiven by his father, this poor man, with the stone still around his neck, dragged himself along the ground towards all the eminent members of the community, apologized and asked them to forget about his past and consider him once more one of them. This was followed by the *kahen*'s blessing, embracing, general celebrations and great excitement around Faitlovitch, who, at the height of his satisfaction and pleasure, added 'I didn't know where to look'.[32]

The younger generation of Falashas was attracted by the novelty of the Protestant mission. Many of the missionary reports published by *London Society Reports* relate that their elderly parents tried everything, including every kind of threat and curse, to stop them from converting to the new faith. The threats often achieved the desired effect, getting them to postpone the decision to abandon their fathers' faith at least until their parents' death. Faitlovitch's success in this case was no doubt partly due to his role as an authority among the Falashas, but also to the prestige and admiration he enjoyed in the villages.

Jona Bogale describes the fascination that Faitlovitch held for the young people in the villages, and the way he preached in the synagogues: 'on the sabbath and in Amharic … [Faitlovitch] told us stories about Jerusalem … and the Jewish people … No one wanted to listen to the priests' stories, only Faitlovitch's.'[33] According to other sources, when preaching, Faitlovitch dressed entirely in white and wore a little black cap on his head in order to command great honour and respect.[34]

RETURNING FROM THE THIRD MISSION

Faitlovitch decided to take a different route back to Asmara so that he could meet the Falashas of Lasta and Belesa, a region where missionary activity was strong. He had been invited to Lasta by Abba Samuel, a priest related to Taamrat. Belesa was infested with malaria and very unhealthy, which was the reason he had not gone there on his second visit to Ethiopia. This time he resolved to go, thanks to the '*importunités*' of the missionaries,[35] who were expanding their activities in that region. Faitlovitch was accompanied on his journey by Gete and his younger brother, who was being trained by Faitlovitch to help Gete in the school in Dembea. Faitlovitch had expected to arrive in Asmara around the end of July, but it was actually mid-August when he got there as he was slowed down by the rainy season and the fevers he had contracted on the way.

Awaiting him in Asmara was a sum for covering his travel expenses with a little extra for the school.[36] Once he had received this, he informed Margulies that he would need additional money[37] for Gete and his brother's return journey.[38] Meanwhile he was waiting for a reply from Addis Ababa giving him permission to send a European to teach in the school that he was about to open.

After recurring fevers had kept him in bed for long periods in Asmara, Faitlovitch told Margulies of his decision to spend the Jewish New Year holidays in Aden and to furnish Gete's brother with the *tefillin* on his return, as he had been giving the young man religious instruction for eleven months. Faitlovitch considered wearing the *tefillin*, as the ritual initiation into Judaism. In his letters Faitlovitch made no mention of any particular rite of conversion, although Margulies had requested it.[39] His intention to perform conversion rituals may have been tacitly understood simply due to the fact that Faitlovitch had asked Margulies to send the *tefillin*.[40] The Orientalist had been unable to obtain phylacteries, *kippot* and *mezuzot*,[41] so he wrote to the rabbi asking him to send everything he needed for the boy from Florence. He praised the boy, noting that

> he can already recite the *tefillot* and reads Hebrew quite well. Next week he is going to start wearing the *tefillin* and then he will be completely *ours* [*author's emphasis*]. This young man ... is very energetic, intelligent and has a very strong constitution ... Always active, he has quickly learnt how to use a sewing machine and a carpenter's tools. He will be the architect of our school in

> Dembea, so to speak, and be responsible for the work inside. He will have huts put up, build the furniture the school needs, make clothes for and look after the pupils, for example getting the corn, having it milled and preparing the food. He can also help Gete teach the alphabet.

In addition to this young man and the European teacher (who, in the end, did not come),[42] Faitlovitch wanted to take on a *debtera* for 'Abyssinian teaching'.[43]

It should be noted that Faitlovitch used to change the names of the boys, as indicated above, giving them Jewish names. He would perform the *tevilah*, a ritual immersion, and impose *bar mitzvah* practices (such as the use of *tefillin*) in order to transform a Falasha boy into a Jew of Ethiopia. He did this on the instructions of rabbis like Margulies, without any doubt about the acts he was performing and without the involvement or consent of the boys' parents. The Falashas had to become western Jews and Faitlovitch acted accordingly.

Gete and his brother left Asmara at the beginning of November to run the small school in Dembea that had opened at the end of 1913 or the beginning of 1914, just on the eve of the war.

Shortly before leaving the colony, Faitlovitch had begun to realize that all of his efforts with the Italian government (and Margulies' at the Ministry in Rome) were useless and started to pursue other routes, first of all England. In an interview for the *Jewish Chronicle* during his second journey, the Sudan had been mentioned as a possible place for a school. In 1913, just before leaving for Italy, Faitlovitch wrote:

> I have the feeling that we will get nothing here without the direct intervention of the Ministry in Rome and this step needs to be taken immediately. If the Italian government is not willing to support us we must find another way. England may be prepared to help and protect us, in which case we would be able to locate our teaching establishment with European teachers in Abyssinia itself. The English are going to appoint a consul in Gondar, I think to counter-balance Italian political and commercial interests, and for that reason they may be interested in the Falashas.

The British consul was M. Armbuster. Faitlovitch asked Margulies to have discussions with the rabbi of England, presenting the Committee as international and not Italian. He later went to London with Taamrat. The First World War broke out shortly thereafter, leaving the school under-funded and preventing Faitlovitch from returning to Ethiopia until 1920. He spent the years of the First World War in Geneva hoping for an opportunity to leave for Ethiopia with Taamrat, who was still living and working in Italy;[44] but there were none, and he taught *ge'ez* at the University in Lausanne while waiting for the war to end.

NOTES

1. 'La solidarietà israelitica e i Falascià', *Rivista israelitica*, 4 (1907), pp. 45–51.
2. See Trevisan Semi, 'From Wolleqa to Florence'.
3. 2,000 lire.
4. The appeal was published by M. Waldman, *Beyond the Rivers of Ethiopia: The Jews of Ethiopia and the Jewish People* (Tel Aviv, 1989), p. 202 (Hebrew).
5. Letter of 28 August 1908, *Fait. Coll.*, f. 120.
6. The report wrote: 'There are barely 6,000 –7,000 Falashas, in groups of 5 to 10 families spread over a considerable area.' See H. Nahoum, 'Mission en Abyssinie: rapport sur les Falachas', *Bulletin de l'AIU*, 37 (1909), p. 35.
7. Letter of 13 July 1909, *Arch. AIU*, Italy, ID4, 7368/6.
8. Letter of 3 August 1909, *Arch. AIU*, Italy, ID4, 7426.
9. In 1912 Margulies asked Rav Kook (in Jafo) to find a suitable teacher for the planned school in Ethiopia and that the latter approached the Sephardim to look for the right person. See Waldmann, *Beyond*, p. 216.
10. Ibid.
11. Ibid.
12. *London Society Reports* (1912), p. 88.
13. Described by Faitlovitch in *Quer durch Abessinien*, p. 89.
14. Letter from Abseghié of 22 May 1913, *Fait. Coll.*, f. 120.
15. *London Society Reports* (1912), p. 88; and Quirin, *The Evolution*, p. 195.
16. Letter from Asmara of 9 February 1913, *Fait. Coll.*, f. 120.
17. Ferdinando Martini, a non military governor, had been appointed after Adua to implement a policy of pacification and economic development in Ethiopia, see L. Goglia and F. Grassi, *Il colonialismo italiano da Adua all'impero* (Rome and Bari, 1981), pp. 102–4.
18. Letter from Addis Ugri of 23 February 1913, *Fait. Coll.*, f. 120.
19. Letter from Gondar of 13 April 1913, *Fait. Coll.*, f. 100.
20. Letter from Abseghié of 18 April 1913, *Fait. Coll.*, f. 100.
21. In the same letter, Faitlovitch added that Ostini 'wasted a lot of words to get across his opinion that Israel is a spoiled child and the cause of much harm to the human race', ibid.
22. Summerfield, *From Falashas*, p. 88, p. 181, n. 121 and n. 122; p. 182, n. 131.
23. Letter from Asmara of 18 September 1913, *Fait. Coll.*, f. 100.
24. Letter from Amba Gualit of 27 April 1913, *Fait. Coll.*, f. 100.
25. Letter from Debra Tabor of 6 May 1913, *Fait. Coll.*, f. 100.
26. Letter from Abseghié of 20 April 1913, *Fait. Coll.*, f. 100.
27. The letter was delivered by a missionary to the Bishop of Jerusalem, Gobat, and not to the 'head of the Jews'. See Quirin, *The Evolution*, pp. 159–60 and p. 278, n 257; D. Kessler, *The Falashas: A Short History of the Ethiopian Jews* (London and Portland OR, 1982), pp. 123–4, shows the translation by D. Appleyard of the letter from Ethiopian. For the Hebrew version see M. Wurmbrand's end note in Faitlovitch, *Masa*, pp. 154–5 (Hebrew).
28. J. Halévy, 'Travels in Abyssinia', pp. 278–9; and Sh. Ben Dor, 'The Journey towards Eretz Israel: The Story of Abba Mahari', *Peamim*, 33 (1987), pp. 5–31 (Hebrew).
29. See Trevisan Semi, 'La rilevazione delle regole del *sanbat* tra gli ebrei d'Etiopia negli inediti di C.A. Viterbo', *Oriente moderno*, 6 (1987), n.s., pp. 79–97.
30. See S. Kaplan, *Les Falachas* (Belgium, 1990), pp. 57–8.
31. Faitlovitch described groups of converts, like the Tabiban, who lived as Christians but secretly continued to practice non-Christians rites.

32. Letter from Abseghié of 22 May 1913, *Fait. Coll.*, f. 100.
33. Summerfield, *From Falashas*, p. 87.
34. Ibid., p. 180, n. 115 (the source is the Italian commercial agency in Gondar).
35. Letter from Tedda of 28 May 1913, *Fait. Coll.*, f. 100.
36. This consisted of 4,000 lire, 3,000 of which were needed to cover travel expenses and 1,000 of which were for the school. L.1,500 came from Ottolenghi and 2,500 from M. Gulenski in Berlin.
37. He asked for an extra 1,000 francs.
38. Letter from Asmara of 18 August 1913, *Fait Coll.*, f. 100.
39. Waldman, *Beyond*, p. 215, n. 9, refers to the *batafat dam berit* and to the *tevilah*.
40. Faitlovitch's diary entry of 30 October 1921. It is not clear which kind of conversion Faitlovitch practiced. For instance, in referring to Abraham Barok, one of the boys taken to Europe, Faitlovitch used the words 'went with Abraham to do the *batafat*'. This could mean *batafat musar* or *batafat dam*, in the last case a sort of circumcision.
41. Letter from Asmara of 18 September 1913, *Fait. Coll.*, f. 100.
42. Faitlovitsh tried many times to have an European teacher come to Ethiopia – including his brother, as indicated in Chapter 7 – but he never succeeded in attaining this goal.
43. Letter from Asmara of 15 September 1913, *Fait. Coll.*, f. 100.
44. See some of the letters sent to Faitlovitch by Taamrat in 1916, 1918, 1919, in Trevisan Semi, *L'Epistolario*, pp. 98–119.

7

Faitlovitch's Fourth (1920–1) and Fifth (1923–4) Missions to Ethiopia: A Schnorrer *in America*

This chapter attempts to deal with the question of Faitlovitch's fundraising activities, which occupied him for most of his life and led to his spending large sums of the money he raised, which really should have been used for his 'holy work'.

Starting with the fourth mission, before each journey to Ethiopia, Faitlovitch made a long trip to the United States in order to raise funds, some of which he spent to support himself while in the United States and to cover his travel expenses. Faitlovitch understood that after the First World War, the United States would assume a larger and more important role internationally, and that American Jewry would be keen to support the Falasha cause, as they strongly supported the European Jews who were suffering because of the war. Consequently, he moved the European Pro-Falasha Committee to the United States and spent a great deal of time there, increasing his fundraising activities.

The point is that, while he would have raised far less money for his work on behalf of the Falashas without these trips, he wasted a lot of money staying there. Being a bit of a *schnorrer*, he took advantage of this situation, while at the same time raising substantial funds for his work with the Falashas. It is difficult to reconcile this rather ambiguous and contradictory activity.

How much money had to be raised to cover the costs of what the Polish missionary used to call 'holy work' – the Atlantic crossings, the ships between Palestine and Massawa, the train journeys between Italy and France and between France and Lodz? What expenses were incurred during his long stays in hotels in New York, London, Paris, and Florence? He spent most of his life travelling, by train or by ship, from one point on the globe to another, always staying in hotels. When not staying in Ethiopia[1] he was travelling to raise funds for the 'Judaization' and education of the Falashas, and for his future journeys. Reit (the president of the American Pro-Falasha Committee) wrote in 1928, '[I] have often wondered why it is necessary for Dr Faitlovitch to make this long trip to America with all its expenses, instead of continuing the program among the Falashas."[2] One could naturally also ask what the deficit in funding might have been if Faitlovitch had not personally visited the Jewish communities around the world, and particularly in America, given the fact that as soon as he left the USA, contributions to the American Pro-Falasha Committee were greatly reduced in comparison to when Faitlovitch was actually there.

Did he feel obliged to play the *schnorrer*, milking the legend of 'the dispersal of Israel' in order to gain funding, or was he a real *schnorrer*, who managed to make ends meet by mobilizing the most diverse Jewish organizations (reform, conservative and orthodox)?

Was the success or failure of an expedition determined by Faitlovitch's personal skill at fundraising, or was the fascination with the myth of a rediscovered lost tribe guaranteed to attract subsidies on its own? For example, the fourth expedition of 1920–21 in Eritrea and Ethiopia, despite being an utter disaster that produced no results, enabled Faitlovitch to obtain the funding to organize a fifth expedition as early as 1923–24 – one that, albeit belatedly, led to the opening of the school in Addis.

The remainder of this chapter deals with the fourth and fifth expeditions to Ethiopia conducted by the 'Jewish Missionary', and the steps he took to raise the funds.

It was after his first three trips to Ethiopia, and during his first trip to the United States in 1911, that Faitlovitch laid the foundations for an American organization to fund his work with the Falashas. On this occasion, he sought the formation of a Pro-Falasha Committee within the Union of American Hebrew Congregations,[3] under the direction of Walter Freiberg (the president of the Union of American Hebrew Congregations).[4] The first funds were not raised until the summer of 1911, once Faitlovitch was actually there.[5] It was clearly due to the presence of the missionary in the United States that interest in the Ethiopian Jews was first cultivated across the Atlantic.

However, it was not until 1915, at the time of his second expedition, that Faitlovitch succeeded in raising a considerable sum. He had set a target of $30,000 and had obtained $8,000. One might have expected Faitlovitch to leave immediately for Ethiopia once the war had ended; but he did not. Instead, in 1919, he set out on a third trip to the United States to appeal to the Americans yet again. This time, he also managed to persuade the Joint, an organization that was actively aiding Jewish victims of the war in Europe, to get involved. The Joint donated a sum of $12,000 to the Falasha cause, $10,000 of which went toward the travel expenses for Faitlovitch and those considered to be his assistants, including a European teacher (actually his own brother, Haim Faitlovitch, whose identity Jacques never revealed),[6] a Jewish physician (Dr Entin, from the Hadassa Hospital in Jerusalem), Taamrat Emmanuel, and Solomon Isaac (the young Falasha who had been taken to Palestine to study in 1909).[7] A sum of $2,000 was set aside for the purchase and shipping of medicines. Faitlovitch had managed to convince the Joint that the Falashas of Ethiopia were also victims of the First World War.[8] Once the funds had been allocated, the directors of the movement, who knew nothing about the Falashas, were very keen to get hold of the book that Faitlovitch had just published in Germany and the *Notes d'un voyage chez les Falachas* by Halévy, in order to learn at least a bit more about the population they were preparing to support through their Humanitarian Aid programme.[9] In all, the Jewish missionary travelled to the United States three times before setting off on his fourth expedition, presumably to secure the funding that would allow him to begin his educational work among the Jews of Ethiopia.

THE FOURTH MISSION

The fourth Ethiopian expedition was organized under the auspices of the American Jewish Committee.[10] The American Pro-Falasha Committee was not founded until 1922.

Faitlovitch left Palestine for Eritrea and Ethiopia with $10,000 to cover travel expenses and the costs of running the expedition, plus $8,000 to start up his educational programme. In addition, 24 cases of medicine were sent directly from the United States to Massawa. This represented a considerable sum of money.

The journey, struck by tragedy at the outset because of the death of the young Solomon Isaac shortly after the departure of the caravan from Asmara, was further complicated by the disastrous relationship between the two brothers, and also by that between Faitlovitch and Dr Entin. To top it all off, the cases of medication that would have enabled them to establish a small clinic arrived in port totally useless.[11]

In a letter he sent to Adler, the vice-president of the Executive Committee of the American Jewish Committee[12] on 19 December 1920, after the group had reached Addis Ababa (on the 6th), Faitlovitch announced that the two Europeans had not managed to become acclimatized and that he had found it necessary to 'release my European companions from the commitment made to me'. In a subsequent report,[13] Faitlovitch wrote that after the six-month journey from Eritrea to Ethiopia, three weeks of which had been spent in Woleka (Gondar), he had hoped

> to leave my two European companions in this part of Abyssinia to advance the work systematically and continuously, but they found the climatic conditions and surroundings too tiring and unfavourable to their health, and in spite of the commitment they had made to me, they urged me to take them to the coast and send them back. I then was compelled to shorten my stay in Woleka.

In a more detailed memorandum to the president of the committee, sent after his return from the expedition and after the establishment of the American Pro-Falasha Committee, he reported, surprisingly, that the expedition had been a success – despite the fact that he had failed to open his clinic, initiate his educational work, or convince his brother to settle in the country.[14] In reality, Faitlovitch was already busy collecting new funding. He also was trying to create a new version of the events. Thus he wrote, with regard to this ill-fated mission:

> Notwithstanding all the adverse conditions, I tried my best to carry my expedition through to a favourable end. The mission for the Joint Distribution Committee was executed successfully ... Drugs were distributed to Jews and non-Jews alike, and hundreds of people came to our post every week to find relief for their ailments.[15]

In the same memorandum, Faitlovitch justified his actions, saying that if he had been unable to establish the educational sector, it was due to the fact that the American Jewish Committee did not want to send him the additional funds. Prior to that point he had simply sent reports to the American committees, which were then edited for use by the American Jewish organizations in raising additional funding.

The travel diary that Faitlovitch kept – in French with annotations in Italian, English, Hebrew, Yiddish, and Ethiopian – is a useful aid in reconstructing an account of the fourth mission, as it provides us with an alternative, less bureaucratic, view. The quarrels between the two brothers are often noted in Yiddish, which would seem to indicate that this was the language in which they customarily spoke to one another. This Yiddish spices up the narrative and gives it a lively, candid flavor. From Faitlovitch's journal, we learn that when the boat left Suez for

Massawa with the five members of the expedition aboard, there were serious disputes between the two brothers. By the time the group arrived in Asmara, the arguments among the three protagonists – the two Faitlovitch brothers and the doctor – had become frequent and violent. More often than not, they had to do with money.[16] The doctor, who according to Faitlovitch was playing hardball, had allied himself with Faitlovitch's brother early on, in an attempt to obtain more money than had been agreed upon, or to get more advance payments. On 24 May, Faitlovitch wrote 'Entin is asking for more financial advances', and a few days later, he noted that Entin and Haim were using blackmail. The climate became more and more oppressive, and as the caravan advanced into the interior of the country, Entin and Haim talked of denouncing Jacques, the idea being one of them would go to the *ras* Tafari, the future Haile Sellassie, while the other went to the American organizations or even the European Consulates. Haim accused Faitlovitch of being an *ausmutzer*[17] (Yiddish for exploiter) and a *rotzeach*.[18] On 10 June, when they were confined to Addi Ugri, Haim said to his brother, 'If you don't let me leave [*Author's note*: Haim may have already decided to do so] and you don't give me 3,000, I will do by force and take 6,000. I'll show you what I'm made of!'] This makes it clear that Haim, from the very beginning, had always intended to abandon the expedition. About twelve days later, while they were waiting in Addi Quala to obtain Italian visas so that they could continue on to Adua,[19] Solomon, who had already been ill for five days, died without ever receiving the attention of a doctor. It is impossible to know where Entin, the doctor of the group, was hiding at this crucial time. On that same day, 21 June 1920, Faitlovitch noted laconically in his diary, 'In the morning, Solomon seriously ill, no doctor, about 9 o'clock Solomon died, did the *qevura*.'

After they reached Adua, the disputes among the three over money and food resumed, violently. On 7 July, Faitlovitch reported that Haim had told him, 'I'm from America, like you', most likely meaning that the American funding was meant for both of them. He also noted that he had overheard his brother and the doctor conspiring against him one evening.[20] 'We will join forces,' said the doctor. 'We will break his bones. Let's hold firm and we will make it.' And Haim said to him, 'I'll ask him for more money, at the moment I want more than just 5,000 francs.'[21] Faitlovitch makes numerous references to his brother's screaming and abuse: 'I don't give a damn about you / I don't give a shit about you [in Yiddish, *Ich schass auf*].[22] I will show you who I am … I will tell the whole world.'[23] This could be interpreted as a threat of blackmail. What both Haim and Entin really wanted was to obtain more money.[24] To this end, ever since June, Faitlovitch had been requesting that the American Committee raise the doctor's annual salary to $2,000.[25] Once they arrived in Woleka, Entin settled in the town of Gondar (27 August), apart from the rest of the group. He ended up being involved in a lawsuit, the origins of which are not clear, and consequently had to present himself at the British Consulate. All along the way, Haim had wanted to lead the caravan instead of his brother, who clearly knew more about the geography and the local customs than he did; if he could not, he said, he would return to Gondar.[26] Faitlovitch wrote, 'Haim waits for me on the road and screams, : "I will not go on, I will go back".'[27] He also recounted a moment in which his brother lost his temper: 'Haim made tremendous scenes.'[28] These scenes continued, reaching a climax at the end of November, when Faitlovitch described his brother as being out of control: 'On the way, Haim is mad all day, he runs ahead, running the risk a fall … and of getting lost.' The sum he demanded had now reached 7,000: 'You will give me 5,000 or 7,000 lire at Addis.'[29] On the night before their arrival in Addis, Haim threatened Jacques, saying that he would go to *ras* Tafari and sabotage his projects, 'and you will have no more business with the Falashas'.[30] Shortly afterwards (on 10 December), Faitlovitch recalled going to the Bank of Abyssinia to exchange currency, which he passed on to Haim along with a check. Haim then announced that he had no intention of remaining in Africa and that he was leaving immediately. In the meantime, Entin had also abandoned Faitlovitch and was living at Doctor Landau's.

It is not surprising that a different version of what happened during this trip appeared in the reports sent to the Minister of Foreign Affairs by the Italian colonial government, which collected evidence in order to discredit Faitlovitch and to prove that he represented a danger to Italian interests in the region. In the version presented by Haim and Dr Entin, which was passed on by Italian sources, both men voiced their objections to Jacques' methods and conduct. Entin went so far as to call him a 'vulgar adventurer' and a 'charlatan who for his own personal reasons has shown the Jews of Europe and especially America that the Falashas' life was one of slavery and of sorrow which … does not correspond to the truth'.[31] Apparently the threat to denounce him and 'tell the whole world' was carried out by Haim and Entin, who may very well have given their own version to the Italian colonial officials. In any case, they succeeded in discrediting the mission and Faitlovitch's initiatives.

It is clear that Jacques Faitlovitch spent a large amount of the money collected in America in order to reach Addis with his companions, but, having arrived there, he found himself alone and without a single project under way.

His next thought was to ask for still more money. Having lost his two companions and wasted so much money, Faitlovitch asked the Joint and the American Jewish Committee for an extra $2,000.[32]

He wrote to the Joint to say that he had been obliged to suspend all health services, and that he would need additional funding in order to open a school in Eritrea under Italian administration.

> For the present I must renounce the medical work here and consequently withdraw my request for the subsidy asked for it in June last year (sic), for at this time I do not have a proper person to leave in charge of it.[33]

He also took the opportunity to inform the president of the Joint that he had been able to distribute all of the medication:

> In Woleka, where we stayed for many months and where I organized a regular clinic and dispensary service, we had numerous daily visits from various parts of Dembea and the surrounding provinces. All the drugs that I received in Massawa … and also a large quantity of medicines I bought in Asmara, I took with me to the interior. Most of them were distributed among Jews and Gentiles along the way.

This seems to be a clear contradiction of what he said in his diary, which indicates that Entin was living not in Woleka but in Gondar, and that most of the cases of medicine had arrived in the port of Massawa completely ruined.

On various occasions Faitlovitch claimed to have offered medical supplies to people in Ethiopia, but there is no evidence that this was ever done. During his fourth trip, he wrote in his journal that the cases of medicine that had arrived were unusable, but he nevertheless declared to the American organization that he had made use of them and not that he had been obliged to suspend the distribution due to a lack of funds. Summerfield writes of the distribution of medical supplies to the Falashas when Faitlovitch arrived in Ethiopia, but this seems to have been a piece of propaganda used by Faitlovitch in the booklets he wrote for American Jewish organizations rather than a reality.[34]

I do not wish to expound on the effect produced by reading the diary in conjunction with this correspondence from the 1920s. The shock provoked by the discovery of Bronislaw Malinowski's diary remains fresh in the memory of generations of anthropologists. Those who studied his theories (and clearly the interest remains) will not forget the feelings expressed by the scholar or the brutality and violence of his reactions to day-to-day activities on the ground. It is also not my intention to discuss each individual's responsibility for the setbacks and the confusion. It is rather to show how, despite the obviously poor usage of the funds he received, Faitlovitch always knew how to obtain new funding. This continued for many years thanks to his own peculiar personal talents as a *schnorrer*. The mediocre results obtained with the sums of money advanced by the American organizations never prevented him from continuing to tap into these organizations, which is exactly what he did after the failure of this particular mission.

With this in mind, it is interesting to consider his arrival in Palestine upon his return from this unfortunate journey to Ethiopia. Now penniless, he was responsible for four young Falashas whom he was taking to Jerusalem to study, plus Taamrat, who had been unable to begin his career as a teacher in Ethiopia since the proposed school had never seen the light of day. He left his five companions at the hotel in Suez and continued on his way to Jerusalem, where he hoped to win the sympathy of the Joint and other charitable concerns that might pay for their travel expenses and for the young men's studies, not to mention his own hotel bill in town.

David de Sola Pool, who at the time was the American representative of the Zionist Commission in Palestine and the Joint's regional director for Palestine and Syria in Jerusalem, sent a telegram to New York on 2 October 1921, announcing the arrival of its man in Jerusalem in the following terms: 'Faitlovitch arrived from Abyssinia without funds bringing a man and four children, please inform American Jewish Committee, telegraph instructions and funds.'[35] The American Jewish Committee responded by disclaiming all responsibility in the affair, but nevertheless sent $695, stating in no uncertain terms that this was to be the last instalment.[36] Faitlovitch's response was to ask for additional money[37] to settle the accounts of his expedition. The Joint refused.[38] De Sola Pool intervened because he believed that Faitlovitch was a true idealist, 'A rare type in our Jewish life. He is perhaps the only missionary we have and I cannot but think that he has devoted himself to the cause of the Falashas in a spirit of real idealism.'[39] In the meantime, Faitlovitch managed to obtain some pounds sterling from other figures in the *yishuv* of the 1920s, £50 from Henrietta Szold[40] and £40 from Menahem Ussishkin, a Zionist from Chovevei Tziyyon.[41] After having made his way across Europe, he disembarked in New York on 13 May 1922, from where he would set off again five months later, on 28 November. While in the States, he tried to prepare for his fifth mission to Ethiopia, during which the Addis school was to open. It was during this trip that the American Pro-Falasha Committee[42] was created, primarily due to the will of Adler, the vice-president of the AJC (who was also responsible for the cultural activities of the Joint, and thus was able to control the use of the funds being collected for the Falashas in the States at that time). In Adler's opinion, Faitlovitch had demonstrated an utter lack of administrative ability. While Adler perceived Faitlovitch to be incompetent, Marshall, the president of the American Jewish Committee, thought he was a profiteer. He spoke in particularly harsh terms about the fourth Ethiopian mission, convinced of the fact that Faitlovitch had misappropriated funds from the cause:

> It is a story of ineptitude. He has taken a number of gentlemen on an excursion to Abyssinia and as soon as they get there paid their expenses for a return trip. He jumped from Italy to Palestine, from Palestine to Abyssinia. Now he is planning to jump back to Palestine and again to Abyssinia. He has the activity of a flea, and so far as I have been able to observe, he likewise possesses some of the annoying qualities of that insect.[43]

Marshall considered Faitlovitch's decision to leave for Palestine with four young people to be that of an irresponsible person: 'I do not understand on what possible theory as gallivanting around the Orient with the children of whom he speaks, [*sic*] or how he can presume to pay £400 a year for their maintenance ... our funds cannot be frittered away.'[44]

THE FIFTH MISSION

During his mission to New York in 1922, Faitlovitch was prepared to ask for a new budget of $15,000 to be granted, to cover the costs of his fifth expedition to Ethiopia – a third of the sum, $5,000 being for his own travel expenses and one year of living expenses in Ethiopia, leaving $10,000 for the opening of a school in Addis or in Eritrea.[45] It was at that point that Adler insisted, as a condition for the donation of the funds, that the institution known as the American Pro-Falasha Committee be created, primarily to oversee the financial management of the expedition: 'He is not a very practical man, and besides, public moneys should not be appropriated to individuals in this way … in other words, we ought to deal with institutions and not with individuals.'[46] In the end, the Joint decided to grant Faitlovitch, to his great disappointment, only half the requested sum, or $7,500.

Faitlovitch's arrogant response to this decision by the Joint caused a stir even within his circle of friends. Adler, expressing his utter annoyance, wrote:

> He seems to take the attitude that all he has to do is ask and we must deliver ... Faitlovitch is so impractical a man that he does not know how to spend money properly, and hence I wanted a real organization to control it, both in Europe and America, and not a paper organization.[47]

As for Schneiderman, the secretary of this new committee, he too felt obliged to remind Faitlovitch (who was preparing to leave the United States) that his 'unbusinesslike proceedings' had gravely damaged the cause. The Pro-Falasha Committee decided that the money collected could not be used until after Faitlovitch had left the States for Ethiopia, in order to maintain control over it and to prevent the sum of money raised from being wasted.[48] In reality, a monthly salary of $250 was paid to Faitlovitch[49] beginning in November 1922, after his departure from the United States, even though he was still in Europe.[50] While the American Pro-Falasha Committee launched itself into a great campaign in order to collect the ambitious sum of $35,000,[51] Faitlovitch decided to remain in Europe, where he spent about $10 a day, no mean sum, as Frisch, the committee's president, noted sarcastically: 'Even tourists travelling for pleasure get along for less.'[52] Thus Faitlovitch cut into the budget granted for his educational work, and it wasn't until the end of April 1923 that the Jewish missionary finally made it back to Addis Ababa. The school did not open until July, and even then it was not completely finished, more than six months past the date set by the American committee. Faitlovitch justified his stay in Europe by claiming that he needed to initiate a pro-Falasha campaign among the Jewish communities of Europe in order to add to the available funds, but when the subject of the budget for his activities in Ethiopia was raised in the United States, these reasons were deemed exaggerated, and this was made clear to him in the following terms: 'It is scarcely worth your while... in view of the work that is waiting for you in Abyssinia to devote your energies to reorganizing committees.'[53] Faitlovitch never failed to astonish the pro-Falasha committee. After spending only two months in Africa, he asked to return to Palestine, or at least, to spend a few weeks in Aden, at the expense of the Committee, on the pretext that the Ethiopian climate was difficult to endure and that the state of his health was not good. Faitlovitch asked the committee 'to permit me to leave the tropical climate for some time and sojourn a few weeks in Palestine for recreation'.[54] The American organization expressed its annoyance, but over the ensuing months Faitlovitch insisted, saying, 'The high temperature has affected me too much; often I am obliged to remain in bed, and staying here I will hardly recover me [*sic*] completely. Had I the necessary means I would leave Abyssinia for some weeks …'[55] One might add that in his diary, where he carefully noted all of his indispositions and all of the days when he had to stay in bed, there is no mention at all of the situation described to the committee. The impression given is that Faitlovitch really could not manage to stay anywhere for more than a few months. After a certain period of time he felt it necessary to wander off again on his travels. However, no one in the States was the least bit concerned about the state of his health, and he did not receive the permission he sought to leave Ethiopia. Instead, Frisch seized the opportunity to criticize the way he had squandered money in Europe:

> An unfortunate impression was also created among the Committee by the fact that you allowed $10 a day for your living expenses while in Europe … When members of the Committee called attention to the fact that only a small proportion of the moneys we expended went to the actual work of education of the Falashas, which is our great object, it was difficult to give a satisfactory explanation.[56]

Faitlovitch justified his actions by arguing about the cost of hotels in Paris and London and the cost of his travels from one town to another. Apart from a few round-trips to Aden, Faitlovitch remained in Ethiopia for the whole year, and it was only at the beginning of June that he was able to embark (again with the four young men) for Palestine. In January 1925, he was back in the United States. This time, in addition to the controversy, he was confronted with the Committee's first financial difficulties. However, his talents as a myth-maker and a fundraiser enabled him to organize a sixth mission to Ethiopia in 1926, on which he was accompanied by his sister Leah in the role of teacher for the girls' school that had recently opened thanks to the funding. Twelve stays in Ethiopia, fourteen trips to the States, long stopovers in Palestine, and above all, several months in Europe during the war – these were all stages of Faitlovitch's lifelong journey of fundraising missions and expeditions.

This chapter began by raising the question of the amount of influence exerted in America by the myth of the search for the lost tribes, and by the personality of Faitlovitch the *schnorrer*, in connection with the funding of the Pro-Falasha work.

The author believes that both the personal attributes of the main protagonist and the fascination with the myth played a part in a history that also involved the eminent personalities and upper-class leaders of American Jewry. It is true that Faitlovitch''s bad reputation risked causing the failure of the entire effort, resulting in the creation of the American Pro-Falasha Committee to guarantee the proper management as well as the continuity of the project. But while Faitlovitch was on American soil, the existence of the Ethiopian Jews took on a mythical dimension. American Jewry would never have considered involving itself in such a venture across Africa in the name of Jewish solidarity until the Jewish missionary in Ethiopia arrived in America. He was, however, a rather special kind of missionary: part adventurer, part colonialist, part *goel*, and also a bit of a *schnorrer*.

NOTES

1. Faitlovitch spent 12 periods in Ethiopia: 1904–05, 1908–09, 1913, 1920–21, 1923–34, 1926, 1928–29, 1930, 1934, 1942–4, 1943–4, 1946. He generally stayed for ten months (with a few exceptions), so he spent about ten years in Ethiopia. Summerfield is incorrect about the continuity of Faitlovitch's time in Ethiopia; '... he had in fact only been present in Ethiopia for a total of 3–4 years', *From Falashas*, p. 89.
2. Letter of 18 December 1928, *Joint*, Joint Abyss, 1921–32.
3. The congregation which united the Reformed Jews.
4. *38th Annual Report of the Union of American Hebrew Congregations*, p. 6, 708 (4 June 1911), *CAHJP*, P3–471.
5. *JTS*, Marx 80–29.
6. At that time, Haim was already married and serving as a rabbi in Lodz. Later he moved to London, where he served as a rabbi and *shohet* (ritual slaughterer).
7. See Weil, 'The Life'.
8. Letter of 5 November 1919, *Joint*, Joint Abyss, 1919–21.
9. Letter to F. Warburg, *Joint*, Joint Abyss, 1919–21.
10. *Fait.* Coll., f. 99.
11. Diary, 11 May 1920.
12. *Fait. Coll.*, f. 141.
13. *Fait. Coll.*, f. 113.
14. *Fait. Coll.*, f. 93.

15. Ibid.
16. Diary, 19 May 1920.
17. Diary, 4 June 1920.
18. Diary, 16 November 1920.
19. The Italian government was hostile to Faitlovitch's expeditions, and put every possible obstacle in his way.
20. Diary, 7 July 1920.
21. Diary, 16 July 1920.
22. Ibid.
23. Diary, 24 July 1920.
24. Diary, 31 August 1920.
25. Letter of 6 June 1920, *Joint*, Joint Abyss, 1919–21.
26. Diary, 24 October 1920.
27. Diary, 25 October 1920.
28. Diary, 17 November 1920.
29. Diary, 4 December 1920.
30. Diary, 5 December 1920.
31. Summerfield, *From Falashas*, pp. 181–2, n 130.
32. Letter from A. Lucas to H. Schneiderman of 2 February 1921, *Joint*, Joint Abyss, 1919–21.
33. Letter of 31 January 1921, Joint, Joint Abyss, 1919–21.
34. Summerfield, *From Falashas*, p. 89.
35. *Joint*, Joint Abyss, 1919–21.
36. Letter of 4 November 1921, *Joint*, Joint Abyss, 1919–21.
37. $1,000 .
38. Letter of 7 November 1921, *Joint*, Joint Abyss, 1919–21 (£50).
39. Letter of 7 November 1921, *Joint*, Joint Abyss, 1919–21.
40. Diary, 10 November 1921.
41. Diary, 19 November 1921.
42. It was created in July 1922: Harry Schneiderman was named secretary *pro tem*, and Rabbi Ephraim Frisch of the Central Conference of American Rabbis was named president. The new president intended to work in conjunction with Elias Salomon, a representative of the conservative movement, and A. Marx, a representative of the reform movement.
43. Letter from Marshall to Schneiderman of 17 August 1921, *Joint*, Joint Abyss, 1921–32.
44. Ibid.
45. Letter of 28 June 1922, *Joint*, Joint Abyss, 1921–32.
46. Letter from Adler to N. Krass of 6 July 1922, *Joint*, Joint Abyss, 1921–32.
47. Letter to W. Mack of 25 July 1922, *Joint*, Joint Abyss, 1921–32.
48. Letter of 14 August 1922, *Joint*, Joint Abyss, 1921–32.
49. One learns that in 1922–3 the annual salaries of Faitlovitch and Taamrat went up to $3,000 and $1,000 respectively, *JTS*, Marx 80–17.
50. Ibid.
51. Letter of 12 December 1922, *JTS*, Marx 80–17. The Committee managed to raise almost the entire amount of this sum.
52. *Fait. Coll.*, f. 99.
53 *Fait. Coll.*, f. 99.
54. Letter to Frisch of 22 May 1923, *Fait. Coll.*, f. 99.
55. Letter of 23 August 1923, *Fait. Coll.*, f. 99.
56. Letter of 22 October 1923, *Fait. Coll.*, f. 99.

8

Faitlovitch's Sixth (1926) and Seventh Missions (1928–29): Jacques and his Sister Leah

The educational programs for the Falashas were relaunched during Faitlovitch's sixth and seventh missions, thanks to the involvement of the Alliance and European Jewry. Faitlovitch expected that many Jewish rabbis, organizations, and committees would welcome young people who had been educated and even personally 'converted' by Faitlovitch in Ethiopia. In 1927, seventeen young people were given accommodations in various European countries and in Palestine so that they could complete the higher education they had begun in the Addis school. During the seventh mission, land for a new school was purchased in Addis with the help of a generous contribution of 5,000 thalers from the Negus. The project was also helped by the fact that Faitlovitch skillfully presented the APFC with a *fait accompli*, thus forcing the American Committee to honour its commitment.

Faitlovitch was accompanied on both missions by his sister Leah, who was never mentioned by name in his official correspondence but simply referred to as 'the woman teacher' or 'the European co-religionist instructor',[1] to be paid by the APFC. Leah taught a class that was opened to Falasha girls in 1926 (although it only lasted a few months) and also taught English in the Addis school. During the 1926 mission, thanks to the presence in Addis of Abel Levi, the son of Sylvain Levi (then president of the Alliance), who acted as an intermediary, Faitlovitch was able to renew his contacts with the Alliance and win back the French Jewish association's participation in the education of young Falashas.

THE SIXTH MISSION (1926)

On his fifth mission (1923–24), Faitlovitch had travelled to Addis via Djibouti and Dire Dawa, which then became his usual route.

Jacques and Leah reached Djibouti on 2 January 1926. By 12 January, they had arrived in Addis by train, where they were met at the station by Taamrat and Nadel, a Jew from Aden who lived in Addis and was a supporter of Faitlovitch's work. Heruy Walda Sellassie,[2] the foreign minister of Ethiopia, and a group of Yemeni Jews living in Addis were also there.

Just a few days after their arrival, Faitlovitch[3] noted that Leah had been to see a *Temqat* ceremony and that she had already begun to teach – two signs of her commitment to her new 'missionary' work.

Faitlovitch began making his usual rounds of the embassies (Italian, German, Austrian, American, and French), and paid a visit to *ras* Tafari and to people close to him. However, the success of the mission was largely due to the fact that Faitlovitch was able to reopen the avenue of a French education for young Falashas. Immediately after arriving in the capital, he began to cultivate a relationship with the French ambassador, Louis Gaussen, with a view to securing a diplomatic guarantee for his project for sending young people to Paris to study under the auspices of the Alliance.

Before Faitlovitch had left for Ethiopia, the APFC had promised to grant him the funds they had already raised, plus those they hoped to raise in the future. Under the terms of this agreement, Faitlovitch was to have received $1,000 (with an annual budget of $15,000) every month, but the sums of money that arrived from New York were far less than promised. As of April 1926, the fundraising appeal had brought in only $1,200, as compared to $,800 raised by the previous April, the year that Faitlovitch had been to America.[4] Faitlovitch's tireless propaganda campaign in the States had produced more generous donations than anyone else had managed to raise. Despite the funds that were raised in 1925, the APFC had not succeeded in narrowing the deficit[5] it had accumulated over the previous two years. Given this situation, some eminent Jews, such as Henrietta Szold, urged Faitlovitch to give up the project and the planned sixth mission.[6] But Faitlovitch, with his usual tenacity, not only ignored those who warned him of the risks, but took his sister, who was also paid by the APFC, along with him. As soon as he arrived in Addis, Faitlovitch began sending heartfelt letters to his sponsors, encouraging them to lobby friends and well-known people in order to guarantee funding:

> I have not yet received even the money to pay the rent for this year ... The teachers have not received their salaries since last May ... Shall this be the end of my life's work, and will Jewry

> leave the Falashas to their own fate, to ultimately fall like prey into the hands of our adversaries and to become forever extinct as Jews? Shall such an end be the destiny of this heroic tribe of our brethren?[7]

The problem of funding during the Addis period became even worse when he lost a case in the court of the British Legation. It was known as the 'landlord court case', and apparently concerned the rent on the Faitlovitch school. It concluded with an injunction ordering Faitlovitch to leave the premises and pay the agreed rent.[8] When Adler learned of this, he commented that the matter might have been resolved differently if only Faitlovitch had been able to act 'with tact and better management'.[9] However, the Executive Committee of the American Jewish Committee decided not to intervene further in the issue, being of the opinion that they had 'no legal standing' given that 'in the new contract which Doctor Faitlovitch authorized, he gave away his rights altogether'.[10]

Since the Joint was primarily committed to providing financial support for the Jews in Palestine and not the Falashas in Ethiopia, and since the APFC did not seem to be sufficiently committed, Faitlovitch again turned to Europe, trying to revive support for his project among the European Jewish organizations. He first approached the Hilfsverein through Eugene Mittwoch, the German Jewish Orientalist who had worked for the creation of a network of schools in Palestine, then appealed to Italian Jewry through Taamrat, and to the Alliance through Abel Levi.

In his correspondence with Mittwoch, Faitlovitch explained that he wanted to involve the Hilfsverein in the school he was planning to organize in the country: 'a school in the country could be managed by them [the Hilfsverein] under German protection, which would certainly be appreciated by many Jews in Germany'.[11] Faitlovitch had no qualms about putting strong pressure on his German Jewish friends in order to ensure that they honoured the commitments they had made in better days to house and educate a certain number of young Falashas. Faitlovitch's correspondence with Germans in 1926 was full of reminders about observance and Jewish honour and warned of the risk of committing *chillul ha-shem*. This showed that he gave no consideration to the difficult financial circumstances of the German Jews or the general economic crisis in Germany. As for the Hilfsverein and the Alliance, since his only concern was to raise much money as possible, he thought he could approach both of these Jewish educational organizations without regard for the ideological differences between them.

Faitlovitch asked Taamrat to speak to the Italian Jews on his behalf. However, when asking for financial contributions, Taamrat was unable to resist expressing his doubts about the work that had been done up to that point. While, in a somewhat ironic tone, he praised the founder of the movement as a man who was 'used to having visions of new skies and land'[12] and asked for a serious commitment from the Italian Jews, he also voiced his doubts about the chances for the success of the Falasha educational programme: 'although I have been closely following the work for more than twenty years, I am still unable to clear up my doubts [*author's note*: regarding the commitment of international Judaism to the Ethiopian Jews]'.[13] This stand, independent of Faitlovitch's, was one that Taamrat never gave up.

In 1926, in spite of all the financial difficulties, Faitlovitch made a new attempt to launch an impressive educational programme. He intended to send about twenty boys to study in Germany, Italy, France, Palestine, and Serbia. A teacher (Goldman) was to come from Germany to the inland town of Dembea to relaunch the educational programme, which had been interrupted many times since 1913, when the first school there was founded. Faitlovitch's sister, Leah, was to teach English in the school at Addis and start a class for girls there.

However, what Faitlovitch wanted most of all was to get the Alliance involved again.

THE ALLIANCE'S INVOLVEMENT AFTER 20 YEARS

The renewal of contact with the Alliance was made possible by the fact that Abel Levi, the AIU president's son, happened to be working in Addis.

In April 1926, the Alliance, under pressure from the son of the AIU president, expressed its willingness to help the Falashas again, an opportunity that Faitlovitch did not want to miss. For this reason he was willing to set aside past differences of opinion ('I hope this positive action marks the beginning of a new era in the work of educating the Falashas'),[14] and to resume relations with the institution: 'I will be happy to see this Jewish humanitarian work start again with the support of a competent organization like the Alliance.'[15] However, the programme that the Alliance had in mind was limited in terms of both objectives and numbers. The young people were to receive professional training, like that offered in the technical college in Jerusalem. The training would be offered to a maximum of four boys between the ages of 15 and 18, who had already reached a certain level of education. The AIU president expressed the same doubts that had been raised previously about the wisdom of the project: 'it is useless to train them on the same level as the students destined for Baghdad or Morocco. It would surely be better to prepare them for a trade, for example as a carpenter, or a mechanic.'[16] It was clear that S. Levi considered accepting no more than two boys and teaching them each just one trade. The following comments in one of the Alliance's publications[17] showed how much resistance there was to the idea of renewed involvement on their part, especially in an educational programme that was not aimed strictly at learning a trade:

> They have had some difficulty in applying themselves to being apprentices of manual trades, saying that they were led to believe that they were going to concentrate on academics. They have had essentially no education. Attempts of this kind in Italy, Switzerland, and by ourselves in Paris have rarely, if ever, succeeded. This may be because these young people were deluded into having ambitions that were too high; the aim was to give them an advanced education, while the Falashas' mentality is still typical of primitive peoples ... it would be wrong to raise them from their present level to that of more advanced Jewish groups.

The argument put forward by the Alliance had not changed in 20 years. Although they had begun to accept some of the students into their school, they did not really expect any change from the Beta Israel. Their mentality was still 'too primitive' for the highly sophisticated Alliance. When he renewed his relations with the AIU, Faitlovitch took full advantage of the lucky coincidence of Abel Levi's presence in Ethiopia. The number of boys to be sent to the technical college in Jerusalem was increased to four, and Faitlovitch insisted that the Alliance accept another six into the Auteuil school in Paris. He maintained that experience had shown that the Falashas were capable of completing not only technical training but also academic studies. He tried to convince the Alliance leaders of the Falashas' intellectual potential: 'the Falashas are capable of pursuing higher education … after such a short time it is astonishing to see, beyond the rough exterior, the specifically Jewish character, with its finesse and such particular taste for works of the spirit.' Moreover, he said, 'I have no doubt that there are some Falashas who are capable of aiming higher, for university studies, with a view to practicing a profession later.'[18] As an expert on eastern Africa, he explained the particular phase that Ethiopia was going through. The country, he said, was becoming a modern society and would soon need professional people. His intuition told him that major changes would take place among the Falashas if they could be educated in the West, and he fought for their acceptance into the most advanced courses of study:

> let our Abyssinian co-religionists take advantage of this opportunity to improve their social and economic position and have the honour and benefit of being some of the first of the indigenous population to practice a profession in this country ... this training is essential for the creation of an educated class capable of leading the Jewish community.[19]

To make his appeal more convincing, he included a note from the French ambassador, Gaussen, which stated 'the need to see young Abyssinians armed with a higher education that allows them to practice a profession in the country'. A few months later,[20] any illusion he may have harboured that the Alliance might accept young Falashas at the Auteuil school was destroyed. Even their commitment to provide accommodation for the four boys in Jerusalem turned out to be quite limited. At the end of July, while preparations were being made in Addis for the departure of Avraham Baruch, Hezekiel Messele, Ezra Worku, and Joseph Teguegne for Jerusalem, Faitlovitch learned that the Alliance had no intention of paying for their travel expenses (although they were willing to send an employee to meet them at Port Said).[21] The four Falashas were described as being about 18 years old, solid, with good religious training and a knowledge of Hebrew and prayers. One of them, Abraham Baruch, who had been to Germany, also knew German and French, and he was the only one in the group who dressed in European style.[22] Faitlovitch noted in his diary[23] that he had performed the *tevilah*, one of the rituals required for conversion, with some of the boys.[24] Faitlovitch, as usual, did not pay much heed to the signs of the Alliance's limited commitment to the project. He concentrated on covering the expenses that were strictly necessary for the four boys to reach Port Said. He was sure that the Alliance would eventually have to help out in some way, which is indeed what happened. He received 1,000 thalers from *ras* Tafari to pay for part of the boys' travel expenses[25] and even an advance from A. Levi,[26] who seemed none the less annoyed by the way things were proceeding.[27] The principal of the Alliance school, for his part, made no attempt to conceal his disapproval of the project, complaining about everything that had been done: the fact that the boys had arrived at the most inopportune moment, in August, when schools were closed, and he had had to organize something for the upcoming religious holidays; the fact that the AIU employee at Port Said had had to pay a sum[28] to stop the authorities from sending the boys back because, surprisingly, they had arrived without any money; the fact that they had very limited wardrobes and wore only khaki clothes and canvas shoes; and the fact that they were too old ('difficult to make them respect any discipline').[29] Faitlovitch insisted that there had been a misunderstanding, making it known that he had understood that the Paris headquarters would pay for their trip: 'I am very sorry to learn that these young people have had such difficulties in Egypt and it is really unfortunate that the Paris office did not give you the relevant information in good time.'[30] Faitlovitch reminded the AIU that in any case they would have to reimburse the Alliance president's son, who had advanced the money.[31] Abel Levi, for his part, complained about the pressure Faitlovitch had put on him in the handling of the matter and the resulting problems he had had with the Alliance.[32] In the end, Faitlovitch had managed once again to involve the Alliance against its will.

But what had Faitlovitch led the boys to expect before their departure? He had probably promised them that they would be able to study exactly what he had in mind for them – that is, academic subjects. In general, Faitlovitch wanted them to study to become doctors, lawyers, and teachers, and although he knew that the institutions they would be attending had other plans, he did not give up on this idea or on his hope that it might be implemented.

Of the four boys sent to Jerusalem, only Hezkiel Messele agreed to start work immediately in a carpenter's shop.[33] Ezra and Joseph refused to work in craftsmen's workshops, protesting that they had gone to Palestine to study, not to learn a trade. Abraham asked for his own room, and refused to take part in communal prayers or to eat the food prepared for him. He also wanted to work only half a day so he could spend the other half studying. Abraham turned out to be suffering from tuberculosis (which he had contracted in Germany) and was sent to Miqwe Israel's school in Jaffa.

On 24 October, after a ten-month stay, Jacques and Leah left Addis and went to Djibouti, and after Jacques had made the usual stop in Aden that he made on every return journey, they set sail from Djibouti for Massawa, Port Said, and finally Haifa. The brother and sister wandered around Palestine and Europe for several months, visiting the young Falashas for whom they had managed to find accommodations with Jewish host families or with various supporters of the Falasha cause.

On 24 March 1927 Faitlovitch boarded a ship in Southampton, bound for New York to start another campaign to raise funds for the 1928 mission.

THE SEVENTH MISSION (1928–29)

Before setting out on his seventh mission to Ethiopia, Faitlovitch spent nearly a year in the United States. During his first few months in New York, he had to face new accusations from Adler, particularly the assertion that he had not submitted reports on the work being done, on the progress of the school in Addis, or on the students' situation.[34] According to Adler, this lack of information could not help but harm the fundraising effort, as contributors wanted to be kept informed about how their money was being spent. Adler went so far as to suggest that Faitlovitch forget the idea of making costly journeys to Ethiopia and find a job as a teacher at the Oriental Institute in Jerusalem. That way, Adler claimed, he could do more for the Falashas' education in Palestine:

> it would be in accord with his plan of educating teachers for the Falashas in Palestine, which would seem to me much more rational than scattering them all over the world to bring back to Abyssinia the indigestion of many cultures. We do not want to make cosmopolitans of the Falashas, but rather simply to give these folk the opportunity once again to know Judaism in their own environment.[35]

Adler had expressed this opinion before; he was convinced that it would be less expensive and more productive to centralize the Falashas' education in a single place in Palestine under Faitlovitch's guidance, rather than get involved in difficult work in Ethiopia. Faitlovitch never agreed with this, as he favoured the idea of maintaining a presence, and guaranteeing 'diplomatic' protection for the Falashas, in the Ethiopian capital. Moreover, he had not given up the goal of expanding his activity inland, like the Protestant missionaries who were a constant thorn in his side. During the months he spent in New York persuading Adler and the members of the APFC of the need to proceed according to the existing plan, Faitlovitch drafted a report on the 17 students then studying in Europe and on the educational work accomplished between 1923 and 1927 thanks to the APFC's action in Ethiopia.[36]

The tensions that arose during Faitlovitch's stay in America also brought about a change in the leadership of the APFC. Hyman Reit, a counselor-at-law in New York, agreed to be president of an Emergency Committee (and later of the APFC) in order to guarantee the continuity of Faitlovitch's work in Ethiopia after the entire committee had resigned.'[37] It was in this role that Reit asked the Cultural Committee of the Joint for an additional contribution of 10,000 dollars, reminding them that the Falasha mission had captured 'the imagination of many of us and has appealed to us because it is one of the few instances in which Judaism of today is called upon to render aid to a separate group that professes its faith'.[38] The request was fulfilled, enabling Faitlovitch to conduct his seventh mission in 1928–29.

It was during this seventh mission that Faitlovitch was able to purchase the land for the school, thanks to a donation from *ras* Tafari, and start work on its construction. The school was officially recognized as an American institution, under the auspices of the US Legation in Addis Ababa.[39] The school's letterhead at that time included bore the inscription, 'Dr Faitlovitch's American School'.

The Cultural Committee, in response to Reit's appeal, had allocated the APFC 2,000 of the $10,000 requested, despite the fact that the Committee's financial situation was critical.[40] When Faitlovitch left New York (on 4 February 1928), the total amount set aside for the mission was $3,600, much less than requested,[41] yet enough to allow him to set sail for Ethiopia. In lieu of the $1,000 per month that Faitlovitch expected to receive from the APFC, he agreed to make do with $500.[42] After spending the usual few months in Europe, Egypt, and Palestine, making sure to be in Palestine in the spring in order to celebrate the *seder* in his Tel Aviv home, Faitlovitch and his sister Leah traveled to Addis (via Djibouti and Dire Dawa) on 24 July 1928, and stayed there until 28 March 1929.

Faitlovitch justified the fact that he was once again being accompanied by the 'woman teacher' (Leah) by telling the APFC that he needed more educational support at the school, as Taamrat had had several heart attacks and needed to rest:

> As soon as I got the news in Palestine of his [Taamrat's] illness, I did all I could to relieve him of his burden and responsibilities;

> I rehired the woman teacher who had been at our school before, to assist with the teaching here.[43]

It is not entirely clear whether Taamrat was really that seriously ill, or in fact ill at all. In a letter he sent to Faitlovitch on 17 March 1928,[44] he wrote that he was in good health. In any case, it is clear that Faitlovitch had decided to take Leah to Ethiopia regardless of the state of Taamrat's health. In fact, in the same letter,[45] Taamrat also indicated that he was aware of the Faitlovitches' imminent arrival in Ethiopia. Given its financial troubles, it is highly unlikely that the APFC would have agreed to the hiring of a new teacher unless there was a valid reason, such as Taamrat's being seriously ill.

The relationship between Taamrat and Faitlovitch was particularly tense at that time,[46] perhaps partly because Taamrat had taken out loans to finance the school, which he then had to repay. This had occurred in spite of the fact that Faitlovitch had pleaded with him a few months earlier not to get into debt.[47] He wrote to him specifically to ask him, in a heartfelt tone, to try to save money and, if need be, to send some boys away:

> Taamrat, I am sorry to have to tell you again that you must not exceed the agreed monthly sum. For the moment I think it is best to send back some pupils and not run up debts … If you really want to save the cause you are devoted to, to assure Judaism of an honourable, useful, industrious future, and if you don't want me to have to dip into my own pocket, try to economize. Think about tomorrow and, if necessary, make some sacrifices now.[48]

Taamrat was obviously unable to comply with these requests.

Whatever the case, when Faitlovitch arrived in Ethiopia, he was informed by Reit that the APFC had no more money to send him.[49] But once again Faitlovitch managed to surprise the APFC with his skills as a *schnorrer*. Ever since August he had been telling Adler about the possibility that *ras* Tafari might donate 5,000 thalers to purchase land for the school.[50] Two months later he reported to Weis, the secretary of the APFC, that *ras* Tafari, in order to mark the occasion of his coronation as Negus,

> has graciously put at my disposal the amount of five thousand Abyssinian Thalers [then equivalent to $2,500] as a contribution toward the purchase of a piece of property here for our school. I

> have a nice piece of land in mind, and I am now trying to get a loan of three or four thousand Thalers; with this money and the contribution from King Tafari I will be able to acquire some property for our institution here.[51]

Given that the Negus was clearly supporting their common cause, Faitlovitch asked the APFC to make a special effort to guarantee the continuity of the education project. A few weeks later, Faitlovitch wrote to Reit to tell him that he might not be able to accept the Negus's offer:

> I am endeavouring at present to get a loan of three thousand dollars in order to bring about this action. I must do it, if only for the sake of our prestige, now that His Majesty the King has so generously contributed.

He asked for extra help from the APFC,[52] and when he did not receive a reply, began to bombard Reit with telegrams, wanting to know: 'How will it end? Are we to perish? Reply.'[53] And then: 'Insist upon having immediate answer as telegraphed. Something must be decided without further delay.'[54] Finally, Reit consulted Adler, pointing out that:

> One of the interesting facts conveyed by this letter [Faitlovitch's letter] is the endorsement and encouragement that Dr Faitlovitch has received from King Tafari. Will it be possible for the Cultural Activities Committee (the Joint) … to supplement its recent grant of $500 with an additional appropriation of $500?[55]

As it turned out, the land had already been purchased on 26 September 1928 for 6,012.50 thalers[56] and registered on 14 December 1928 in Taamrat's name, on behalf of Faitlovitch, as executive director of the APFC. There were 4,090 square metres of land, on which there was an existing building, but in the following months Faitlovitch decided to demolish it and have a new one built. Faitlovitch left this land to his wife in the will that he drew up in 1952.[57]

In the end, Faitlovitch managed to turn a mission that initially did not augur well at all into a reasonable success, thereby allowing the school that had been established in 1923 to continue. The school that Faitlovitch had in mind is probably similar to one that appears in a drawing which may have used as an illustration for fundraising purposes. The school seems to have come straight out of *The Arabian Nights*. Underneath the picture is the caption 'Dr Faitlovitch's School, Addis Ababa, Abyssinia'. It looks like a picture of the Temple of Jerusalem, made up of a very wide courtyard with a perimeter formed by small low buildings. At the front is an Oriental-style door and at the back a sort of temple, accessible from adjacent land, with an expanse of water, gardens, and buildings in Versailles style, which would probably have housed the school.

This picture is in striking contrast to the one we are used to seeing in photographs, which show a desolate-looking school, and to Taamrat's description of September 1932:

> what can I say about 'Faitlovitch's School'? The outside looks like a camp of Abyssinian caravans, or rather a camp of Redskins like one I once saw in a museum in New York .... During the rainy season, as the roofs leak badly, people and household objects all collect in a corner, and the rest of the space virtually becomes a lake. The flooring is dust in summer and mud in winter. If the few pupils are unhealthy, it is due to their rashness in coming to stay here and to my illusion that I would one day have a school. In terms of teaching, I do what a single person can, often without books and other items indispensable both to the teacher and to those learning.[58]

Not surprisingly, a school for the Falashas next to the Temple of Jerusalem would long remain one of Faitlovitch's dreams.

NOTES

1. Letter from Taamrat to the Journal *Israel*, February 1926, *Fait. Coll.*, f. 99.
2. Heruy Walda Sellassie (1878–1938) was a writer and intellectual as well as the Foreign Minister of Ethiopia. In 1923 he was a member of the Ethiopian delegation in Geneva. He also accompanied *ras* (later Negus) Tafari's wife to Jerusalem in 1923 and 1934. In 1931–32 he went on a mission to Japan, see Hideko Faerber–Ishihara, *Les premiers contacts entre l'Ethiopie et le Japon (1923–1936)* (Paris, 1998); and more generally, S. Tedeschi, 'La carrière et les idées de Heruy Walda Sellassie (1878–1938)' in L. Fusella, S. Tedeschi and J. Tubiana, *Trois essais sur la litterature éthiopienne* (Antibes: Aresae, 1984), pp. 39–104.
3. Diary, 19 January 26.
4. Letter of 12 April 1926, *JTS*, A. Marx 80–17.
5. Totalling $6,000.
6. Letter from Faitlovitch to H. Szold of 28 February 1926, *Fait. Coll.*, f. 99.
7. Ibid.
8. Letter of 5 October 1926, *Fait. Coll.*, f. 99; diary, 30 August 1926 and 11 September 1926. In his diary, 6 September 1926, he noted: 'Taamrat talked from 10.30 to 2.00' and on 8 September 26 he wrote that they said to him in court, 'You brought lawyers.' Sentence was passed on 23 September 1926.
9. Letter from Adler to Chajes of 25 May 1927, *JTS*, Adler 26.

10. Letter from Adler to Weis of 5 May 1926, *JTS*, Adler 26.
11. Letter from Faitlovitch to Mittwoch of 11 June 1926, *Fait. Coll.*, f. 99.
12. Letter of February 1926, *Fait. Coll.*, f. 99.
13. Ibid.
14. Letter of 7 May 1926, *Fait. Coll.*, f. 100.
15. Letter of 7 May 1926, *Fait. Coll.*, f. 100 .
16. Letter to his son, *Fait. Coll.*, f. 99.
17. *Paix et droit*, 6, 9 (1926), p. 5.
18. Letter of 7 May 1926, *Fait. Coll.*, f. 100.
19. Ibid.
20. Diary, 18 June 1926.
21. In diary, 24 July 1926 he records that Bigart, the AIU secretary, had said he did not want to 'pay the expenses'.
22. Letter from A. Levi to Lupo, principal of the Jerusalem school, of 27 July 1926, *Fait. Coll.*, f. 99.
23. Diary, 29 March 1926.
24. The diary entry did not specify which boys, but they may have included those who were about to go to Europe.
25. Diary, 29 July 1926.
26. Letter from Faitlovitch to Lupo of 28 September 1926, *Fait. Coll.*, f. 99.
27. Levi, who disagreed with Faitlovitch, had suggested that the boys work on board to help pay their way, diary 3 August 1926.
28. 1,156 Egyptian piasters.
29. Letter from Lupo to Faitlovitch of 29 August 1926, *Fait. Coll.*, f. 99.
30. Letter from Faitlovitch to Lupo of 28 September 1926, *Fait. Coll.*, f. 99.
31. Ibid.
32. Diary, 19 September 1926.
33. In Taamrat's correspondence, he is mentioned as a labourer working on the construction of Adventist hospitals, see letter of 1 September 1933, in Trevisan Semi, *L'epistolario*, p. 165.
34. Letter from Adler to Weis of 5 May 1927, *JTS*, Adler 26.
35. Letter from Adler to Chajes of 25 May 1927, *JTS*, Adler 26.
36. *JTS*, Marx 80–17.
37. Letter from Faitlovitch to Taamrat of 26 October 1927, in Trevisan Semi, *L'epistolario*, p. 138.
38. Letter from Reit to the Cultural Activities Committee of the Joint of 4 November 1927, *Joint*, Joint Abyss, 1921–32.
39. Letter to Reit of 26 August 1927, *JTS*, Marx 80–29.
40. Letter of 4 November 1927, *Joint*, Joint Abyss, 1921–32.
41. Letter to Adler of 28 August 1928, *JTS*, Marx 80–29.
42. Letter from Faitlovitch to Adler of 28 August 1928, *JTS*, Marx 80–29.
43. Letter to Reit of 26 August 1928, *JTS*, Marx 80–29.
44. See letter of 17 March 1928, in Trevisan Semi, *L'epistolario*, pp. 145–6. The next in the series of letters is from 26 July 1931.
45. Ibid.
46. See the diary entries for those months.
47. See letter of 26 October 1926, in Trevisan Semi, *L'epistolario*, pp. 137–40.
48. Ibid.
49. Letter from Faitlovitch to Reit of 26 August 1928, mentioning the telegram received from Reit on 23 August, *JTS*, Marx 80–29.
50. Letter of 28 August 1928, *JTS*, Marx 80–29.
51. Letter of 12 October 1928, *Joint*, Joint Abyss, 1921–32.
52. Letter of 5 November 1928, *Fait. Coll.*, f. 127.
53. Letter of 22 November 1928, quoted in the letter from Weis to Adler of 6 December 1928, *Joint*, Joint Abyss, 1921–32.
54. Ibid. This refers to the telegram of 30 November.
55. Ibid.
56. Affidavit of 9 January 1929, *Fait. Coll.*, f. 117.
57. See H. Admor, 'Le testament de Jacques Faitlovitch' in D. Friedmann (ed.), *Les Juifs éthiopienss*.
58. See letter of September 1932, in Trevisan Semi, *L'epistolario*, p. 152.

9

Faitlovitch and His 'Students': A Troubled Chapter

In the early 1900s, twenty five young Falashas, some of whom were related to each other, journeyed from Abyssinia to Palestine and Europe to be educated in Western Judaism and the ways of modernity. Once there they had to cope with the demoralization and loneliness that is typical of immigrants who must adapt to a new environment without the support of their community. Many suffered from depression, or became ill with pleurisy or tuberculosis. Some overcame these problems; others died.

The boys who came to Europe were received by local Jewish communities and individual rabbis in different ways. At times they strongly supported the youths' efforts to adapt to the Western world, and at other times they abandoned them due to a lack of money, interest, commitment, or continued financial contributions.

Some of the young people were educated in Palestine, but the majority were scattered throughout France, Italy (including the colony of Rhodes), Germany, Austria, Switzerland, England, Serbia, and Egypt. Sometimes they were moved from one country to another; this was usually due to the fact that they had contracted illnesses and were thought to need a change in climate.

Ten boys were educated in Palestine, six of them beginning in 1909 at the Lemel school in Jerusalem, which belonged to the Hilfsverein der Deutschen Juden.[1] The other four boys were entrusted to the Alliance's Professional School in Jerusalem, starting in 1926. These boys generally remained in touch with the Ethiopian Christian community in Jerusalem, and were less isolated than the boys in Europe because they lived with other Falasha youths.

Faitlovitch was unconcerned about the fact that he was expecting the boys he brought to Europe to abandon their entire culture, just as Daniel, the boy brought back by Halévy, had been expected 'to break through the rigorous customs of their sect'.

Only the presence of a group to which they could belong, or at least one companion from their country of origin, provided a sense of support and eased their feeling of being uprooted. Moreover, when local Jewish communities strongly supported these young men's efforts to adapt to the Western Jewish world, substituting to a certain extent for their original communities, the results were positive. This was the case with Taamrat Emmanuel, Gete Yirmiahu, Jona Bogale, Abraham Adgeh, Tadesse Jacob, and others. However, when the local Jewish community was not very committed, the results were disastrous.

JEWISH COMMUNITIES IN EUROPE AND THE US AND THE QUESTION OF THE BOYS' EDUCATION

Faitlovitch, being aware of the complex political framework within which he would have to operate and caught between the rival aspirations of the European nations meddling in the region, attempted from the beginning to involve the various European Jewish communities. This continued through the period immediately following the First World War. In the late 1920s, he would turn to the United States, but up to that point, he found considerable support for the education of the young Beta Israel in Germany, at least until economic conditions in the country became so serious that maintaining support was increasingly difficult.

In 1927, Faitlovitch wrote to the head of the school in Frankfurt attended by Jona Bogale,[2] one of the young men who would later become a great leader of the Ethiopian community:

> For 22 years I have considered the aim of my life to be to awaken the Jewish population all over the world to the Falasha question. Both at home and abroad, committees have been formed to provide significant means, both from the Jewish viewpoint and from the generic cultural view, to actively promote the Falasha question. The war destroyed the work so laboriously carried out and devalued the money collected in Germany … Two and a half years ago I managed to have a Falasha boy settled in your institute. With enormous pleasure I noted that, even though the boy had no cultural education and very little preparation in any field, and did not even know how to count from 1 to 10, today he is sufficiently educated as to master the German language and has also reached a certain mastery in other scientific subjects that corresponds to [the ninth year of] secondary school … Leaving aside the boy's scientific progress, he has also laid the foundation for a religious education so that, once he has finished his schooling and

> returns to Abyssinia, he will be able to live and demonstrate the Jewish religion to his fellows and attract, or re-attract, numerous Falashas as brothers of world Judaism.[3]

These were the arguments that Faitlovitch used to get Jewish institutions involved in pro-Falasha work. However, he did not hesitate to use more meaningful and convincing expressions, for example invoking the *chillul ha-shem* when faced with a refusal, or conversely, the *qiddush ha-shem* when he received a positive response.

Faitlovitch used all of his personal contacts, especially among the Orthodox rabbis of Europe, to convince them of the importance of the task he had taken on in the name of Jewish solidarity – including his battle to thwart the work of the Protestant missions that were actively converting Falashas in Ethiopia – and of its implications for Jewish honour and prestige.

Faitlovitch eventually began to pursue financing from the United States, as the difficulties he was encountering in Europe were enormous. He sought the help of the United States because it was a country he considered more uninvolved and neutral.

In actual fact, while the United States agreed to fund the Addis Ababa school, along with its director, Taamrat Emmanuel, and Faitlovitch, it did not get directly involved in the education of the Beta Israel boys. Only Taamrat Emmanuel went to New York for a year, after he had already become the director of the Addis Ababa school. It was not until the post-war period that any Beta Israel went to the United States.

Faitlovitch tried to get the United States more involved in the educational programme. In 1929 he wrote,

> I may informally opine that an American education would be very desirable for the more capable of your students and that such students upon their return to this country could be of material assistance in expanding American culture and prestige in Ethiopia.[4]

However, he did not succeed.

The reasons for the limited American participation had to do with the greater distance – and the resulting higher cost of transporting the young people – and with disagreements over the educational policies to be implemented and doubts regarding Faitlovitch's organizational capabilities.[5]

When Cyrus Adler, the chairman of the American Pro-Falasha Committee, explained the Americans' lack of interest in increasing their involvement in educational activities, he expressed his opposition to the path being taken. He made it clear that he was against the dispersal of the young people and that he believed they would be better off being concentrated in a single area, in Palestine.[6]

Adler's view may simply have stemmed from his not wanting to get too involved in Falasha matters, but he was right about the plan to scatter the boys all over the world, which gave rise to many problems and created ill health, bitterness and disappointment among them.

According to the first essays published on Solomon Isaac[7] and Gete Yirmiahu,[8] the two boys trained in Palestine, they seemed to feel a little less lonely than the boys who were trained in Europe. The strong impact that the symbolism of Jerusalem and the myths linking it to the Ethiopian culture must have had on the young Ethiopians was certainly a determining factor in limiting their sense of loneliness and alienation, and in reinforcing their feelings of pride in their identity. Gete Yirmiahu was particularly affected by the symbolic fascination that the holy city and *Eretz Yisrael* held for many at the beginning of the last century.

When Faitlovitch decided to take Gete back to Ethiopia with him (on his third mission), the latter, who was trying very hard to remain on an equal footing with the other students at the Hilfsverein's school in Jerusalem, wrote to him:

> I read about the trip with contrasting feelings and I thought: if I do not understand myself yet, how can I go and teach others? Therefore, I am very surprised, and I beg you, dear teacher, to allow me to stay in Eretz Yisrael for two more years, so I can study the Torah and the Hebrew language: I shall be very happy to make progress in my studies and, within this time, I could achieve a deep knowledge of the Talmud and the *halakot*.[9]

Later, in a letter written to Rabbi Margulies after he had returned to Ethiopia for good, Gete revealed how nostalgic he was for Palestine:

> My dear teacher, I came back home without seeing you. On Sunday 12 of Tevet 1913, I left our source of life, Eretz Yisrael, and the Holy City, Jerusalem. When I left the city, I was full of yearning, I was unsure what to do and my heart was broken … The city taught me the living Torah that cures whoever needs to be cured. I shall kiss its dust in my dreams and when I awake I shall be upheld by the hope that all its lost sons will reach the Holy Land.[10]

Some of the boys who had been settled in Europe also wanted to move to Jerusalem, but the bad climate and the difficult social and economic conditions in Palestine prevented Faitlovitch from satisfying their wishes.

On several occasions, Faitlovitch considered the possibility of opening a school for the Falashas in Palestine, but the idea was never pursued. In a memorandum presented in New York as early as 1922, he had stated:

> It is my view that the best place for such a school would be Palestine. This is not very far from Abyssinia, and contact with the Jews of the Holy Land would be a tremendous advantage in the training of Falashas for teaching their people at home. This school may later develop into a centre of instruction for Jews from other isolated countries.[11]

However, we know that when Adler suggested this solution to Faitlovitch in 1927, he refused to accept it. It is true that Faitlovitch began to reconsider this hypothesis seriously in 1938, as the situation in Ethiopia, then under Italian occupation, had become critical.[12] But the difficulties in Palestine were no less significant than those encountered elsewhere. In Palestine, it was very difficult to count on help from individuals and institutions; moreover, the school in Jerusalem where the first boys had been educated had closed.

Had Faitlovitch decided to send all of the Falashas to Palestine and prepare them to settle there, they might have been better able to adjust. But the idea of gathering them in Zion and creating a Falasha *aliyyah* movement to the *yishuv* was far from Faitlovitch's intention during the first decades of last century. It was only after the Second World War and the creation of the State of Israel that he seriously considered the possibility of a mass *aliyyah*.

PATERNALISTIC AND AUTHORITARIAN

Faitlovitch was paternalistic and authoritarian in his decisions regarding the fate of the young people from Ethiopia. He paid no attention to the wishes expressed by the young people in his care and made decisions that would alter their fate, sometimes dramatically.

One example is the case of a young man who was taken to Italy at the end of the fourth expedition in 1921. In this instance, Faitlovitch acted without listening to the opinions of those who had looked after the boy in Italy and presumably knew him better, and ignored the desperate appeals made by the Falasha boy himself, Hizkiahu Finkas.[13] Individual needs counted for nothing compared to the goals of the 'holy work', which had to be pursued at all costs. Hizkiahu Finkas arrived in Italy in December 1921 and died in Alexandria, Egypt, in February 1931.

HIZKIAHU FINKAS' STORY

Faitlovitch, returning from his fourth journey to Abyssinia, brought four boys back with him. Two of them were to be placed in the Hilfsverein school in Jerusalem (Yona Bogale and Abraham Meir), a third (Abraham Barok) would be sent to Switzerland, and the fourth (Hizkiahu Finkas) to Italy. Faitlovitch wanted to place the last boy in Margulies' care, in the hope that the Florentine rabbi would educate him as he had Taamrat and Gete. But Faitlovitch did not take into account the recent changes in the Florentine Jewish community, then infected by a poisoned atmosphere; nor did he consider the Italian political climate on the eve of fascism. In fact, Margulies had written to Faitlovitch about the difficulties he was having in the Florentine Jewish community due to his religious, cultural, and, most importantly, Zionist initiatives.[14] The climate was so poisoned that he felt forced to resign in the face of the hostility shown to him. He ended up dying from a stroke on the eve of Purim in 1922. Margulies refused Faitlovitch's request to take responsibility for the education of the boy, who was then 10 or 11 years old, since he was not even sure that he would stay in Florence. But in December 1921 Faitlovitch arrived in Florence with the child, and after some unsuccessful appeals to the rabbi of Livorno and Pisa, he succeeded in forming a committee of four of Margulies' former students, who agreed to take complete responsibility for the young man's education and training. Margulies died just two months after Hizkiahu's arrival. The child was placed in the small house of the rabbinical college's librarian, who received a salary from the committee. We know from correspondence that during the three years he spent in Florence, Hizkiahu was underfed, forced to live in a confined space full of stored furniture, and subjected to an extremely intensive study regime. The greatest difficulties he had in those years, according to his letters, were in learning Italian, a language he was expected to master, while he would have preferred to learn more

Hebrew. He also suffered from the lack of a companion from his own world. He had grown extremely homesick by the time that Faitlovitch arrived in Florence in 1924 with four Beta Israel boys that he was accompanying to Germany and Austria. Two of them had been his traveling companions during the journey from Abyssinia; they had been studying in Jerusalem and were now being moved to Germany and Austria, as three boys fresh from Abyssinia had just arrived in Jerusalem at the Hilfsverein school. The librarian eventually refused to keep Hizkiahu with him any longer, officially due to insufficient means, a lack of space, and the behavioural difficulties of an adolescent, but probably also due to the fact that he, too, had been abandoned by the Jewish community, with a 'stranger' in his home whom he never mentioned by name in his letters, but simply referred to as 'the Falasha'. Hizkiahu felt very lonely and depressed, and he insisted on being allowed to join the other boys in Europe or Palestine. In Florence, the four people who had agreed to support the boy's education had been reduced to one person, the lawyer Alfonso Pacifici. Pacifici did not want to take responsibility for what might happen to this intelligent, but also rebellious and problematic, adolescent, and he tried unsuccessfully to persuade Faitlovitch to take the boy with him. Hizkiahu was sent to Turin to the orphanage run by Rabbi G. Bolaffio. But Faitlovitch would not change his views or his plans for the boy: Hizkiahu would have to become a doctor in Italy and return to Abyssinia to work, at any cost.

But life in Turin was even worse for Hizkiahu than in Florence. At one point, he was charged with homosexuality and the school did not want him to stay there. Most likely, he had been victimized by someone, as Faitlovitch himself said after an investigation. Right up to the time of Hizkiahu's death, there are records of the many problems that resulted from keeping the young man in Italy, where nobody felt responsible for him or wanted to contribute to his expenses, especially once Hizkiahu fell ill with tuberculosis. This refusal to take any financial responsibility was merely an external sign of an even deeper feeling of unwillingness among Italian Jewry (at all levels) to be involved in this matter. All of the documentation examined by the author[15] gives evidence of this feeling. Pacifici was the only one who felt obligated to care for the boy, but he acted alone, and reluctantly. Hizkiahu was sent to sanatoria in Davos, Switzerland, where his health improved, but he was soon forced to leave because of a lack of payment, and was sent to the Jewish Sanitorium in Merano, Italy. He was also discharged from the Merano facility, again because no one would pay for his care. The rabbi of Turin complained that nobody wanted to be bothered with the boy – neither Pacifici, nor the Chief Rabbi of Rome Angelo Sacerdoti, nor Angelo Sereni, the president of the Union of Italian Israelite Communities – and said that the young man

> can no longer stay in Merano because he is almost cured. We have started procedures with the Committee for emigrants in Trieste to try to arrange for the youth's emigration to Palestine, but there are insurmountable difficulties; he has no documents, passport, birth certificate, nothing. Meanwhile there are enormous expenses to be sustained … we have no more funds. If you want to prevent the youth from being handed over to the police as a homeless person you must, as soon as possible, send news, money, show an interest. You can also write to the Jewish Sanatorium in Merano directly by telegram to prevent the young Hizkiahu from being discharged.[16]

Faitlovitch went to see him, but the young man was nevertheless discharged from Merano and sent to Turin – and from there back to Florence, to Pacifici. Not much is known about Hizkiahu's last few months in Italy before embarking for Egypt, but we do know that he was delivered, like a parcel, to the rabbi of Alexandria, Davide Prato, who protested against the disastrous idea of sending a tubercular patient to the hot, humid climate of Alexandria, the city where Hizkiahu died on 7 February 1931. It is clear that everyone in Italy had tried to get rid of the boy and that Hizkiahu felt very lonely, unappreciated, and misunderstood. Moreover, he could not understand why he was made to repeat classes because of his poor Latin and Greek. Was he supposed to go back to Abyssinia and teach these subjects to his brethren? Hizkiahu's feelings of inadequacy in the face of the great effort required of him, combined with the meagre support offered by the Italian Jewry, had very serious consequences. He was aware of the connections between the somatic and psychological levels of the disease that struck him down, and in a letter to Faitlovitch written from Alexandria, he mentioned the role that his environment had played in his illness: 'the main cause which has obliged me to interrupt my studies has been the illness; almost as if to vindicate an unsatisfied and ill-contained burning desire'.[17] This unsatisfied burning desire, bursting out of the confines of his superego, which could no longer control the impulse, was identified by the boy as the cause of his somatic illness. Discontent and loneliness seem to have been Hizkiahu's only companions as he moved through various Italian cities before ending up to Alexandria. His misery was relieved only by the arrival of his companions as they passed through Florence on the way from Jerusalem to Germany or Austria, whom he desperately hoped to join. But Faitlovitch was not interested in his individual case, except in the context of the work he intended to accomplish. His strong personality and his authoritarianism stood out against the background of an Italian Jewish community that was not very committed to Faitlovitch's 'holy work'. Only a highly esteemed person such as Margulies might have been able to change the course of events. But he was already dead.

MAKONNEN LEVI'S STORY

By contrast, the case of Abraham Adgeh and Makonnen Levi, two young men taken to study in London in 1927, is an example of how the commitment of the host family and the community in general could help a young person to identify with the culture of his adopted country.

Abraham Adgeh spent nine years with the Levy family, of whom Shalva Weil wrote: 'Mr Levy was a respected dentist in the community and he and his family took complete responsibility for him [Abraham] and arranged for his education.'[18] In her paper dedicated to Abraham, Weil illustrated the boy's effective integration ('one of the more successful students of Dr Faitlovitch')[19] into a prestigious school in Highbury (St John's College) and noted that: 'Abraham, more than Makonnen, was very popular and developed real friendships with members of the community.'[20] This was a great achievement from the point of view of his integration into British-Jewish culture. However, it surely made it difficult for the young man to re-adapt when he had to return to an Ethiopian context, as by then it had become impossible for him to live in a rural environment without running water, books, and newspapers. Abraham took part in the resistance against the Italians in Ethiopia and obtained a position with the Ministry of Commerce when Haile Selassie returned to power. As Weil concludes: 'The picture that emerges is one of a gifted individual, who acquired the manners and education of his hosts and continued to place great importance on education. In Ethiopia, he would fondly recall his days in England.'[21]

The story of Makonnen Levi, Taamrat's nephew, is quite different. The four years he spent in London must have been extremely difficult for him. One year after his arrival, Samuel Levine, who was housing him and providing for his education, went bankrupt and was forced to close down the Townley Castle School, of which he was headmaster. Levine then tried to free himself of the irksome responsibility the boy had become.[22] When Levine approached Faitlovitch to impress on him the seriousness of the situation, the latter did not reply for two years, which only made things worse. Levine even turned to the Ethiopian Embassy and asked them to pay for the boy's return journey, explaining that he 'had been involved in the matter by Faitlovitch and had been a supporter of the Falasha movement in 1925'. He said he had agreed to take a Falasha boy at his school after being assured that there was 'a small committee in London that would supervise the education of the boy and generally see to his interests and welfare'. He declared that he had been misled, 'as there was no committee at all'.[23] As in the case of Hizkiahu Finkas, the small committees created to support the actions undertaken on a boy's behalf were not always competent. Moreover, most communities did not consider this work a high budget priority. As soon as they ran into difficulties, community leaders would turn to Faitlovitch, who in the meantime had usually moved on to other initiatives, or become involved in fundraising for the Addis Ababa school, and preferred to ignore their entreaties in the hope that they would find a solution by themselves. Faitlovitch handled Hizkiahu and Makonnen's cases at the end of the 1920s in much the same way, leaving it to their respective communities, Florence and London, to procure funds and assume full responsibility for the troubled boys. With his prolonged silence, Faitlovitch seemed to be trying to force the Jewish world to speak with his voice and take on the 'holy work' that he had initiated, assuming responsibility for the commitments he had made to the boys' families and the Falashas of Ethiopia. This was Faitlovitch's usual behaviour: he would create awkward situations and leave the individuals who had become involved in the pro-Falasha programme to work them out as best they could.

TADESSE JACOB'S STORY

Tadesse Jacob, another nephew of Taamrat's, arrived in Cairo in 1931 thanks to the chief rabbi of Cairo, the same Nahum who had been sent by the Alliance in 1908 to counteract the results of Faitlovitch's mission during that same period. In the meantime, relations between the two of them had become friendlier, due to the intervention of various people, including a special role played by Wolfenson (Ben Zeev),[24] as Tadesse himself testified.

After having studied for a few years at Faitlovitch's school in Addis, Tadesse had been singled out because of his remarkable learning abilities. In fact, his correspondence in French from Cairo between 1937 and 1939 is admirable for its masterful language. Quotations and educated references to French literature and philosophy fill his letters, showing the excellent learning abilities that distinguished this young man.

During an interview at his house in Addis in 2000, the author noted the reverence with which Tadesse still regarded Faitlovitch, whom he considered to be a kind of 'saviour', the man who had enabled him to attend the school in Addis, and with the help of a scholarship, to finish his studies at the French *lycée* in Cairo, with the help of Nahum and the Jewish community there. The education he received would have a profound influence on the rest of his life, from his participation (with Taamrat) in the Ethiopian resistance in Egypt, to his entry into Ethiopia from Sudan as he accompanied Emperor Haile Selassie on his return from exile, to his appointment to a position in the Ministry of Customs that was important in terms of social prestige as well as financial reward. Tadesse was not tormented like his uncle Taamrat. He was more affable and inclined to find ways to compromise rather than let a situation reach the breaking point. He managed to take advantage of what Faitlovitch had been able to offer him without being overwhelmed by his patron's authoritarian character, and he fully enjoyed all of the benefits received.

There were varying reactions towards Faitlovitch from the young people he had introduced into the European Jewish world. He had mapped out a future for this segment of the Falasha community, and at the same time initiated a period of discontinuity from the original environment. Some of the young people were more successful than others in reconstructing the various components of their identity and finding ways to integrate. Others paid for their success with difficulties in reconstructing an identity for themselves in a world of disparities that led to feelings of alienation. Still others, such as Hizkiahu Finkas, Makonnen Levi, and Solomon Isaac, were unable to cope and suffered breakdowns. A unique case, due to the complexity of his character, was Taamrat Emmanuel, to whom the next chapter is devoted.

Some of Faitlovitch's students accused him of taking control of their lives and fates, while others appreciated his efforts and took advantage of the opportunities they were offered. For others still, there is not yet enough biographical documentation to allow a full analysis of the issue.

NOTES

1. One of these boys was Solomon Isaac (Yitzhak). See Weil, 'The Life', pp. 40–9.
2. See Sh. Weil, 'In memoriam: Yona Bogale', *Peamim*, 33 (1987), pp. 140–3 (Hebrew).
3. Letter of 7 March 1927, *Fait. Coll.*, f. 99.
4. Letter from the Legation of the United States of America in Addis Ababa to Faitlovitch, dated 13 January 1929, *Fait. Coll.*, f. 117.
5. Letter to Chajes in Vienna of 25 May 1927, *JTS*, Adler 26.
6. Letter of 25 May 1927, *JTS*, Adler 26.
7. Weil, 'The Life'.
8. See C. Guandalini, 'Gete Yirmiahu and Beta Israel's Regeneration: A Difficult Path' in T. Parfitt and E. Trevisan Semi (eds), *Jews of Ethiopia the Birth of an Elite* (London-New York, 2005) pp. 112–129
9. See Guandalini, 'Gete Yirmiahu'.
10. Ibid.
11. *Fait. Coll.*, f. 93.
12. Report of the Chairman of the American Pro–Falasha Committee, Elias Solomon, *Fait. Coll.*, f. 127.
13. For Hizkiahu Finkas, see E. Trevisan Semi, 'From Wolleqa to Florence: The Tragic Story of Faitlovitch's Pupil Hizkiahu Finkas', in Parfitt and Trevisan Semi (eds), *The Beta Israel in Ethiopia*, pp. 15–39.
14. See A. Astrologo and F. Del Canuto, 'Firenze 1920: storia del "comune ebraico"', *La rassegna mensile di Israel*, 44 (1978), pp. 6–42.
15. It can be found in *Fait. Coll.* and in the *CAHJP*. The author also had a private interview with Alberto Benaim, Hizkiahu's Italian playmate in Florence.
16. Letter from Bolaffio to Faitlovitch of 28 February 1928, *Fait. Coll.*, f. 100.
17. Letter from Hizkiahu Finkas to Faitlovitch of 18 May 1929, *Fait. Coll.*, f. 118.
18. Sh. Weil, 'Abraham Adgeh: the Perfect English Gentleman' in Parfitt and Trevisan Semi (eds), *Jews of Ethiopia the Birth of an Elite*, pp. 101–111.
19. Ibid.
20. Ibid.
21. Ibid.
22. See E. Trevisan Semi, 'Ethiopian Jews in Europe: Taamrat Emmanuel in Italy and Makonnen Levi in England' in Parfitt and Trevisan Semi (eds), *Jews of Ethiopia the Birth of an Elite*, pp. 79–100.
23. Ibid.
24. See brief autobiographical note written by Tadesse Jacob the year after he arrived in Cairo (1932), 'The Story of my Life', *Fait. Coll.*, f. 138 (Hebrew).

1. Faitlovich's family (*Faitlovitch Collection, Sourasky Central Library, Tel Aviv University*)

2. Faitlovitch's family sitting on their balcony in Tel Aviv in the late 1920s (*Faitlovitch Collection, Sourasky Central Library, Tel Aviv University*)

3. Faitlovitch sitting with the four boys standing: Hizkiahu Finkas, Abraham Meir, Jona Bogale and Abraham Barok in 1921 (*Faitlovitch Collection, Sourasky Central Library, Tel Aviv University*)

4. Taamrat Emmanuel (*Viterbo's family*)

5. Faitlovitch sitting with his brother Haim, Taamrat Emmanuel, Dr Entin and Solomon Isaac standing, in Jerusalem in 1920 (*Faith's family*)

6. Faitlovitch with Taamrat Emmanuel and Gete Yirmiahu (1907–08) (*Faitlovitch Collection, Sourasky Central Library, Tel Aviv University*)

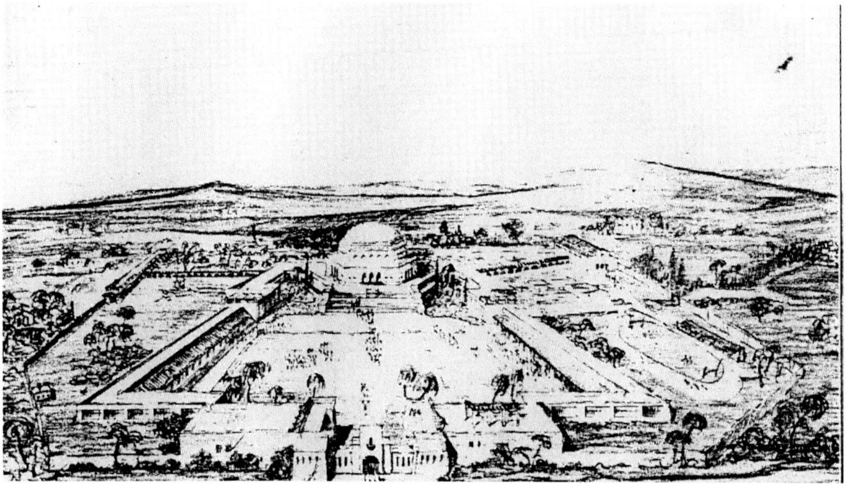

7. Faitlovitch's imaginary school in Addis Ababa (*Faitlovitch Collection, Sourasky Central Library, Tel Aviv University*)

8. Faitlovitch's real school in Addis Abeba (*Viterbo's family)*

9. Faitlovitch with his sister Leah at the Addis Ababa school in 1926 (*Faitlovitch Collection, Sourasky Central Library, Tel Aviv University*)

10. Faitlovitch and Taamrat Emmanuel (*Faitlovitch Collection, Sourasky Central Library, Tel Aviv University*)

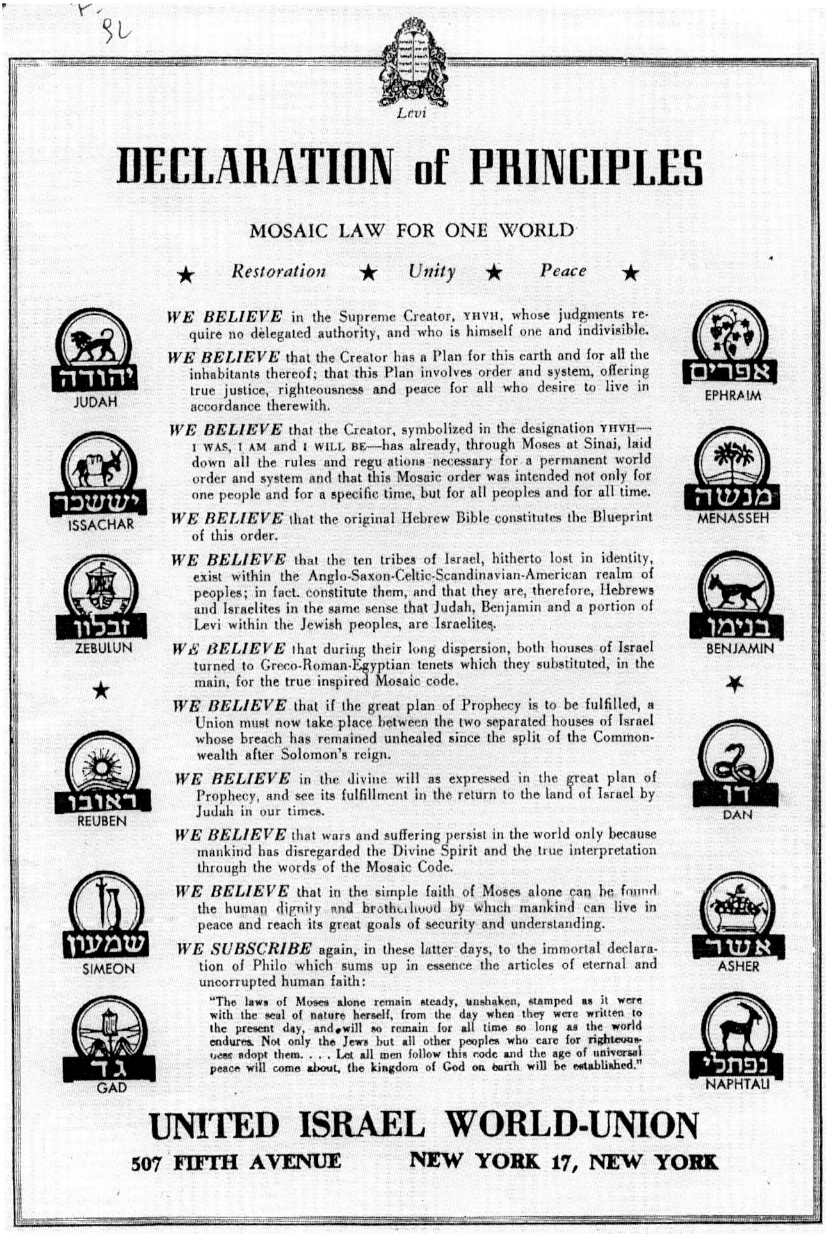

Levi

DECLARATION of PRINCIPLES

MOSAIC LAW FOR ONE WORLD

★ *Restoration* ★ *Unity* ★ *Peace* ★

WE BELIEVE in the Supreme Creator, YHVH, whose judgments require no delegated authority, and who is himself one and indivisible.

WE BELIEVE that the Creator has a Plan for this earth and for all the inhabitants thereof; that this Plan involves order and system, offering true justice, righteousness and peace for all who desire to live in accordance therewith.

WE BELIEVE that the Creator, symbolized in the designation YHVH—I WAS, I AM and I WILL BE—has already, through Moses at Sinai, laid down all the rules and regu ations necessary for a permanent world order and system and that this Mosaic order was intended not only for one people and for a specific time, but for all peoples and for all time.

WE BELIEVE that the original Hebrew Bible constitutes the Blueprint of this order.

WE BELIEVE that the ten tribes of Israel, hitherto lost in identity, exist within the Anglo-Saxon-Celtic-Scandinavian-American realm of peoples; in fact. constitute them, and that they are, therefore, Hebrews and Israelites in the same sense that Judah, Benjamin and a portion of Levi within the Jewish peoples, are Israelites.

WE BELIEVE that during their long dispersion, both houses of Israel turned to Greco-Roman-Egyptian tenets which they substituted, in the main, for the true inspired Mosaic code.

WE BELIEVE that if the great plan of Prophecy is to be fulfilled, a Union must now take place between the two separated houses of Israel whose breach has remained unhealed since the split of the Commonwealth after Solomon's reign.

WE BELIEVE in the divine will as expressed in the great plan of Prophecy, and see its fulfillment in the return to the land of Israel by Judah in our times.

WE BELIEVE that wars and suffering persist in the world only because mankind has disregarded the Divine Spirit and the true interpretation through the words of the Mosaic Code.

WE BELIEVE that in the simple faith of Moses alone can be found the human dignity and brotherhood by which mankind can live in peace and reach its great goals of security and understanding.

WE SUBSCRIBE again, in these latter days, to the immortal declaration of Philo which sums up in essence the articles of eternal and uncorrupted human faith:

"The laws of Moses alone remain steady, unshaken, stamped as it were with the seal of nature herself, from the day when they were written to the present day, and will so remain for all time so long as the world endures. Not only the Jews but all other peoples who care for righteousness adopt them. . . . Let all men follow this code and the age of universal peace will come about, the kingdom of God on earth will be established."

UNITED ISRAEL WORLD-UNION

507 FIFTH AVENUE NEW YORK 17, NEW YORK

11. Declaration of Principles of the Mosaic Law for One World (*Faitlovitch Collection, Sourasky Central Library, Tel Aviv University*)

12. Faitlovitch's last house in Tel Aviv, Vitkin street 21 (*photo by author*)

Faitlovitch versus Taamrat: A Western Colonialist versus a Disappointed Native

Taamrat Emmanuel (c. 1888–1963) was born in Azazo, a village near Gondar. He was the son of Terunesh – a woman described by his cousin Tadesse Jacob as a Coptic noblewoman,[1] and by others as a converted Falasha – and Fanta Dawit, a Falasha[2] who converted to Christianity and took the name of Gabra Maryam.[3] Taamrat was 'discovered' as an adolescent in the Swedish mission in Asmara and converted to Judaism by Jacques Faitlovitch during his first trip to Abyssinia in 1904–05.

The meeting of Faitlovitch and Taamrat in the Abyssinia of the early 1900s was a coming together of two extremely distant universes, rich in shared mythological symbols and representations, and it set in motion certain processes that continue to unfold today.

Taamrat had been approached by Westerners before, through the Protestant missionaries and their schools in the city of Asmara, which were infused with the Italian culture of the colonies. Later, when he was sent to Paris to continue his studies, he soon fell under the influence of the European Jewish culture he encountered at the École normale of the Alliance, a culture that was not without its share of racism.

While on his way to Paris to pursue his education, Taamrat stopped in Marseilles, where he arrived on 11 August 1905: he was seen as living proof of the existence of a mythical African Orient. At the time, he was not fully aware of the ramifications of the regeneration project in which he, his companion, and many other young men to follow would be involved. After only two years in France, he was sent to Florence as a result of a disagreement regarding the nature of his education.

In Florence, Taamrat earned the title of *maskil* in 1915, and that of *shochet* in 1916. In those years the values of democracy and liberalism, which had been proclaimed and taught by great statesmen such as Giuseppe Mazzini and Carlo Cattaneo in the mid-nineteenth century, were still considered a positive heritage and a common good. Trapped in Italy by the outbreak of the First World War, Taamrat remained in the country until 1920, an eyewitness to the unrest and upheaval of the period.

The world in which Taamrat lived was the Jewish Zionist world of Margulies (1858–1922), Chajes (1876–1927) – the future rabbi of Vienna – and Faitlovitch; but it was also a world defined by an assimilated Italian Jewish culture and the Italian values of the period. The mythical 'West' of Taamrat's imagination could not be reconciled with the rapid changes taking place, first in Italy and then in Ethiopia, and the image ended up being shattered, leaving him with nothing but disillusion and disappointment.

TAAMRAT AND FAITLOVITCH

Taamrat Emmanuel was Faitlovitch's favourite student, and he became a great Ethiopian intellectual. Taamrat was the number one escort, informant, mediator, and interpreter for the Europeans who came in search of the Falashas. He was especially close to Faitlovitch, with whom he had a privileged relationship. But it was also a relationship in which he was continually torn between obedience and rebellion, and it ineluctably altered his life.

Faitlovitch and Taamrat's personal relationship mirrors the relationship between their two cultural universes. Faitlovitch, a strong, autocratic, and determined personality, observed the Ethiopian reality through the Taamrat's eyes, yet he insisted that his own interpretations were more correct than those of his informant, whom he described at different times as 'obstinate', 'disobedient', 'indifferent', and ''infantile'. Taamrat frequently rebelled against his 'master', acting on his own convictions and passions. He always chose to uphold what he considered his most precious asset, his dignity, especially when his Abyssinian identity was at stake. For example, he translated an anti-fascist article into Amharic, participated in the Resistance movement of the Ethiopian political exiles in Egypt, and was active in Sudan in helping the Negus return to his country. These choices were strongly criticized by Faitlovitch, for whom the only values worth upholding were Jewish honour and his 'holy work', i.e. the regeneration of the Falashas. When prevented from taking action, the 'student' would simply make dispirited remarks from the corner to which he had been sent, and whenever possible, he would brandish the weapon of irony, to his 'master's' endless agitation.

Taamrat was named head of the school that Faitlovitch founded in Addis Ababa in 1923, and he continued to observe with great discernment and disenchantment the ideological developments in Italy and their repercussions in Ethiopia, under the shadow of a utopian vision that would loom over him for the rest of his life. He felt himself to be isolated, as though interned in the school in Addis Ababa. He attempted to flee the city on more than one occasion, without ever completely managing to escape. C. A. Viterbo, the Italian lawyer who was closest to him during his Florentine days, wrote in an article commemorating his death, 'his spirit was restless and ranged above and beyond the confines of the School'.[4] Taamrat himself described it in 1932 as 'a simulacrum of a school'.[5] From that neglected, inadequate space, Taamrat watched as the West paraded in front of him.[6] The Italians had become Fascists and conquerors; the Jews, though philanthropists, were penniless; and the Italian Fascist colonial regime soon began to flex its muscle in Ethiopia. Censorship and control of the press created trouble for Taamrat, not only in terms of his dealings with the Italian authorities, but also in terms of his relationship with Faitlovitch. One episode in particular, described by Grinfeld,[7] led to the closure of the Falasha school in Addis Ababa in March 1927, with unpleasant repercussions. Taamrat translated an anti-Fascist article that had been published in France into Amharic,[8] adding a brief introduction of his own on Mussolini. This unleashed a furious reaction from the Italian Legation,[9] and resulted in the closure of the school. Faitlovitch, too, reacted harshly to the news, but for different reasons. He feared that the incident would seriously compromise his work of Jewish outreach among the Falashas of Ethiopia in the eyes of the Italian authorities. He treated Taamrat like a rebellious child, threatening him with 'punishment' and abandonment, and emotionally blackmailing him with such phrases as 'your foolishness has caused me to become indisposed and stay in bed for a few days. Despite this carelessness I won't dismiss you for the moment … I don't want to abandon you.' In the same tone, he reminded Taamrat of the priority of his commitment to what Faitlovitch called the 'holy work'. Faitlovitch demanded that his student identify fully with the Falasha cause and forget his feelings of solidarity with his own people, despite the fact that they were threatened by a foreign country dominated by what Taamrat called a 'stupid and inhuman regime'. The rules were clear: 'keep out of political questions, no matter what they are for or against. Don't get involved in other people's business … your name must not be associated in public with any action that isn't related to our work.'[10] Faitlovitch closed the subject with a quotation from Jeremiah 2:2 that implied his forgiveness: 'I remember thee, the kindness of thy youth … when thou wentest after me into the wilderness in a land that was not sown.'[11] Taamrat had expected his master to get angry; in fact, in a letter he wrote to inform him of the episode, he declared himself ready to step down if the episode had compromised Faitlovitch's future work:

> If because of this event I have become a disturbance for your work, I sincerely prefer to save your holy work rather than myself, and I will accept it gladly … despite my prudence I find myself dragged into such affairs; as you always declare, you must have no pity when it comes to saving your work.[12]

Taamrat may have hoped deep down that he would be released from the commitment that had been a burden to him ever since his time in Florence, and about which he had become extremely sceptical. His scepticism came to play an important role in his decisions to oppose Faitlovitch. In response to the initiatives that Faitlovitch had pursued in Switzerland in the middle of the First World War, Taamrat wrote:

> I congratulate you for your work ... However I lack the animating force, perhaps also the faith, to follow in your giant footsteps; it seems beyond my forces to undertake the affairs of the Falashas, not to mention your titanic projects … We will discuss it after the war, let us for now try to live.[13]

Yet while shirts were changing colour in Italy and military uniforms were being donned, Taamrat remained a product of the liberal education he had received at the beginning of the century and he interpreted the 'Fascist madness' through those eyes. Writing to Faitlovitch just days after the end of the Italian occupation of Addis Ababa, Taamrat, with subtle irony, deplored the changeability of human beings.

TAAMRAT'S DOUBTS, DISAGREEMENTS, AND ACCUSATIONS OVER FAITLOVITCH'S 'HOLY WORK'

In truth, Taamrat strongly doubted that Faitlovitch's 'holy work' would produce any successful results, despite his enormous efforts. In a letter to the director of *Israel*[14] in February 1926, he freely expressed his reservations when he wrote:

> as much as the founder of the movement [Faitlovitch] has new skies and new lands in his visions, where the people to whom he has dedicated his whole energy will one day form a single body of universal Judaism and will go forth together sharing their joys and their sorrows, I who have followed him closely for over twenty years, am unable to abandon my doubts.

He was not sure whether Judaism, in this case Italian Judaism, really wished to recognize that there were Jews in Abyssinia. His conclusion was that if the work continued to languish or ceased altogether, 'starting it [would be] more damaging than fruitful'.[15] Taamrat never shared Faitlovitch's utopian vision, especially when it was beset by controversy. In the letters and reports he sent to the American Pro-Falasha Committee, Taamrat continually decried the lack of funds sent for the education of the Falashas and what he considered a lack of interest among the Jews in the future of his people.

Faitlovitch and Taamrat's initial views of each other's worlds in the early 1900s, which were inevitably idealized, gradually deteriorated over the years into mutual disappointment, accusation, and recrimination. After observing how many times Faitlovitch lost any possibility of cooperating with other people wishing to help and support the work on behalf of the Falashas because of his tendency to quarrel and to impose his opinion and his 'lack of harmony' with people,[16] Taamrat lost any hope that something could ever change. In 1949, when he was in Paris as *conseiller culturel* of the Ethiopian Embassy, he accused Faitlovitch of being the only one responsible for the failure of all the work on behalf of the Falashas, and wrote:

> you have had all the means and the facilities to travel and to stay in touch with the Falashas and with those who could be interested in them and help them. This was only up to you … nobody came to put obstacles to your work and if there were differences of opinion these were secondary. By this you can see how much responsibility you do have and on whom was put all the weight … I must admit that your dynamism distances any person wishing to cooperate. Even I couldn't cooperate with you![17]

So much so that when they met again in Israel late in their lives, these two protagonists of 50 years of Falasha history had no easy relationship. In 1951, Taamrat declined an invitation to a party at Faitlovitch's house, organized to promote the activities on behalf of the Falashas,

justifying his refusal with these bitter words: 'my participation at that banquet, half informal, half academic, in other words rather idle, would only seem to be a kind of advertisement. The clamour made will always be greater than the result obtained.'[18] Taamrat already preferred silence and study to clamour. One month later, he received a tribute from the Brit Ivrit Olamit in Jerusalem, and in a letter sent afterward to Ben Zvi, the president of the Brit, it was noted that it was fortunate that Taamrat had spoken in French and that Rabbi Gold had not understood his speech.[19] Taamrat was no longer hiding his feelings.
He settled in Jerusalem permanently in 1955[20] and was in Israel when Faitlovitch died,[21] taking part in the *sheloshim* ceremony held at the residence of President Ben Zvi.[22]

Taamrat had never shared Faitlovitch's utopian vision, especially in view of the cataclysms of history: the outbreak of the First World War, which for six years blocked the use of the funds collected in Europe and the United States (part of which was for Taamrat's living expenses in Italy) and halted the activity of the Pro-Falasha Committee, which had moved to Frankfurt;[23] the economic crisis of 1929 and the resulting difficulty in collecting funds from American Jews; the rise of Hitler and the disappearance of German Judaism, which had shown more solidarity with the Falashas than other groups; the occupation of Ethiopia by a racist and anti-Semitic regime; and, of course, the *Shoah*. Taamrat often spoke of the misfortunes that befell the Falashas and those who tried to help them. In 1918, he wrote, 'As soon as one begins to talk about the Falashas, wars break out and if anyone ... becomes particularly interested, something terrible happens to them.'[24]

TAAMRAT'S RESISTANCE TO A WESTERN JEW'S ARROGANCE

Taamrat reproached Faitlovitch for insisting on a project that was too ambitious and unrealistic with respect to the education of young people. Faitlovitch believed the educational programme should be geared towards the liberal professions rather than the trades. He wanted to train future teachers, rabbis, doctors, and lawyers, and he proposed an educational approach based on a strictly Western Jewish model. Taamrat also criticized Faitlovitch for not giving full recognition to the ancient Falasha traditions, and tried to resist the changes that Faitlovitch wanted to introduce into Falasha culture and religion.

Taamrat often used the arguments put forward by Viterbo – who did not approve of the short- and medium-term pro-Falasha projects –

as counter-proposals to Faitlovitch's ideas. He declared himself in favour of moving the school from Addis Ababa to Gondar so that it would be closer to the hinterlands inhabited by the Falashas. He also believed in the idea of a trade school that could guarantee the gradual development and survival of his people.

Viterbo had expressed concern over that fact that the Falasha school was located in Addis Ababa, a long way from the students' families. He criticized Faitlovitch's decision, in which, he said, 'the convenience of a delegation before an emperor prevails', and faulted him for his lack of concern for the consequences of the student's distance from their places of origin.[25] In his report of his trip to Ethiopia, Viterbo wrote that the Falashas

> must not become little Europeans. They cannot all become knowledgeable or great scholars. Instead the school must be designed for a large group of students and must take into account the fact that they must return to be, like their fathers and grandfathers, peasants, shepherds, blacksmiths, and artisans. The aim of the school must not be to transform the lives of the Falashas, but to help them to improve, both for their personal and for general benefit.[26]

On this question, Taamrat quoted Viterbo's opinions in his letters to Faitlovitch: 'the school that Viterbo sees for the Falashas concentrates on agriculture and manual labour'.[27] Taamrat added that the Italian lawyer had not been shocked by certain local customs, and had even appreciated their uniqueness. Thus, using Viterbo's opinions, he expressed his own thoughts on the issue, recalling that Viterbo

> was by no means scandalized over certain customs ... which would seem to be in open contradiction to some post-biblical or talmudic institutions, as an extremist would be. On the contrary, open-minded as he is, he wishes some of the particularly good customs could be developed. And I agree with him, especially regarding the prayer ceremonies.[28]

His praise of Viterbo's open-mindedness suggests an accusation of radicalism and intolerance on the part of Faitlovitch. The argument over where the school should be located became most bitter when the disagreement between Faitlovitch and the Union of Italian Israelite Communities reached its peak in April 1937, after Viterbo had returned to Italy.[29] It was not until his trip to Ethiopia in 1942–44 that Faitlovitch changed his mind and tried to build a school near Gondar, but by then the Palestine committee charged with funding the educational work was insisting on the reopening of the Addis school[30] and Faitlovitch gave up, leaving Ethiopia for Egypt.

Viterbo thought it was important to maintain the traditional Falasha customs, a view that was completely shared by Taamrat, who tried to use the Italian Jew's authority to counteract his master's authority.

From the very beginning, Faitlovitch had tried to change important Falasha cultural traditions such as the use of monasticism and of sacrifices, which were deeply rooted in their religion. In this matter he aligned himself with the Protestant missionaries who, a few decades before, had waged a strong campaign to stop this practice, which clearly disturbed the Westerners arriving in Ethiopia. Quirin has reported a discussion between Faitlovitch and a monk on the subject of sacrifices, in which Faitlovitch succeeded in demonstrating that it was forbidden to perform sacrifices anywhere except in Jerusalem.[31] In reality, however, the practice of sacrifices had become much rarer, as Deborah Lifschitz discovered on her journey in 1932 when she was obligated to pay for the performance of a Falasha sacrifice.[32] The decline of the custom, as mentioned by Lifschitz, was partly due to difficult economic conditions, but also, as Viterbo stressed in 1936–37, 'the use of sacrifices has diminished because of the contacts in the last thirty years between the Falashas and talmudic and rabbinical Judaism'.[33] Viterbo also wrote that 'it is a fact that after thirty years of influence exerted by world Jewry, especially through Dr Faitlovitch, the Falashas have been very influenced by talmudic and rabbinical Judaism'.[34] Faitlovitch tried to impose the talmudic tradition, then unknown to the Falashas, and to remove any deviation from rabbinical Judaism from their practices. Viterbo remarked in his unpublished notes, made during his travels among the Falasha villages with Taamrat, that some light could be seen in the villages after sunset on Friday, despite the fact that the Falasha custom was to extinguish their fires at night – a common practice in all African villages due to the fear of wildfires – and he attributed this to Faitlovitch's influence. Earlier, Aeskoly had compared the Falashas to the Karaites (who rejected the Talmud) who extinguished their fires by sunset on Friday and spent the night in the dark. It is possible that Faitlovitch convinced the Falashas to change this practice because it might be interpreted as evidence of a sectarian influence. Unlike Faitlovitch, Viterbo tried to explain many of the Falasha religious traditions, especially those related to the celebration of festivals and rites, saying that they were based on ancient and abandoned Jewish customs, and felt they should continue to celebrate them according to their ancient ways.[35] This attitude was completely foreign to Faitlovitch, who did everything he could to induce the Falashas to make rapid changes and assimilate Western Judaism. Summerfield has observed, based on interviews with Jona Bogale and a few priests who had met Faitlovitch, that 'Faitlovitch was sufficiently respectful of their traditions as, when he discussed the issue of modifying their religion, he said it in such a way as to not offend the community, the priests or the people'.[36] But this approach could also be interpreted as merely a good way to get people to accept the changes without arousing any great resistance.

One view that Faitlovitch and Viterbo shared was the importance of changing the Falasha calendar. The Falashas used both a lunar calendar and the Ethiopian solar calendar and had a very complex religious year. Viterbo agreed with Faitlovitch that a new calendar should be prepared in order to match their festivals to Jewish feast dates and avoid confusion. The calendar was in fact introduced by Shmuel Be'eri, an emissary of the Jewish Agency who, along with Jona Bogale, directed the school that opened in Asmara in December 1953. This calendar was officially adopted in 1954, when 400 Falashas gathered in Wusaba to declare their acceptance of it.[37]

Taamrat and the other youths educated in Europe were expected to become completely assimilated into Western Judaism and its practices, in order to introduce them to the Falashas in Ethiopia. As shown in the previous chapter, there were varying responses from Faitlovitch's students, forced to cope with this abrupt change. Taamrat tried to resist some of the changes, especially those involving festival celebrations and prayer ceremonies. He completely disagreed with the way in which the Falasha youths were being educated; he would have preferred that the school be more vocational than intellectual, in keeping with its location. But Faitlovitch was too strong. Taamrat could do little more than complain, which he continued to do throughout his life. He also objected to the major task that Faitlovitch had set for himself at the end of his life: to bring about a mass migration of Falashas to Israel. Taamrat opposed this plan because he feared that if the Falashas arrived in Israel without sufficient preparation, 'they would become *schnorrers*'.[38] He expressed himself openly on this topic because he thought that a minimum of twenty to thirty years' preparation would be required to prepare the Falashas for a transfer: 'in the conditions they are under today, Falashas can not abandon Ethiopia; nor can they live and fight for life like the Jews coming from all over the world to Israel.'[39] The issue of a possible immigration to Israel caused problems for Taamrat in Ethiopia. In fact, having most likely been pushed by Faitlovitch, contrary to his own opinion he tried to convince the Negus that in some very distant future it might be possible for Falashas to migrate to Israel in order to avoid the appearance of a 'Jewish question' in Ethiopia. Because of this statement, Taamrat was obliged to leave Paris for a time in order to discuss the issue with the emperor.[40] Although he disagreed with Faitlovitch, he was unable to oppose him outright, and this state of dependence on his mentor was a cause of great frustration and disappointment.

Unfortunately, even the work he had hoped to accomplish in Faitlovitch's library after his former mentor's death was made impossible by a paralysis that struck his left side, leaving him unable to write. Taamrat died in Tel Aviv in December 1963.

Taamrat managed to combine the best of the values he had gleaned from the two cultures. He was supportive of and loyal to the teacher who had introduced him to European and American Judaism, and to those who had exposed him to the liberal, democratic Italian culture. However, he was also loyal to himself and respectful of his own dignity. Taamrat never forgot that he had been born an Ethiopian, and he could not tolerate the contempt shown towards his fellow countrymen by occupying foreigners from a country caught up in 'Fascist madness'. He refused to join Faitlovitch in Palestine, even when, after much difficulty, he had managed to obtain an entrance visa from the British Mandate. Instead, he chose to work for his own country, and along with other Ethiopians who had taken refuge in Egypt, to help the Negus return to Ethiopia.

Faitlovitch had the authority and power to impose his will on Taamrat, who had been his student for most of his life. Taamrat's choice to fight for Ethiopia against Italian colonialism, and to stay in Ethiopia after the Negus' return, were the kind of radical steps that a 'native' Ethiopian Falasha had to take in order to avoid being Faitlovitch's pawn.

NOTES

1. Private communication, Addis Ababa, May 2000.
2. Taamrat used the term 'Falasha' with no negative overtones.
3. See also Chapter 2.
4. C. A. Viterbo, 'Note tristi Emmanuel Taamrat', *Israel*, 9 January 1964.
5. Letter to the American Pro-Falasha Committee, September 1932, *Fait. Coll.*, f. 137.

6. For the school during the Italian occupation, see Y. Grinfeld, 'The Hebrew school in Addis Ababa at the beginning of the Italian Occupation (1937–37)', *Dor le-dor*, 5 (1992), pp. 51–2 (Hebrew).
7. T. Grinfeld, 'Taamrat Emmanuel – Forerunner of the Revival of Ethiopian Jewry', *Peamim*, 22 (1985), pp. 67–8 (Hebrew). This article also lists Taamrat's scientific publications.
8. The article was translated by *Revolution prolétarienne* and published in *Berhanna Salam*, 17 March 1927.
9. According to Grinfeld, 'Taamrat', p. 67, this episode cost Taamrat two days in prison, but the author found no trace of this in the letters. In his letter of 9 April 1927, *Fait. Coll.*, f. 137, Taamrat says that the Legation had at first believed that the translator was Weinziger, the former Austrian consul and editor of the journal, but once the real identity of the translator was known, they demanded his arrest. The *Ras* instead responded with the arrest of Ghebre Krestos, not for having published the article but for having broken the law that declared that the *Ras* was to inspect each article regarding foreign affairs before it was published. Taamrat added: 'Thanks to the personal intervention of the *ras*, nothing has happened to me … I had to close the school for a day.' The one who was held responsible and punished was Ghebre Krestos, who was fined a hundred thalers and imprisoned for a month while, according to Taamrat, 'I returned to celebrate Purim', which ironically is the feast of those who have escaped danger.
10. Letter of 31 May 1927, *Fait. Coll.*, f. 137.
11. The quotation is in Hebrew. This is one of the very few surviving letters from Faitlovitch in New York to Taamrat, of 31 May 1927, *Fait. Coll.*, f. 137.
12. Letter of 9 April 1927, *Fait. Coll.*, f. 137.
13. Letter of 4 June 1918, *Fait. Coll.*, f. 137.
14. Letter of February 1926 to the Journal *Israel*, *Fait. Coll.*, f. 99.
15. Ibid.
16. Letter of 11 April 1949, in Trevisan Semi, *L'epistolario*, p. 335.
17. Ibid., p. 334 .
18. Letter from Jerusalem of 7 September 1951, *Fait. Coll.*, f. 137.
19. Letter from A. Rosenfeld to Ben Zvi of 7 October 1951, *CZA*, A116/156. Rav Zeev Gold was president of the Department for Educational and Hebrew Culture in the Diaspora of the Ha-Histadrut ha Tzionit.
20. The news was reported in *Africans Israelites* (organ of the Union of Ethiopian Hebrew Congregations, a movement of black Americans converted to Judaism, see Chapter 12), June 1955: 'Professor Taamrat Emmanuel, our Honored President, has been transferred to the Ethiopian Consulate of Jerusalem, Israel; we hope we will be successful in bringing him to America on a speaking tour. We hope to have articles by Dr. Jacques Faitlovitch and Professor Emmanuel in the near future.' *Fait. Coll.*, f. 142. Grinfeld ('Taamrat', p. 61) instead claims that Taamrat settled permanently in Israel in 1957. Also in an interview published in *Ha-aretz*, 23 January 1956, Taamrat is described as being resident in Jerusalem and cultural counsellor to the Ethiopian Consulate.
21. It was Taamrat who informed Viterbo of Faitlovitch's death in a telegram from Israel. See letters from Viterbo to Taamrat of 18 October 1955 and 13 November 1955 (Viterbo private archives). In them Viterbo begged Taamrat to break his long silence.
22. In an article L. Levi (*Israel*, 15 December 1955) referred to the funeral tribute given to Faitlovitch and wrote that Taamrat: ' now attaché to the diplomatic–cultural service of the Negus … in Jerusalem– replied to the questions put forward by the participants'.
23. Faitlovitch, in a letter of 15 June 1915 to Cyrus Adler of the Executive Committee of the American Jewish Committee, wrote: 'Italy's entrance into the war has materially affected our work for the Falashas, because it has completely paralysed the section of our headquarters in Germany', *Fait. Coll.*, f. 141.
24. Letter of 15 January 1918 from Rome, in Trevisan Semi, *L'epistolario*, pp. 104–5.
25. C. A. Viterbo, 'Relazione al Ministero dell'Africa italiana dell'opera svolta in A.O.I. in rappresentanza dell'Unione delle Comunità Israelitiche Italiane', in F. Del Canuto (ed.), *Israel 'Un decennio 1974–1984'* (Rome, 1984), pp. 87–8.
26. Ibid., p. 88.
27. See letter of 15 February 1937, in Trevisan Semi, *L'epistolario*, p. 234.
28. Ibid., p. 233.
29. See letter of 21 April 1937 in Trevisan Semi, *L'epistolario*, pp. 239–40.

30. See Chapter 14.
31. J. Quirin, *The Evolution*, p. 195.
32. D. Lifschitz, 'Un sacrifice chez les Falachas, juifs abyssins', *La terre et la vie*, 9 (1939), pp. 116–23.
33. Viterbo private archives.
34. Ibid.
35. See the chapter on Viterbo in Trevisan Semi, *Allo specchio*, pp. 107–23.
36. Summerfield, *From Falashas*, p. 88.
37. Ibid., p. 124.
38. Y. Etan, 'The Falasha Number One', *Ha–aretz*, 23 January 1956 (Hebrew).
39. Letter of 11 April 1949, in Trevisan Semi, *L'epistolario*, p. 335 .
40. Ibid.

11

Faitlovitch's Work Among the San Nicandro Converts in Italy: Lost Tribes Enthusiasm

This chapter deals with an event that occurred in Italy in the 1930s, which may be seen as an interesting but incidental episode in Faitlovitch's life story. However, the event is relevant because it shows the depth of Faitlovitch's commitment to every issue involving people who claimed to be Jews or were willing to convert to Judaism – even when they came from a tiny village in the south of Italy. It is the story of Faitlovitch's role among the followers of Donato Manduzio in San Nicandro in the early 1930s. About fifteen years later, the conversion of the Italian group and its subsequent immigration to Israel took place under the banner of Jewish universalism and messianism.

The events that surrounded the birth of Zionism created fertile ground for a messianic interpretation. It has frequently been noted that many elements of the Zionist vision were essentially messianic: social justice, liberation from foreign slavery, and the gathering in of the exiled. Signs of the fulfilment of prophetic visions were sought in everyday life and were interpreted in the light of a more general process of redemption and progressive Judaization. The redemption process that had begun with the rebirth of Israel in the Land of the Fathers and the convergence of the 'dispersed of Israel' from around the world was read as a universal event of cosmic importance that would led to the redemption of all humanity.

The history of the converts in San Nicandro was considered a concrete example of these messianic signs by the Zionist pioneers of the Palestine Brigade, who made contact with the group while crossing the Apulia region in tanks flying the blue-and-white banner that was to become the Israeli flag.

A group of people claiming to be Jews in San Nicandro, a small village in the Gargano area not far from the city of Foggia,[1] interested Faitlovitch right from the start. On one of his journeys through Italy, he decided to visit the small village with the intention of observing this phenomenon and including it in his 'missionary' plans.

The story of the conversion of a small group of inhabitants of the village of San Nicandro unfolded between the two world wars in an area in which there was intense proselytism by itinerant Italian American missionaries – Evangelicals, Pentecostals, Baptists, Adventists – travelling throughout the region. These missionaries were former Italian immigrants to America who had converted to Protestantism in America and returned to Italy to preach Protestantism.

The first person to recount the story of these conversions, romanticizing it and interpreting it as a miraculous messianic event, was P. E. Lapide[2] (Major Spitzer) of the Jewish Brigade, a member of the British Eighth Brigade led by Montgomery, who discovered the converts while he was crossing the Gargano area with his military convoy at the end of 1943. Once the existence of the converts was known, the members of the Jewish Brigade established increasingly close contact with them and attempted to send some of the converts to Bari, where they would have the opportunity to study Hebrew.[3]

According to Elena Cassin,[4] the prospect of migration to Palestine, warmly supported by the Jewish Brigade, led to the consolidation of the converts, who had at first not seriously considered the possibility of emigration.

THE STORY OF THE CONVERSION

Donato Manduzio (1885–1948), a charismatic leader and the founder of the movement, was born into a peasant family, and learned to read and write when he joined an infantry regiment during the First World War. He was sent home after being wounded, but received a disability pension which enabled him to devote himself to the reading of works that interested him, including books about magic.

In 1930 he had a vision, which he later described in his diary (in 1935). In it, he was in the dark, when he heard a voice telling him it had brought him light. Looking more carefully, he perceived a man holding an unlit lantern in his hand who, when asked why he did not light it, replied that he could not because he had no matches. Manduzio looked at his hand and realized he was holding a match, with which he proceeded to light the lantern, after which the vision disappeared. He wondered the following day about the meaning of the dream, but was unable to explain it until he met an acquaintance who had received a Bible from a Protestant preacher and gave it to him. When he opened the Bible, he discovered, to his great surprise, the story of the creation of the world, which greatly fascinated him. It may seem surprising that a person raised as a Catholic had not heard the story of Genesis, but, in fact, Catholicism as taught by the Italian Catholic Church was limited to a few stories from the New Testament and contained almost nothing from the Old Testament. This was especially true in rural areas, where people did not know the alphabet.

Manduzio believed that God the Creator, the same God that led Adam to Canaan and made promises to Isaac and Jacob, wished to call upon him to rekindle the light of the biblical religion. In subsequent visions he heard himself called Levi, and he decided to assume this name and have his followers call him by it. Manduzio thought of himself as a new Moses, who would lead his people into the desert towards the Promised Land. From 1932 onward, the children born into the community were given biblical names to affirm their new identities, despite the opposition of the registry office clerk.[5]

There were no Jewish communities in the Apulia region, the closest being Naples. Thus the fact that a peasant of San Nicandro would think that the Jews had been extinct for centuries and consider himself the founder of a new Jewish people met with little surprise. However, there was great astonishment the following summer when, on a market day, Manduzio met a travelling merchant who revealed to him that there were many representatives of that people in other cities. Manduzio obtained the addresses of some Jews in Florence and Turin from the merchant and immediately wrote to them. A reply came from Turin, inviting him to contact the Chief Rabbi in Rome, Angelo Sacerdoti. The start of this correspondence, at the end of August 1931, opened up a new chapter in the story.

According to Manduzio, the Rabbi of Rome – who initially thought this was a joke – did not reply until he had received his third letter.[6] 'How can all this have taken place', the Rabbi wanted to know, 'in a town where no Jews live and where Judaism, as a way of life, must be completely unknown?' The Rabbi's next question concerned the possibility that they had been descended from converted Jews: 'Do you have no tradition that you are descendants of Jewish families forced in the past to convert to Catholicism?'[7] It must indeed have seemed strange to the Rabbi in Rome that a simple reading of the Bible had produced a movement for conversion to Judaism. The possibility that a group of descendants of converts, or Marranos, belonging to the mysterious group called the *nidhei Yisrael*, had been 'lost' in southern Italy sounded more credible to the Chief Rabbi in Rome.

That movement, like other charismatic movements, was based on the interpretation of Manduzio's 'visions'. Interpreting them became a technique for analyszing everyday life and, thanks to a belief in premonition, a strategy for the future. The charismatic activities of the head of the movement and of those followers who also had the gift of 'visions' – including many women – further consolidated the group. The charismatic leader was also gifted with thaumaturgic healing powers and thus acquired considerable authority.

The group was initially called *i sabbatini* (from the Italian word *Sabato*, meaning Saturday) because of their practice of observing Saturday as a day of rest and holding their meetings on that day in Manduzio's house, which acted as a place of prayer. There they learned biblical verses and texts, set to the tunes of popular songs, by heart, which permitted the followers, many of whom were unable to read or write, to commit them to memory. Other texts were written and set to music by the followers themselves.[8] In all, there were about fifty converts, including women and children.

FAITLOVITCH'S VISIT

Until 1936, the Jewish communities in Rome and Florence maintained informal contacts with San Nicandro.[9] Therefore the phenomenon was known to Jacques Faitlovitch, who was undoubtedly struck by the story, which was often discussed in Italian Jewish circles.

Faitlovitch went to San Nicandro in January 1935 in order to learn whether these people could be considered *nidhei Ysrael* or *gerim* and made some notes of the visit in his diary.[10] According to the author of an article in commemoration of his death, Faitlovitch had first been to see Manduzio in 1931.[11] However, no confirmation of this has been found in his diaries, and it seems unlikely that Faitlovitch paid an initial visit to the Gargano area in that year. The first certain visit by Faitlovitch was in 1935. Nevertheless, from his brief description we get a clear impression that Faitlovitch had already met some of the *sabbatini*, although we do not know where.

In 1935, after two days in the town, Faitlovitch departed for Rome, satisfied that he had spent 'a good day with the proselytes'. From that moment on, Faitlovitch referred to them as proselytes – or to use the Hebrew word, *gerim* – indicating that he thought they represented a people who wished to convert rather than a case of marranism. His stay had been briefly disturbed by the police, who had come to investigate the presence of a foreigner – a Polish Jew who was well known to the Italian authorities as someone who hated Fascism – in an isolated village in Italy. A different version of the visit can be read in another volume of Manduzio's diary, written in 1938.[12] In this version, a doctor 'Falto Luigi', an amusing distortion of the surname 'Faitlovitch', whose imminent arrival had been announced in a letter from Pacifici (who had recently emigrated to Jerusalem), arrived at Manduzio's house at 9 p.m. on 28 January 1935, carrying a 'small suitcase'. The diary goes on to say:

> The doctor said, 'As you can see, I've come from Jerusalem and I bring best wishes from Alfonso Pacifici and all the brethren in the Holy Land' … [and] after he'd told us a lot of interesting things, he was astonished to know how we'd come to be, and I told him everything.

Manduzio also recalls that Faitlovitch

> left us Hebrew numbers and letters written in the Hebrew alphabet, as well as four books he had written about the Africans, and after he left he sent us three Hebrew–Italian spelling books. We were also told to allow one of our boys to go and study the Hebrew language, and I don't know how it happened, but as of today, 21 May 1938, no-one else has taken up these studies.

The promise made during that visit, to pay for a young man from the group to pursue Hebrew studies, could not be kept because of bureaucratic complications and red tape, for which Italy continues to be famous.

A few days later, Faitlovitch presented the proselytes' case to the Union of Israelite Communities in Rome, and in particular to Dante Lattes, a Zionist and editor of *La Rassegna Mensile di Israel*, the Italian official journal of the Union of the Israelite Communities.[13] In early September of the same year, Cerrone, one of the proselytes who apparently had more initiative than the group as a whole, went to Rome, where Faitlovitch was staying. Cerrone spent a few days with Faitlovitch, who took him to see various key members of the Italian Jewish community (Umberto Cassuto, Dante Lattes, and David Prato) and to attend services at the Rome synagogue. At the beginning of December 1936, Faitlovitch stopped in Foggia before setting sail for

Egypt from Brindisi. On this occasion he had only half a day to spend with Cerrone and another proselyte.[14]

It is certain that Faitlovitch, who travelled more than once to the Gargano area to visit the proselytes, and who introduced Cerrone to the official Jewish institutions in Rome, maintained a certain interest in this tiny group of converts. It was therefore not at all surprising that the following year, he became involved in enrolling young converts in a Jewish institution in Europe (as he had done with the young Falashas of Ethiopia) and helping to organize the group's emigration to Palestine. This is discussed in greater detail below.

Nineteen thirty-six was a watershed in the lives of the *sabbatini.* The new Chief Rabbi in Rome, David Prato, who had studied at the school run by Zvi Margulies, established official contacts with the converts through his personal envoy, Raffaele Cantoni. Cantoni came to San Nicandro in July 1937 for the purpose of regularizing the converts' rituals, opening a small synagogue, and integrating the group into the Jewish community in Naples. Cantoni also paid for one of the boys to spend the summer of 1937 in a Jewish summer camp. It must be remembered that the Jewish summer camps were becoming hotbeds of emigration to Palestine.

In 1937, official Italian Jewry seemed to have decided to get involved in this unusual conversion story. Raffaele Cantoni, representing the new Rabbi in Rome, visited San Nicandro again on 22 October with 22 *tallitot*[15] – which, as Cassin suggests, indicates the number of male converts at the time – plus an eight-armed menorah, a smaller menorah, a chalice and a container for incense. Authorization from the Ministry of Religion, which had been requested the previous year, had not been granted them; nor had they received permission to practice religious rites from the Fascist political authorities, which is not surprising given that the anti-Semitic press campaign that would culminate in the racial laws of 1938 was being planned during this period.

In 1938, the converts of San Nicandro were brought before the police chief and interrogated about their claims that they were Jewish. In the same year, Cantoni informed Manduzio of the decision temporarily to suspend the regularization of their conversion due to the difficulties faced by other Italian Jews who had been 'born into the faith', encouraging him to wait for better times.

The period of open persecution began in 1940. The converts would later demonstrate their solidarity with Italian Jewry by helping Jews from northern Italy who were trying to reach the Allies in the south.[16] In 1940, when news reached San Nicandro that Raffaele Cantoni had been interned – as a Zionist and anti-Fascist – in the Sforzacosta camp[17] in the Marche region, Manduzio sent him affectionate letters of solidarity and, more importantly, managed to arrange food parcels for him when he was later confined on the Tremiti islands.[18]

The meeting with the Jewish Brigade at the end of 1943 was undoubtedly a particularly important moment for the future of the group. Even Enzo Sereni visited the group just a few days before he parachuted into northern Italy (later to be captured and executed by the Nazis), and taught them to sing the *Ha-tiqvah*.[19] The commitment that the members of the Brigade made to the converts did not cease with the end of the war. On their return to Palestine, they managed to have the story of the conversion brought to the attention of the Jewish authorities in Palestine and interpreted as a sign of the great messianic times that were anticipated.

After the Liberation in 1945, Rabbi Prato returned to Rome and Raffaele Cantoni became the president of the Union of Israelite Communities. The issue of the converts could finally be resolved. On 26 July 1946, Rabbi Alfredo Ravenna was sent to San Nicandro to organize a ritual circumcision, which was performed on 13 adult proselytes between 4 and 8 August by *mohel* Arnaldo Ascarelli.[20] Raffaele Cantoni and Spitzer were present at the ceremony. The *tevilah* took place in the Mediterranean Sea, at Torre Maletta.[21]

During 1948 and 1949, the first groups immigrated to Israel and a few of them went to visit Faitlovitch in Tel Aviv. Most of the converts settled in Alma, a *moshav* not far from Safed in Galilee. Manduzio himself died in San Nicandro in 1948. Like Moses, in whose footsteps he had hoped to tread, he never saw the Promised Land. According to information acquired by Elena Cassin, Manduzio thought that emigration could only take place once the messianic promises had been fulfilled, when 'the hour of the golden age had struck in Israel'.[22]

In subsequent decades, the Italian converts were considered a particularly successful example of integration in Israel.[23]

ITALIAN *GERIM* AS LOST TRIBES

While Europe was in the grip of the *Shoah* and Jewish communities throughout Europe were being increasingly devastated by Nazism, a group of Christian families in Fascist Italy decided to convert to Judaism. When this news began to circulate at the end of the Second World War, it was interpreted as a 'miracle'.

Israel Ben Zeev wrote an article on the *gerim* of San Nicandro, whom he had visited in Israel in 1952.[24] In it he described the enthusiasm with which the strange news of the conversion, spread throughout Israel by members of the Jewish Brigade, was received in those dark times. Faitlovitch himself called this story 'a miracle of the Creator' when it was recounted to him first-hand by Manduzio during one of his visits to San Nicandro.[25] In his diary, Manduzio noted that Faitlovitch's reaction was rapturous: 'Because in such a dark place has emerged a light similar to our Father Abraham who leaves his Father and Mother to carry out the will of the Holy One.' In Jewish circles, the myth of the Lost Tribes and of people of Marrano descent was quite readily applied to the case of the Italian converts, and was used to justify their new status as members of the Jewish people. The Italian immigrants were classified as 'tribes of Israel' in the series of monthly meetings that Ben Zvi, president of the State of Israel, devoted every *rosh chodesh* to the 'dispersed of Israel' in the 1950s.

As mentioned above, the converts of San Nicandro attracted Faitlovitch's attention early on, and he mentions them in his diary, using the term *gerim.* Faitlovitch was trying to develop Judaism, transforming it into an active missionary religion, dedicated to spreading that light throughout the world and to all of the people on earth. During a speech he gave to one of the 'missionary' committees he had created,[26] he explained that the 'light' had hitherto been buried, but that the time had now come to uncover it and to illuminate all the corners and peoples of the earth. He added that it was a question of regaining ancient glory and honour, of recovering the knowledge of the Jewish people's role in the world, and of propagating the Jewish faith and sharing its wealth with other countries.[27]

The numerous visits that Faitlovitch paid to San Nicandro indicate how interested he was in this story. In addition to journeying to this distant village in the Gargano area while traveling through Italy on his pro-Falasha activities, he also welcomed one of the followers (Cerrone) in Rome, helping him to obtain financial aid from the Rome community[28] as well as books such as the Talmud and *L'Apologia dell'ebraismo*,[29] and facilitated the group's emigration to Palestine.

The circle of people who shared Faitlovitch's universalist vision and supported his pro-Falasha activity were interested in the conversion of Manduzio and his followers. The dozens of letters written to Faitlovitch by one of the converts (Cerrone) from 1935 to 1937[30] mention others who worked on the converts' behalf, particularly the key people mentioned above, all of whom were part of the group that collaborated on the journal *Der Ruf*, such as Alfonso Pacifici, M. Asher and Rabbi David Prato. In his letters to Faitlovitch, Cerrone used a scribe or another proselyte, who left blank spaces so that Cerrone could add the Hebrew letters. The use of Hebrew in the letters is curious: it is used for people's names (the new biblical Jewish names given to the followers), for festivals, and for place names in Palestine. At times, when it is Cerrone himself who is writing, it is simply used to transcribe the Italian. The considerable importance given by the various pan-Hebrew movements to the spread of the new Hebrew language being revived in Palestine is well known. Hebrew was considered an important means for communicating Jewish values and unifying communities from different backgrounds. In the case of San Nicandro, the language took on a strongly symbolic role, and the converts undoubtedly considered it a particularly important element in their identification with Judaism.

Faitlovitch's previous experience with educating Falasha youths in Europe to be future proponents of Judaism and modernity was repeated at San Nicandro. Cerrone's second son (Josef) was accepted to study at Dr Asher's school in Switzerland. Asher had offered to finance the education in his school of a boy of eleven or twelve, chosen from the poorest of the *gerim*'s children, with the suggestion that a second boy might be added later. However, just when everything appeared to have been arranged, Cerrone's son was unable to leave, despite Asher's aid. Cerrone approached Taamrat for help, asking him to pick up his son in San Nicandro and take him to Switzerland.[31] In the end the formalities of Italian bureaucracy,[32] which required innumerable official papers (listed with precision in a letter) that were impossible for a poor shoemaker such as Cerrone to obtain, proved to be an insurmountable barrier, and the project was abandoned.

Faitlovitch's commitment to the group's emigration to Palestine was also significant. He even wrote out a list of the families that were to emigrate, along with a file that listed the number of people in each family, their ages, and their professions. In his letters to Faitlovitch, Cerrone insisted that the emigration process be speeded up, primarily for economic reasons (the presence of eight children, imminent evictions, and increasing hunger), but also in the hope that the children would receive an education that would free them from poverty. But as time passed, his hope grew fainter: 'I had hoped one day to see my son sitting at a desk concentrating on his studies, to see him perhaps one day learned in the Torah. Today I see him covered in dust and sweat, wielding a hoe.'[33] Cerrone had a brother who had emigrated to the

United States some time earlier (and whom Faitlovitch had visited during his trips to New York) and was therefore well aware that emigration would mean improved economic and social conditions.

In his letters, Cerrone also mentioned alternatives to emigrating to Palestine, such as moving to Rome or to other cities with Jewish communities:

> I trust in your willingness to help me to move to Jerusalem or Rome, or elsewhere, or to recommend me to a good community because here I shall certainly starve to death. I am subjected to considerable humiliations and everyone asks me why I do not turn to my fellow Jews rather than to pagans. I am therefore forced to do this, and you my brothers must help me as you are able, unless you wish to see me lost. I cannot hope for help from the few brethern here as they too are poor.[34]

The story of the poor shoemaker is an important illustration of the expectations that the converts of San Nicandro had developed. In those years, the only way to obtain better living conditions or a better education for one's children was to emigrate, and large waves of Italian emigrants left Italy for America, Canada, and Australia. Palestine became yet another opportunity for social change. The followers of Manduzio looked forward to emigrating, partly thanks to the solidarity of Italian Jewish communities, and hoped that with the intercession of some Jewish patron, they would be able to benefit economically. In another letter[35] he wrote, 'if Rome refuses to accept me I would always wish and hope that I will be welcomed and housed in the Holy City where peace and justice reign'.

One of Cerrone's expectations was that Faitlovitch would find a wife for his first-born son, who had turned 14 and who he felt should 'pass according to our tradition into the state of matrimony'. In particular, he asked that 'a companion be found for him in America, or elsewhere, to distance him from the idolaters from whom with great sacrifice I have taken him, to see him among fellow worshippers and the saints of Israel'.[36] The future of this follower's family was therefore placed entirely in Faitlovitch's hands, including the education and marriage of his sons and the emigration of the entire clan.

A verse in Cerrone's uncertain Hebrew lettering, found in a letter he wrote in Italian, reads, 'The Eternal One welcomes the children of Israel from all the corners of the world'; Faitlovitch added, in his own hand, a transcription of the verse into the Latin alphabet. This is one of the most oft-quoted excerpts from the Faitlovitch's documents, and his efforts to ensure the spread of Judaism were based on this philosophy.

Clearly, there was a strong desire to emigrate to Eretz Yisrael – the meeting place for the dispersed of Israel – among the proselytes of San Nicandro themselves as early as 1935, so that by the time the Jewish Brigade arrived nine years later, it was merely a question of completing a process that had already begun, a process to which Faitlovitch had contributed.

NOTES

1. For an analysis and interpretation of the story of the San Nicandro conversion up to the present day, see Chapter 5 in T. Parfitt and E. Trevisan Semi, *Judaising Movements: Studies in the Margins of Judaism* (London, 2002), pp. 66–85.
2. P .E. Lapide published a book that had been translated into the main European languages. See *Les Compagnons de San Nicandro ou retour aux sources* (Paris, 1961).
3. This proposal was not encouraged by Manduzio, the founder, who believed that the Hebrew primers the group already possessed were sufficient.
4. E. Cassin, *San Nicandro: histoire d'une conversion* (Paris, 1957), p. 113. It was reissued by Quai Voltaire in 1993 with a 'Postface de l'auteur'. All quotations are taken from the second French edition. The English version is entitled *San Nicandro: The Story of a Religious Phenomenon* (London, 1959).
5. E. Cassin, *San Nicandro*, p. 39.
6. Angelo Sacerdoti replied on 8 October 1931. The entire text of the letter was published in G. Cividalli, 'Ritorno a San Nicandro', *La Rassegna mensile di Israel*, 39, 4 (1973), pp. 233–4.
7. Ibid.
8. Some of the songs from San Nicandro were recorded and sold.
9. G. Cividalli, 'Ritorno a San Nicandro', *La Rassegna Mensile di Israele*, 39, 4 (1973), pp. 233–4, relates that several Italian Jews had previously become interested in the group in San Nicandro and had sent them some books.
10. Diary, Sunday 27 January 1935 Faitlovitch arrived by train in San Nicandro at 19:10 after having disembarked a few days earlier in Brindisi (coming from Haifa). He noted in his diary 'allé directement chez Manduzio, l'ai trouvé et aussi il y a les autres'. On 28 January, he wrote that 'hotel Italia': Den Topf in ein Stube'. It was the only hotel in San Nicandro, probably the same one Elena Cassin recalled 20 years later, see her 'Postface', *San Nicandro*, p. 252.
11. *Israel*, 15 December 1955. Leo Levi, the author of the obituary and a Zionist from Turin who had been very active in the affairs of the Italian Jews in that period, may be considered an accurate source, but he may have mistaken the year. In Faitlovitch's diary of 1931, made up of extremely careful daily entries, the author found no reference to a visit to San Nicandro. Faitlovitch may have first heard of San Nicandro during a very short visit to Rome and Florence in December 1931, on his way from Palestine. Indeed, Rabbi Sacerdoti knew of the situation and had already replied to one of Manduzio's letters. In December 1932 and again in 1934, Faitlovitch visited Italy. During one of these trips he may have paid a first visit to San Nicandro or he may have met some followers in Rome or Florence, where he usually stayed during his visits to Italy.
12. This diary is slightly different from the one known up to now and was given by a relative, Eliezer Tritto (a convert who had settled in Israel), to the Longanesi publishing house (which was publishing the Italian edition of Cassin's essay). The publishers sent the copy to Elena Cassin, whom the author thanks for granting her permission to consult it.
13. Diary, 31 January 1935.
14. In his diary he wrote on 6 December 1936: 'Cerrone and his friend at the station. We chat

about things and they give me letters from Manduzio.' In his letter Manduzio expressed his regret that Faitlovitch had not come to San Nicandro and that he had not heard from Pacifici for a year, and asked Faitlovitch to send his best wishes to 'our brothers in the world and in the Promised Land', letter of 6 December 1936, *Fait. Coll.*, f. 92.

15. E. Cassin, *San Nicandro*, p. 55.
16. M. N. Pierini, 'Il movimento neo-ebraico di Donato Manduzio' in A. Moscato and M. N. Pierini (eds), *Rivolta religiosa nelle campagne* (Rome, 1965), p. 200.
17. In the beginning, the Sforzacosta camp was a camp for prisoners of war, but Jews accused of being pro-Zionists or anti-fascists were interned there as well. In the autumn of 1943, and spring of 1944, many anti-fascists were also interned.
18. See Cividalli, 'Ritorno', pp. 231–2. Manduzio composed a canticle to be sung on Friday evenings as a prayer for the release of Cantoni; the first two verses were published by Cividalli (ibid., p. 232).
19. Lapide, *Les Compagnons de San Nicandro*, p. 232.
20. See the review by A. Ravenna on the English translation of the work by E. Cassin that appeared in the *Jewish Journal of Sociology*, 2, 2 (1960), pp. 244–9.
21. Cassin, *San Nicandro*, p. 255.
22. Ibid., p. 88 and Ravenna, p. 248.
23. M. Roshwald, 'Marginal Jewish Sects in Israel', *International Journal of Middle East Studies*, 4 (1973), pp. 219–37, 328–54. In his survey, the American sociologist defined them as a model group; they spoke good Hebrew and had assumed Israeli first names, but they retained their surnames and married members of other groups.
24. I. Ben Zeev, 'My encounter with the Italian *gerim* in Upper Galilee', *Am va-sefer* (May 1952), pp. 33–4 (Hebrew).
25. Pierini, 'Il movimento', p. 308.
26. See Chapter 13.
27. *Fait. Coll.*, f. 114 (Hebrew).
28. In a letter of 15 September 1935, *Fait Coll.*, f. 92, Cerrone thanked Nella Luzzatto of the Rome community.
29. This was a book by Dante Lattes (*L'apologia dell'ebraismo*, Rome, 1923).
30. *Fait. Coll.*, f. 92.
31. See letter of 1937 from Taamrat who was in Cairo to Cerrone, in Trevisan Semi, *L'epistolario*, p. 245.
32. Letter of 28 April 1937, *Fait. Coll.*, f. 92.
33. Letter of 4 March 1938, *Fait. Coll.*, f. 92.
34. Letter of 28 May 1935, *Fait Coll.*, f. 92.
35. Letter of 15 October 1935, *Fait. Coll.*, f. 92.
36. Letter of 1935, *Fait Coll.*, f. 92.

12

Faitlovitch's Work Among the Blacks of Harlem: The Invention of a New Identity

The genesis of a Jewish-Ethiopian genealogy for African Americans in Harlem, in which Ethiopia was the shared locus, took shape between the 1920s and the 1940s, resulting in a process of identification that this author has called elsewhere 'the "Falashisation" of the blacks of Harlem'.[1] Ethiopia, the country known in the Bible as Cush and associated with the glories of ancient Egypt and the Queen of Sheba, was well suited to represent a common birthplace.

In 1929, Gordon MacCreagh, a non-Jewish explorer who had just returned from Abyssinia, was invited by the secretary of the American Pro-Falasha Committee (Max Weis) to publish an article in support of the Falasha cause.[2] The title of the article, 'The Falashas: The So-called "Black Jews of Abyssinia"', was significant, and in it the author complained about the scant attention paid by American Jewry to the Abyssinian Jews. MacCreagh thought that this lack of interest was due to the incorrect use of the word 'black' to describe the Falashas, and he made a point of explaining that they were not 'black' but, rather, 'brown' Jews. 'In the Broca colour scale', MacCreagh wrote, 'they would range, say, between six and seven; that is to say, brown tone overlaid by many generations of African sun burn. Black is the skin tone associated with the negro races. And there is nothing at all negro about these very remarkable people, the Falashas of Abyssinia.'[3] The explorer thought it would damage the Falasha cause if Judaism were to be associated with blackness. Moreover, MacCreagh considered Judaism to be a purely 'ethnic' concept.

In that same year, the director of a Jewish school in Esslingen, Germany,[4] expressed a different opinion. Not only was he willing to accept young Falashas into his school, but he would also be happy to open it up to black Jews from North America. He considered Judaism to be a religious community, not an ethnic one. He wrote that he had not only been in touch with the *Neger Juden* of North America, but had written a long letter to a well-known black rabbi, Josias Ford. Ford – a central figure in the development of the identity of black Americans – was at that time about to move from New York to settle in Ethiopia.[5] These contacts and exchanges between Jews and blacks on both sides of the Atlantic reflected a movement of men, news, and metaphors and the development of a concept of Judaism that was no longer connected to ethnic-tribal descent.

At the beginning of the century, the question of skin colour became an important variant that gave rise to a reflection on the characteristics of the people that made up the Jewish diaspora, who at that time were divided between nationalism (Zionism) and transnationalism (diaspora universalism). The dividing line was extremely ambiguous. Rabbi Matthew, one of the black Jewish leaders, recognized the signs of this ambiguity in Faitlovitch when he wrote:

> Even Dr Jacob Faithlovitch [*sic*] who has since died, said the American black Jews were no part of the Ethiopian Jews, for though their skin is dark, they [Ethiopian Jews] are still white … His was indeed a strange statement since the whole world knew and still knows that the Ethiopians are as black as any other black people in the world.[6]

In the America of the Great Depression in the 1930s, the black populations that had migrated over the previous decades, mainly from the West Indies and the southern states, were experiencing extreme social discontent. Unemployment, illiteracy, and poverty were all exacerbated by the phenomenon of exclusion with which they were faced.

THE CONSTRUCTION OF A NEW IDENTITY

The need to create a new identity free of humiliating undertones, one that could endow them with a recognized social status, was something they had in common with other black movements.

The search for a historical heritage, and the possibility of recovering a past rich in traditions and symbols, certainly appealed to a people attempting to redefine itself and to identify sources of pride it could present to other communities. Judaism, the religion of the Book, with its spiritual and intellectual tradition, also represented an opportunity to inherit a written tradition. Thus the teaching of Hebrew became an integral part of the activities of black congregations. The importance given to education in Judaism undoubtedly constituted an attraction for people who had only just begun to taste freedom.

A black man from Harlem named Matthew, later known as Rabbi Matthew, began a campaign against the use of the hated term 'negro', proposing that blacks be known as 'Hebrews of Ethiopian descent'.[7] In this new definition, the use of the term 'Hebrews' instead of 'Jews' indicated a distinction – and a distancing – from white Judaism, while the term 'Ethiopian' emphasized common origins and reunification. It was a process of identification with a group that enjoyed the acceptance of American Jews even though it was black-skinned and based in Africa, and at the same time, a process of Judaization. This process grew and developed as the propaganda work of the "white" Jew Jacques Faitlovitch, the spokesman for the Falashas in America, proceeded to attract interest and approval and obtain financial aid. The identification with the Falashas created intense solidarity, support, and concern for this people, particularly in the 1950s, when black American Jews began to perceive an attitude of discrimination and rejection in the Israeli government's policies toward the Falashas.[8]

It is worth noting that Ruth Landes, the first person to conduct a field survey in Harlem in the 1920s and 1930s, referred to the work of 'the Polish archaeologist and Zionist, Dr Jacques Faitlovitch, who had rediscovered the contemporary Falashas early in this century' among the blacks in New York.

Faitlovitch's presence among blacks in Harlem in the 1920s and 1930s is of considerable interest. On the one hand, he was looking for traces of ancient Jewry and remnants of the lost tribes; on the other, he was waiting to see whether the moment for Judaism 'to disseminate its light everywhere"[9] had truly arrived. Faitlovitch was extremely ambivalent, at least at the beginning, in his attitude towards the Black Movement in Harlem. Ruth Landes had already noticed this when she wrote, 'He [Faitlovitch] was moved, if also skeptical, when the group's leader or "rabbi" declared that the African Hebrew Heritage belonged to blacks only and included Falashas, the Queen of Sheba, and tribes of West Africa.'[10] Faitlovitch believed that the movement ran the risk of monopolizing the African Jewish genealogy, thereby distracting attention from the Falashas, his own personal cause. He also feared that the movement might produce a hostile attitude among American Jews, who were very reluctant to integrate the black communities of Harlem,[11] and might therefore be tempted to exclude the Falashas from the project of reuniting the 'dispersed' of Israel. Despite these reservations, Faitlovitch showed great interest in these movements, as indicated by the fact that some of the documentation on the black Jews of America is housed in the Faitlovitch Archive in Tel Aviv.

Various rabbis and Jewish organizations, as well as the American Pro-Falasha Committee, sent Faitlovitch documentation on the pseudo-Abyssinian Jews of America in the hope of obtaining clarification on the genuineness of their claims and requests. Acting on behalf of Faitlovitch, the Jewish Agency investigated the congregation of the Church of the Living God in Philadelphia and its leader, the prophet F. S. Cherry,[12] as well as Matthew's congregation.[13] The Jewish community in Baltimore had requested financial aid for the purpose of helping so-called black Jewish children from New York return to Abyssinia so that they could complete their religious training,[14] and Faitlovitch was consulted for more precise details.

Various studies have dealt with the possibility of a link between American blacks and the Jews of Ethiopia, but the question has always been considered little more than a curiosity, and not much attention has been paid to the formation of the movement or to its continuity as a Judaizing movement in America. A. Ehrman, an author who specifically examined the movement of the Commandment Keepers,[15] wrote, 'In the early 1920s Matthew learned of the romantic story of the Falashas (authentic Jewish Negroes of Ethiopia) and immediately "discovered", that he himself was a Falasha.' H. Brotz,[16] (later quoted by many others) added that the knowledge of the Falashas's existence was, for the blacks of Harlem, 'the "missing link" which for them fundamentally settled the question of their identity in a scientific manner'.

The construction of a myth, and more importantly, of a myth of origin, is a complex operation. Because the various parts of which it is formed are often contradictory, it takes a great deal of time to dissect, reconstruct, and systematize them. Yet sometimes, even when coexisting elements appear to contradict each other, once the various odd pieces are put together as if in a puzzle, they acquire the inner coherence that was initially missing. Given all the different versions and small pieces of history presented by the leaders of those movements (and by historians of the same movements in recent years), what is evident is how complex the development of a myth is. In this case, the myth expressed the depth of a people's longing for liberty and served to justify the construction of a new identity that offered an escape from a history of stigma and prejudice.

S. Howe[17] recently examined the process of the Africanization of American blacks, of which the Falashization process considered here is a part. He traced the history of the African American political texts that provided the theoretical basis for the identification with Ancient Egypt as a great black civilization that gave life to the Ethiopians and other 'Cushites' or 'sons of Ham'. From Africa, this civilization allegedly moved to Greece and from there to the rest of the world, generating 'a source both of racial pride and of hope for future achievement'[18] among American blacks.[19]

Many black ideologues, especially those of Caribbean origin,[20] theorized with respect to blacks' identification with the Ethiopians that since the Ethiopians were none other than the Jews of the Bible, the only true Jews were black, and those whites who declared themselves Jews were false.

Marcus Garvey, the founder of the Universal Negro Improvement Association, was one of the most important figures in these movements, which continued to influence the black theorists of this century. Josias Ford, a Barbadian by birth and a central figure in the phenomenon examined here, was the choirmaster of the Universal Negro Improvement Association[21] and played the piano and the violin.[22] He was so invested in the creation of a new Ethiopian Jewish identity for himself and for American blacks that he actually moved to Ethiopia on the crest of the 'Back to Africa' movement created by Marcus Garvey, which invited American blacks to return, as Zionists did, to the continent of their origin, in order to revive ancient and glorious African cultures in Africa itself.

Ford taught that 'The black man is really the Ethiopian Falasha and the Bible Hebrews, who were stripped of their name and religion during slavery.'[23]

Some years later, another story, which claimed origins that were even more intertwined with the history of East Africa, was put forward by Matthew, who had succeeded his teacher Ford as the leader of the movement. In his story, the rivalries that arose after the death of Solomon forced two of the tribes to leave and emigrate to East Africa, while the other ten were conquered by the Philistines and dispersed. The only people to retain a real Jewish identity were the two tribes that remained in Africa, and therefore the only real Jews were those who came from Africa.[24] According to this theory, white Jews today would be the descendants of Esau (red-haired) and black Jews would be the descendants of Jacob. This is an inversion of the traditional story, which says that the tribes of Judah and Benjamin remained in the south of Israel while the other ten were dispersed.

In 1941, a painting of the 'Lion of Judah' – the Emperor of Ethiopia, Haile Selassie – held a prominent place on the wall of Matthew's synagogue. That year, which was also the year that the emperor returned to Ethiopia, not only was Ethiopia represented prominently inside the place of prayer, but Rabbi Matthew – who we know was from the West Indies – was described as having come from a small Falasha village in Lagos (Nigeria), and as being the grandson of a 'very famous Falasha preacher'.[25] A newspaper article reported that he knew a little 'Sephardic Hebrew', which he had spoken in that African village.

A description of Rabbi Matthew's synagogue of the Royal Order of Aethiopian Hebrews dating from the late 1950s still listed among its furnishings a portrait of Emperor Haile Selassie, an Ethiopian flag, and a piano.[26] The symbols that evoked the myth of origin were as prominent as ever.

Rabbi Cragg, who later took over from Matthew in the same congregation, was also given a Falasha grandfather. It was said that he was born in New York, but that his father and grandfather had been 'of Falasha extraction'.[27]

In his well-known book *We the Black Jews*,[28] Yosef Ben-Jochannan, who was probably Puerto Rican but claimed to be of Ethiopian Jewish extraction,[29] did not distinguish between Falashas and black Jews, since the Commandment Keepers claimed to be descended from King Solomon and from the Queen of Sheba, just like the Falashas. Ben-Jochannan even went so far as to claim that Mussolini had exterminated four-and-a-half million Falashas in the 1930s,[30] perhaps in an attempt to revive public support for the Falashas.

In a recent publication, *The African Origins of Modern Judaism*, José Malcioln, another Afrocentric writer, who was described by Howe as being 'more coherent, better documented, though little more persuasive … than Ben-Jochannan',[31] claims that Abraham and all of the populations he converted went to Ethiopia, where they were called *falashim* (exiled), and that the *falashim* are direct descendants of the people of Cush.[32] So the myth has now become history and the genealogies are supported by history.

HARLEM

Between 1919 and 1931, eight black Jewish sects were formed in Harlem.[33] As has been noted,[34] Harlem at that time was a large Jewish immigrant neighborhood, and the future black leaders probably worked occasionally as *shabbes goyim*, non-Jews employed on the Sabbath to perform the activities forbidden to observant Jews.

During this period, the population of Harlem was undergoing enormous transformations. Jews who had improved their economic conditions left the neighbourhood to settle in new areas, and due to the Federal Immigration Laws of 1921 and 1924, no new waves of Jewish migration arrived to replace them, as in the past. Of the 178,000 Jews who lived in the area during the period of its greatest growth, only 88,000 were still living there in 1927.[35] The departure of the Jewish population was hastened by the great influx of blacks, who were escaping violence at the hands of whites in other areas and seeking less crowded places to settle, as well as better-quality housing. The Jews who remained in Harlem, most of whom were businessmen who made a living from the trade brought in by the new wave of black residents, soon became a minority. By 1930, about 165,000 of the 328,000 blacks in New York were living in Harlem.[36] Thus Harlem was in the midst of immense social change.

It was in Harlem, which had become a symbol of black pride and honour and the focal point of American black nationalism, that the two main leaders of the black Jewish movement, Rabbi Matthew and Josias Ford, both of whom came from the West Indies, chose Ethiopia as the second pole of their mythical-political universe as early as the late 1920s. There were three congregations of black Jews in Harlem in 1929; one of them was the Commandment Keepers, then led by Rabbi Matthew, the second was Beth B'nai Abraham, headed by Rabbi Ford, and the third was Talmud Torah Beth Sion, led by Rabbi Israel ben Newman.[37]

JOSIAS FORD AND TAAMRAT EMMANUEL IN HARLEM

The Commandment Keepers of the Royal Order of Aethiopian Hebrews, led by Matthew and later joined by A. J. Ford, was the group that was most influenced by the 'Falasha' discourse.

Ford had no links with Ethiopia except for his longing to identify with and belong to a group geographically situated in that area, and his interest in the possibility of sharing a myth that spoke of royal descent, lions of Judah, and Abyssinian princes. This enabled him to invent a past that, although it included phases of slavery, could be linked to a path of freedom and redemption. Josias Ford's move to Ethiopia, and his life and eventual death there, represented the missing link in the mythical fantasy reconstruction of a glorious past, and crystallized the myth of origin. His journey, which was of vital importance to the history that followed, was until recently fiercely contested by scholars of these movements, who were troubled by the idea that a mythical genealogy might be transformed into an ethnic link. Recently discovered documentation now allows us to place this event in the context of the relations established between America and Ethiopia.

Gerber gives various possible dates for Ford's departure for Ethiopia, opting in the end for 1930 – the year of the coronation of Haile Selassie. Ford was sent to Ethiopia by his congregation 'to represent them at the coronation of Emperor Haile Selassie and to help found a settlement there'. In Gerber's opinion, this took place after he had met a 'Falasha who had toured the United States a year or two earlier'.[38] Recent publications[39] have continued to support the idea that a meeting took place between a Falasha (Taamrat) and Ford in New York before his departure, and that this meeting was influential in Ford's decision to move to Ethiopia. Taamrat was indeed the first Falasha to visit New York,[40] but as far as we know, he did not arrive before 24 February 1931, a year after the emperor's coronation. He arrived with Faitlovitch, and on his return from the United States, landed in Plymouth on 14 January 1932. Ford, who was in Ethiopia for the emperor's coronation, where Faitlovitch and Taamrat were among the guests, must have gone there without having met any Falasha before his departure.[41]

In the summer of 1919, the *Kantiba* Gabru Desta, a member of an Abyssinian diplomatic mission to the United States, met Ford during a visit to Harlem and encouraged him to persuade his followers to move to Ethiopia.[42] This was on the initiative of *Ras* Tafari, who was hoping to modernize Ethiopia by offering favourable conditions for the settlement of skilled labourers. Some years later, in 1927, Warqneh Eshetu Martin[43] informed Ford of an agreement with the J. G. White Engineering Company in New York to employ African-American workmen in the construction of the proposed dam at Lake Tana and of *Ras* Tafari's agreement to pay the skilled workers.

Ford came to Ethiopia for the emperor's coronation accompanied by three other members of the black American community, one of whom was the well-known singer Eudora Paris. He taught music to Warqneh's children, repaired musical instruments and even played at Haile Selassie's court.[44] The fact that he was in Addis Ababa in 1931 is proven by a document in the Schomburg archive.[45] In a three-page letter, Ford told Rabbi Matthew that he had sent him a 'certificate of ordination', and that he was enjoying the confidence of important dignitaries at the court of Haile Selassie and had obtained land on which to build farms and houses for blacks from New York. Ford said he was worried about finding the money required for the construction work:

> We have the land (not bought) given. We need money for building and development. Do make up. These most wonderful gentlemen of ancient Aethiopia want to see what Aethiopian America is going to do for the development of a modern Aethiopia ... I have told them, we want homes for ourselves and our generation for ever, we want religious freedom, we want farms, horses, mules, cattle, poultry and opportunity for work on the great dam, we want land in the vicinity. All of these things they have granted us ... Now with all this bigness I have got the responsibility of building a headquarters to house Americans here. Do help me. I have got seven with me now. Some landed without a cent ...Try and wake up interest in building homes here among Americans who want to come.

The teachings of the 'Back to Africa' movement were being put into practice.

Between 1932 and 1933, about ten more black Jews arrived in Ethiopia, including Mignon Innes, also from Barbados, who later married Ford.[46] In 1941, Mignon Ford opened the Princess Zenebwork secondary school, which is still there today.[47] When Ford's message reached Harlem, Taamrat was in New York and Rabbi Matthew was leading the Harlem congregation. The documentation of Taamrat's presence among black Jews in Harlem is evidence of real, and not just mythical, links between Harlem blacks and the Falashas.

Taamrat's second visit to Harlem[48] was described with great pomp:

> A man of medium stature with a beautiful beard arrived at 8:50 pm, the congregation stood in his honor and the carnet [*sic*] led the strain, 'Ethiopia, the Land of our Fathers'. After he was escorted to his seat, a short prayer was led by Rabbi W. A. Matthew and the right hand of fellowship was extended to the distinguished visitor.

Taamrat gave his speech to Matthew's congregation in French, and 'He apologized for not being able to express himself in English although he had been studying English at Columbia for a short time.' His talk was preceded by a brief introductory speech on Africa by Almammy Deau, a member of the congregation who was originally from French Guinea.

One document tells of a declaration made by Norman Salit that created a scandal among Harlem blacks, which it defines as an 'attack on the Negro Jews of Harlem'. Salit, a Zionist counsellor-at-law in New York, had declared publicly that the Falashas belonged to Judaism, but on various occasions, and particularly in the press, he had also stated that there was no link between the Falashas and the black Jews of Harlem.[49] Matthew then took advantage of the presence of Taamrat, who was seen as an authentic representative of the people that masses of black Americans in the 1930s were beginning to recognize as part of their history, to ask him for an official statement. Taamrat was said to have replied diplomatically that 'Mr Salit is a friend of his, but when he made the statement he was indeed surprised because he is sufficiently educated to know that he has neither historical nor biblical proof for his statement.' Taamrat begged them to drop the incident and forget about it. With great tact, he pointed out the lack of a scientific basis for such a debate, without which it was better to leave the question alone. The ceremony closed with the singing of the Ethiopian national anthem. Hymns and songs honouring Ethiopia, 'the land of our fathers', had already entered the rituals of the new tradition.[50] These compositions invoked syncretist themes referring to Christianity, Judaism, and Islam.

Ford died in Addis Ababa in 1935 at the age of 58, after an illness.[51] When the Italians arrived in Addis Ababa, all his property was stolen, as Taamrat reported in a letter to Faitlovitch (who was then in Palestine). Taamrat, then the head of the Falasha school in Addis Ababa, referred to the departure of Ford's widow for New York in 1936, but he had confused this with the departure of Eudora Paris.[52] Taamrat observed:

> Poor Ford's wife ... is taking with her her mother [?] and another woman who lived with Ford, plus a little two-year-old Abyssinian whose mother is mentally ill. She is also taking with her a lovely *sefer Torah* parchment that she miraculously managed to save when she lost all her belongings.[53]

Eudora Paris' departure[54] from Addis with a 2-year-old Abyssinian and a parchment *sefer Torah* was a highly symbolic event. In light of what was to follow, it came to represent the thread of continuity with the rest of the story. The 2-year-old took Paris' name. He would later become known as Hailu Moshe Paris, the leader of the black Jews in the Bronx.

The vital link in the story's development was precisely the fact that Eudora Paris, the singer who had accompanied Ford to Ethiopia, took Hailu back to New York to the congregation led by Matthew, who in 1931 had received investiture as a 'Rabbi of Ethiopia', receiving his 'certificate of ordination' directly from Ford.[55] The certificate, which came from Addis Ababa and bore both Hebrew and Amharic titles, was to become a symbol of the authenticity of these traditions. The parallel between the little Moses saved from the waters who became the saviour of the Jewish people and a little Falasha, also named Moses, saved from Ethiopia by the congregation of the Royal Order of Aethiopian Hebrews of New York, who would later become the leader of the Ethiopian Jewish people in America, became the centrepiece of their mythological history.

Faitlovitch, as mentioned above, visited black communities and their rabbis, looking for traces of links to the ten lost tribes. Faitlovitch had friendly relations with Rabbi Matthew, and during the months he spent in New York in 1950, he passed whole days with Matthew's congregation in Babylon.[56] Cragg, the leader of the Union of Ethiopian Hebrew Congregations and Rabbis, invited him to become a member of the congregation's Advisory Council, whose honorary president was Taamrat Emmanuel. Faitlovitch did not accept this invitation because as an Orthodox Jew he could not be a member of a Reform association.[57] After the Second World War, Faitlovitch seriously considered the idea of a mass conversion of black Americans. He supported the work of David Horowitz, the founder of Mosaic Law for One World,[58] the man who had chosen Cragg to be president of the Union of Ethiopian Hebrew Congregations and Rabbis. The brief references to East Africa, Abyssinia, and Ethiopia that were found in local newspapers in the early 1900s, in stories about the origins of black Jewish leaders and the members of their congregations, not only became more frequent and consistent over the years, but were gradually synthesized into more complex stories.

FAITLOVITCH AND THE CIRCULATION OF INFORMATION ON THE FALASHAS IN THE USA

In the United States, readers of the *Jewish Comment* had been informed of Faitlovitch's trips to Abyssinia and the discovery of the Falashas since the beginning of the 1900s.[59] In early 1900, The *American Jewish Year Book*[60] reported that Jews in Germany wished to send a mission to the Falashas in Abyssinia, and up until 1921 or 1922, American Jews were fairly regularly informed of the progress of their activities on behalf of this group.[61] In 1905, Moise Schwab[62] published an article whose title referred to them as African Jews: 'The Falashas of Abyssinia: An Authentic Report of African Jews'. Schwab claimed that while 'African Jews' did exist, they did not have the physical traits of black people. He published photos of two of Faitlovitch's pupils (Gete Yirmiahu and Taamrat Emmanuel) and asserted that their faces 'do not resemble those of negroes'. The meaning of the message was clear: black-skinned African Jews might exist, but they did not have 'negro' features. Faitlovitch arrived in the United States for the first time on 9 April 1911[63] and stayed until 12 August. During those months he began a propaganda tour among the American Jewish communities in order to draw attention to the Falashas and raise funds.[64] He got the Board of the Union of American Hebrew Congregations to nominate Walter Freiberg, the president of the Board, to be the person in charge of creating a pro-Falasha committee, to be headed by Freiberg himself, 'to preserve for Judaism the Falashas of Abyssinia'.[65]

There were some who questioned Faitlovitch's pro-Falasha activity in America. A pamphlet by Rabbi George Zepin,[66] in particular, gave rise to a fierce polemic. Zepin declared that he accepted the Nahum report,[67] hence the opinions expressed by the Alliance Israélite Universelle, which opposed any educational initiative toward those whom Zepin defined as 'people of primitive intelligence ... in a semi-civilized country'.

At the end of 1914, Faitlovitch arrived back in the United States and stayed there until 28 August 1915. In his many letters to Alexander Marx,[68] he referred to the difficulties he was encountering during his long tour through Jewish communities in America, but he also mentioned the enthusiastic response to his trip. Faitlovitch had left Europe in the middle of the First World War to continue his pro-Falasha work among the Jews in America, trying to convince them to take on the commitment that until then had been fulfilled by the Jews of Germany, Austria, and Italy.

Faitlovitch took advantage of the fact that the convention of the Union of American Hebrew Congregations was to be held in Chicago that year, and asked to give a speech there, which was widely reported in the press. An editorial in the *Reform Advocate*[69] announced that 'among the men of parts and power who attended the session of the Council of the American Hebrew [?] Congregations held in the city last week, none was as prominently in the center of curiosity as was Dr

Jacob Feitlovitch [*sic*].' At this event, Faitlovitch launched his long conference tour for the Abyssinian Jews, with the aim of arousing the interest of American Jews and collecting $30,000, an amount he considered essential for the 'Jewish counter-mission'.[70]

Faitlovitch also participated in the Central Conference of American Rabbis[71] and managed to set up a special committee, headed by Rabbi Samuel Schulman, who, at the end of a fact-finding investigation, declared himself a supporter of pro-Falasha work.[72]

During Faitlovitch's second trip to America, the *American Hebrew*[73] published a long article, 'The Black Jews of Abyssinia', written by Faitlovitch himself, in which the black Jews were introduced as 'a remainder of an old Jewish tribe' whose origins were traced back to the Jews who had arrived in Ethiopia from Egypt:

> By reason of the scarcity of Jewish women, these Jews, being at first only wanderers and adventurers, were compelled to intermarry with the daughters of the land, whom they converted to Judaism. In addition to this, the influence of the climate, the heat of the burning Ethiopian sun, darkened the skin of these immigrants. They preserved, however, the traits characteristic of their race. Their bodies were assimilated but their soul survived.

He did not fail to mention the heroism and the strength shown over the centuries by the 'Jewish tribe' in warding off Christian attacks:

> Like all Jews, the Falashas have undergone centuries of misfortune and persecution. But through all these bloody persecutions they have shown the steadfastness which is characteristic of the Jew ... They can say with pride, 'I am black, but comely'.

The idea of the possibility of a separation between body and soul and between ethnic Judaism and religious Judaism, and the possibility of being black-skinned yet still attractive, found its supporters in certain spheres, both Orthodox and reform. However, in other American Jewish circles, it gave rise to misgivings. Doubts about the 'Jewishness' of the Falashas led Faitlovitch on more than one occasion to publish information and propaganda that stressed the recognizably Jewish characteristics of the group. Finally, as a last resort, he brought to America his most trusted and educated student, Taamrat Emmanuel, who had been educated at the rabbinical college in Florence and had lived in Europe for 16 years.

The *American Jewish Year Book* of 1920–01 reported Faitlovitch's third visit to the United States in 1919.[74] The article explained that he had not been able to travel to Abyssinia because of the war, and that he was calling upon 'the co-operation of other national Jewish Organizations in the United States, for the promotion of efforts on behalf of the Falashas'.[75] Faitlovitch was hoping to enlist the participation of the Jewish National Fund.

THE MEETING BETWEEN FAITLOVITCH AND FORD

The meeting between Faitlovitch and Ford assumed great importance in the retelling of the events that followed it, and was in many ways mythologized. Gerber noted that:

> From then on, he [Ford] and 'Rabbi' Wentworth Matthews, whom he had ordained and who became the best known of all black Jewish leaders, seized upon this new information to bolster their identity as Ethiopian Hebrews. It certified to them not only that blacks had been Jews, but that they are the original Jews.[76]

Thus the visit was not simply a meeting between two important figures, Faitlovitch and Ford, but was the beginning of a process that involved meetings and exchanges, one that developed out of a mutual need. The mythical interpretation of that meeting, however, became part of a more general process of delegitimizing the black Jewish movement.

The history of the black Jews in America has been influenced by the backgrounds and ideologies of those who recorded it. Often, when documentation was lacking, a history was invented that was no less mythical than the history that was supposedly being demythologized. Graenum Berger went to great lengths to disprove the Falasha origins of American blacks.[77] In his study of the phenomenon of the Judaization of black Americans, Berger tried to show that there were no links between the two worlds, and ridiculed the idea that any might have existed. Most importantly, he denied the fact that there was any thread of continuity. He wrote: 'There is no history of mother or son continuing any identification with Judaism either in Ethiopia or in the United States.'

When Haile Selassie returned to Ethiopia in 1941, twenty or so black Americans went to settle in Ethiopia.[78] While visiting the Falashas in 1951, Alexander Rosenfeld, the president of the Brit Ivrit Olamit, came across a black Jewish couple from Harlem living in Addis Ababa. They were followers of Matthew who had decided to settle in Ethiopia precisely because of their identification with the Ethiopian Jews.[79] The couple gave him their account of the Jewish origins of the Africans. After spending time in Addis, Rosenfeld worked among black Jews in Harlem,[80] giving speeches and offering his help to the black movement. Thus elements of continuity were found both in Ethiopia and in the United States.

Other examples of this were the Mount Horeb congregation in the Bronx led by Hailu Moshe Paris, and the founding of Hatzaad Harishon ('The First Step'), a movement created by Hailu Moshe Paris and Jacob Gladstone (a professor of Hebrew), which lasted until 1972.[81]

Berger took his cue from a 1927 article by B. Z. Goldberg[82] in which the author claimed that there was a Falasha community 'on the outskirts of the colored belt of New York'.[83] After a brief, confused, and somewhat contradictory description of Faitlovitch's activities, Goldberg added, 'Some of these Falashas have found their way to America.' Berger described the role attributed to Faitlovitch in the article as follows:

> Some believe that this was the origin of black references to their aboriginal association with the Falashas. When Jacques Faitlovitch … discovered that there were black Jews in New York, he called Arnold Josiah Ford, to see if they were Falasha. He decided in the negative.[84]

In the end, he concluded, the American Pro-Falasha Committee 'apparently had no interest in making the connection with the black Americans, including black Jews, or in encouraging blacks to identify with or to help support the overseas philanthropic venture'.

As Eric Hobsbawm wrote, 'Inventing traditions … is essentially a process of formalization and ritualisation',[85] during which ritual and symbolic complexes are created. In the invention of an Ethiopian tradition and the foundation myth that illustrates it by the black movement of 'Hebrews of Ethiopian descent', the existence of a population in Ethiopia about which very little was known, in a mythical 'elsewhere', known in the Bible as Cush, was of great importance. The black Jews of Ethiopia, a people about whom information (albeit somewhat vague and ambiguous) had begun to circulate in the United

States in the early 1900s, permitted the black community to assert a glorious past and claim a genealogy of kings, not slaves. This was achieved through the symbolically potent construct of Ethiopian Judaism.[86]

The purpose of Ford's trip to Ethiopia was to create new myths and rituals to connect ancient Ethiopia and modern Ethiopia with Ethiopian America. His purpose was to awaken and energize black Americans with the promise of land and the possibility of a new life. 'We want religious freedom, we want farms, horses, mules, cattle, poultry,' wrote Ford in 1931. In the end, history prevailed over myth, and the continuation of the thread was guaranteed by the return to America of Ford's friend with a *sefer Torah* and a 2-year-old child who, in the popular imagination, simply had to be a little Falasha. This marked the start of a new phase in the construction and formalization of black Jewish identity.

Faitlovitch, the man who had 'rediscovered' the Jewish tribe in East Africa, took it upon himself to establish links between American blacks and the Jews of Ethiopia, albeit in an ambiguous and contradictory manner.

NOTES

1. See E. Trevisan Semi, 'The "Falashisation" of the Blacks of Harlem: a Judaising Movement in 20th Century USA', in T. Parfitt and E. Trevisan Semi, *Judaising Movements*, pp. 87–110.
2. Letter of 8 October 1929, *JTS*, Marx 80–17.
3. In the article, MacCreagh quoted the opinion of Jacques Faitlovitch, whom he had met in Addis Ababa, regarding prejudices related to skin colour: 'Dr Faitlovitch in Abyssinia expresses a fear that because his people are dark skinned, because they have been miscalled the "Black" Jews; that therefore there has been no greater interest shown by the Jews of America', *Fait. Coll.*, f. 112.
4. Letter by Stern from Stuttgart to Faitlovitch of 5 October 1929, *Fait. Coll.*, f. 100.
5. Arnold Josia Ford, a piano and violin player of Jamaican origins who was influenced by the 'Back to Africa' movement. Ford became the leader of the Commandment Keepers of the Royal Order of Aethiopian Hebrews and immigrated to Ethiopia in December 1930, where he died in 1935 at the age of 58.
6. *N.Y. Age Defender*, 11 May 1958 (microfilm in Schomburg).
7. *Sunday News*, s.d. (microfilm in Schomburg).
8. See Chapter 14.
9. Programme of the Society for the Knowledge of Judaism and the Spreading of Torah, created by Faitlovitch, *Fait. Coll.*, f. 114. See Chapter 13.
10. R. Landes, 'Negro Jews in Harlem', *Jewish Journal of Sociology*, 9, 2 (1967), p. 176. Landes was to have published a long article on this topic in *Sociologus* in Berlin in 1933, but the rise of Hitler had led to the discontinuation of the journal, and the manuscript was later lost (ibid., p. 175).
11. A study carried out by E. Wolf was commissioned by the Jewish Board of Guardians of New York in 1933 to assess whether the black congregations that defined themselves as Jewish should be included among those aided by Jewish social services. The reply was that 'the problem resolves itself into a Negro one and, therefore, outside of the realm of Jewish social service, except for the broader humanitarian and internationalistic viewpoint.' See Wolf,

'Negro "Jews": a Social Study', *Jewish Social Service* (June, 1933), pp. 314–19 (:319).
12. A report on this congregation was written by for Faitlovitch by Abraham Hirsch on behalf of the Jewish Agency for Palestine of 5 May 1950, *Fait. Coll.*, f. 108. The conclusion was that it was a community made up of black Jews who claimed that they were exiled slaves from Ethiopia.
13. Report of the Jewish Agency of 11 April 1950, *Fait. Coll.*, f. 108.
14. The letter had been sent by Mordekai (the signature Mordekai is in Hebrew), agent of Modikia Herrmans (*sic*) of 21 October 1928, *Fait. Coll.*, f. 108.
15. A. Ehrman, 'The Commandment Keepers: a Negro "Jewish" Cult in America Today', *Judaism*, 8, 3 (1959), pp. 267–8.
16. H. Brotz, *The Black Jews of Harlem* (New York, 1964), p. 49.
17. *Afrocentrism: Mythical Pasts and Imagined Homes* (London and New York, 1998).
18. Ibid., p. 36.
19. See M. Bernal, *Black Athena: The Afroasiatic Roots of Classical Civilization* (New York, 1989).
20. Ibid., pp. 73–86.
21. Landes, *Negro*, p. 180.
22. For Ford, see K. J. King, 'Some Notes on Arnold J. Ford and the New World Black Attitudes to Ethiopia', *Journal of Ethiopian Studies*, 10, 1 (1972), pp. 81–7. From the *New York Amsterdam News*, 23 December 1925 (microfilm in Schomburg): 'Rabbi Ford comes from South America. To show his Hebraic training he spoke in Yiddish to Justice Panken. He asserted the congregation (Beth B'nai Abraham) has a large membership of people who were born Jews. Most of them come from east Africa and from South America.'
23. J. H. Boykin, *Black Jews: A Study in Minority Experience* (Miami, 1996), p. 32.
24. *Afro-American*, 8 February 1936 (microfilm in Schomburg).
25. *The Jewish Advocate*, 28 February 1941, *Fait. Coll.*, f. 92.
26. A. Sherman, 'Appendix: Black Jews of America' in *L'Afrique païenne et juive* (Lezay, 1956/7), pp. 366–70.
27. *N.Y. Age Defender*, 22 January 1955 (microfilm in Schomburg).
28. Y. Ben Jochannan, *We the Black Jews* (Baltimore, 1983), p. 315.
29. Howe, *Afrocentrism*, p. 226.
30. Ibid., p. 226.
31. Ibid., p. 227.
32. Malcioln, *The African Origins of Modern Judaism* (Trenton/Asmara, 1996).
33. Brotz, *The Black*, p. 10.
34. Ibid.
35. J. S. Gurock, *When Harlem was Jewish 1870–1930* (New York, 1979), pp. 144–6.
36. Ibid., p. 149.
37. According to J. Dorman, *Hatzaad Harishon: Integration, Black Power and Black Jews in New York, 1964–1972* (BA Thesis, Palo Alto, CA 1996), p. 31, this congregation was the Jewish school of the Moorish Zionist Temple.
38. I. J. Gerber, *The Heritage Seekers: American Blacks in Search of Jewish Identity* (New York, 1977), p. 15.
39. See what W. R. Scott wrote in *The Sons of Sheba's Race: African-Americans and the Italo-Ethiopian War (1935–1941)* (Bloomington, 1993), p. 182: 'In 1928 or 1929 Professor Tamrat Emanuel [*sic*], a European-educated Falasha on tour in the United States under the auspices of a white Jewish philanthropic organization – the Pro-Falasha Committee – got in contact with Rabbi Ford.' Earlier, King, 'Some Notes', p. 84, also wrote: 'The chance meeting [with Taamrat], perhaps in 1929, seems to have determined Ford on emigration to Ethiopia.'
40. For Taamrat Emmanuel, see Chapter 10.
41. The links between the Emperor of Ethiopia and the black Jews of Harlem are well documented. In particular see King, 'Some Notes'; Scott, *The Sons*, pp. 179–91; J. E. Harris, *African-American Reactions to War in Ethiopia 1936–1941* (Baton Rouge and London, 1994). Rabbi Matthew, who on several occasions had condemned Italy for its occupation of Ethiopia, was invited as Guest speaker to the Ethiopian World Federation on 10 May 1942 to celebrate the first anniversary of the liberation of Ethiopia from Fascist dominion. See the letter by Lij Araya Abebe of 1 May 1942, Schomburg, SCM 97–9
42. Scott, *The Sons*, p. 182.
43. An Ethiopian medical doctor, diplomat and advocate of pan-Africanism.
44. Ibid., p. 183.

45. Document of 5 June 1931, Schomburg, SCM 97–9.
46. Scott, *The Sons*, pp. 183–4.
47. J. E. Harris, in *African American*, p. 151, recalls that the school, first called Beit Ouriel School, and later, in 1943, Princess Zenebwork school, was 'the first coeducational school in the country, began with ten students, including Ford's two sons'. The school was nationalized in 1975 by Menghistu. Mignon Ford returned to the United States in 1984. She returned to Ethiopia during Harris' study mission. Harris called her 'the sole living link to the African American settlers of the 1930s'. Ibid., p. 152.
48. Document of 23 December 1931, Schomburg, SCM 97–9.
49. Berger, *Black Jews in America* (New York, 1978), p. 84.
50. For the hymns to Ethiopia composed by Ford, see King, 'Some Notes', pp. 83–7, which includes some verses.
51. Harris, *Afro-American*, p. 151.
52. Eudora Paris was a well- known singer among black nationalists in Harlem, who emigrated with Ford and two other people to Ethiopia. She worked as a musical entertainer at an Addis Ababa hotel frequented by diplomats. She left Ethiopia with her mother Nancy in 1936 for safety after the Italian occupation. They left with a small Ethiopian boy they had adopted and named Hailu after *kantiba* Gabru's son (Hailu Moshe Paris). See Scott, *The Sons*, pp. 184–5.
53. Letter of 12 June 1936, in Trevisan Semi, *L'epistolario*, p. 219.
54. Scholars agree that Ford's widow remained in Addis Ababa with their children. See also Gerber, *The Heritage*, p. 16, Ford's widow: 'Mignon Ford, together with two other West Indian women, founded the Princess Zenebwork school in Addis Ababa in 1940. Recently … Ford's son Joseph, returned to America to raise money to promote literacy in Ethiopia.'
55. The certificate is mentioned in a letter from Ford to Matthew in Schomburg, SCM 97–9, in which the investigation conducted by the Jewish Agency in Matthew's congregation is also discussed. It reads: 'Matthew showed them a hand-written (in English) document dated at Addis Ababa and signed by Rabbi Ford there, certifying Matthew as a Rabbi of "Brith Avraham". The words "Brith Avraham" were written on top of the document in Hebrew and in Tigre.' (he probably means Amharic) Letter of 11 April 1950, *Fait. Coll.*, f. 108.
56. Diary of 1950.
57. The letter of 31 May 1955, *Fait. Coll.*, f. 108, which was written on the letterhead of the association, bore the slogan 'Dedicated to Kelal Israel and the Falasha Jewish Tradition'. The manifesto, signed by Martin Wurmbrand, listed the purpose of the association: 'To become the voice of Falasha Jewry on the national level in all matters affecting the American Jewish Community.'
58. David Horowitz showed great commitment in the field of Jewish proselytism. He had an Orthodox Jewish background and his missionary activity began in California. He established ties with Jewish groups in Israel. See Chapter 13.
59. Berger, in *Black*, p. 59, notes that as early as 1872 Rabbi Sabato Morais of Philadelphia had announced that 'The Board of Delegates joined similar organizations which originated in Europe ... in sending a missionary to rescue the Falasha Jews from heathenism.'
60. *American Jewish Year Book*, 3 (1901–02), pp. 21–2.
61. *American Jewish Year Book*, 9 (1907–08), p. 551, reported that 'Dr Faitlowitch [*sic*], who visited the Falashas of Abyssinia a few years ago, approached the government, through Baron Franchetti, in the interest of proposed schools among them, under Italian auspices' and continued to report information on the initiatives undertaken. From Volume 10 on, Abyssinia had a separate entry: 10 (1908–09), p. 203 and p. 216; 11 (1909–10) p. 67; 15 (1913–14) p. 275; 16 (1914–15) p. 167. Volume 18 (1916–17), pp. 301–2, announced that the American Jewish Committee had appropriated $5,000 for relief for the Falashas, and that Cyrus Adler and J. L. Magnes had been co-opted as members of the International Pro-Falasha Committee. In Vol. 22 (1920–01), pp. 413–14, it was announced that Faitlovitch had returned to the United States 'to endeavor to organize in this country a committee to collect funds for the work and supervise his activities in Abyssinia … At his request, your Committee has agreed to endeavor to secure the cooperation of other national Jewish organizations in the United States..' Volume 23 (1921–22), p. 355, announced that 'Shortly after our Thirteenth Annual Meeting last November, Doctor Jacques Faitlovitch left the United States for Abyssinia for the purpose of pursuing there, under the auspices of this Committee, the work of establishing a system of Jewish and secular education among the Falashas.'
62. *Jewish Comment* (Baltimore), 21, 6 (1905), s.i.p.

63. Diary of 1911.
64. Letter of 4 August 1911 to A. Marx, *JTS*, Marx 80–29.
65. Thirty–Eighth Annual Report of the Union of American Hebrew Congregations, p. 6708, *CAHJP*, P3–471.
66. G. Zepin, *The Falashas: A Report Concerning the Advisability of Establishing a School for Hebrew among the Falashas of Abyssinia* (Cincinnati, 1912).
67. See T. Parfitt, 'Rabbi Nahoum's Anthropological Mission to Ethiopia' in T. Parfitt and E. Trevisan Semi (eds), *The Beta Israel*, pp. 1–14.
68. The correspondence is in *JTS*.
69. E. G. Hirsch, *The Reform Advocate*, 30 January 1915.
70. Faitlovitch obtained only $5,000.
71. *Central Conference of American Rabbis*, 25 (1915), p. 75, 90 and 114.
72. Some of the people whom Faitlovitch involved in his pro-Falasha activities in the United States were the same people who generally supported conversions and Jewish missionary work. Samuel Schulman, for example, in 1919 spoke in favour of actively proselytizing Judaism. The president of the Hebrew Union College of Cincinnati, Caveman Kohl, was favourable to Faitlovitch's work and was a strong advocate of the need for Jewish missionary work, holding the opinion that 'God sent Israel among the nations that it might win a rich harvest of proselytes.' See A. Shusterman, 'The Last Two Centuries' in D. M. Eichhorn (ed.), *Conversion to Judaism: A History and Analysis* (New York, 1965), pp. 157–9.
73. *The American Hebrew*, 20 August 1915, p. 382.
74. According to the authors of works devoted to the history of black Jews in America, it was during this third journey to the United States that Faitlovitch met Josias Ford. Ruth Landes, however, mentions Faitlovitch as having been in Harlem only between 1929 and 1931. Unfortunately, Faitlovitch's diaries from 1916 to 1919 are missing. Faitlovitch left the United States in November 1919, and his next visit was in 1925. In any case, when Faitlovitch mentioned in his journal that 'Rabbi Ford' had come to his office, we get the impression that they were old acquaintances: see diary 17 December 1929.
75. *American Jewish Year Book*, 22 (1920–21), p. 414.
76. Gerber, *The Heritage*, p. 16.
77. He based his reconstruction partly on his correspondence with Jona Bogale, one of Faitlovitch's students, who specified that the only Falasha in New York at that time was Taamrat. See Berger, *Black*, p. 61, n 14.
78. King, 'Some Notes', p. 86.
79. Y. Ahi Efraim, *Trip to the Falashas*, in Y. Eisenberg (ed.), *The Duties of the Emissary* (Tel Aviv, 1985), p. 152 (Hebrew).
80. H. Gavriahu, 'For the *nidhei Israel*' in Y. Klausner, A. Tartakower and A. Ramba (eds), *The Wandering Hebrew Ambassador: Dr Alexander Rosenfeld* (Tel Aviv, 1957), p. 212 (Hebrew).
81. Dorman, 'Hatzaad'.
82. Goldberg, 'A negro bris', *B'nai B'rith Magazine*, 16, 11 (1927), pp. 445–66.
83. Berger, *Black*, p. 60.
84. Ibid.
85. E. Hobsbawm, 'Introduction: Inventing Traditions' in E. Hobsbawm and T. Ranger (eds), *The Invention of Tradition* (Cambridge, 1983), p. 4.
86. D. Friedmann, *Les enfants de la reine de Saba* (Paris, 1994), pp. 386–93, *Annexe V*, recently described the case of Ulysses Santamaria, a scholar of the black Jewish movement and the Falashas who died young. Santamaria, a Black from Santo Domingo, had invented a false identity and claimed that he was Jewish (on his mother's side), the grandson of a rabbi and born in the United States. After Santamaria's death, Friedmann, who had worked with him researching the Falashas, wondered about this 'généalogie baroque' and about his need for a 'mythologie identitaire', which had annoyed him during their research together. Santamaria never felt the need to 'confess' his invented identity to his co-researcher or to admit that it was false. After he died, Friedmann decided that the meaning of the research he had conducted lay precisely in his identification with the Falashas: 'Les Beta Israel étaient des Noirs qui se voulaient juifs et furent reconnus comme tels par ceux qui détenaient le pouvoir de les reconnaitre. Entre cette analyse de l'histoire des Juifs éthiopiens et de leur processus de changement dans l'immigration et la quête identitaire voilée et d'Ulysses il y a avait une réfraction, comme dans un miroir' (p. 393). I think that the case of Ulysses is perhaps the best example, admittedly a very particular one, of what happened *en masse* in the United States.

13

From Diaspora to Zion: Faitlovitch's Homecoming and the Committees for the Lost Tribes

FROM DIASPORA TO ZION

Faitlovitch married on 11 April 1937. The ceremony took place in Tel Aviv, at one of the hotels along the seashore. His bride, Mara Halevi Davidov, received a gold ring from the former minister of Ethiopia.[1] Mara, described as a sweet, patient woman,[2] came from a family of merchants from Riga, most of whom died in the *Shoah*; only one sister had survived Auschwitz, and the experience had scarred her for life. Faitlovitch's family had left Lodz for Eretz Yisrael near the end of the 1920s, and thus they were spared from the *Shoah.* At the time of his wedding Faitlovitch was not yet living at 10 Vitkin Street – the house that was to become the library and the nerve center of the associations for the *gerim*[3] – but at 26 Mea Shearim Street. The first member of the family to settle in Palestine was probably his sister Hana, who, after marrying in 1926, went to live in Natanya. Moshe, Jacques's father, died in 1931; his mother, with whom Jacques had a close but sometimes conflicted relationship, lived much longer.[4] As for Jacques' three brothers, Haim, a member of the 1921 expedition to Ethiopia, had settled in London, where he served as a rabbi and a *shohet* (ritual slaughterer);[5] he was joined there by Eliezer.[6] Yehoshua, who had settled in Paris, would die young, without ever marrying.[7] Meanwhile, the other two sisters had married in Palestine and, with the exception of Leah, had had children. Jacques relationship with Leah changed greatly over the years; the intense feelings that the young Faitlovitch had for his sister[8] turned stormy after she married. Leah's first marriage was in 1933 to professor A. Halevi Gulak,[9] but she was widowed after only seven years. She later married an Orthodox rabbi (Berman), the director of a *yeshivah* in Rehovot. The relations between the two siblings deteriorated over the years to such an extent that for long periods of time they avoided seeing each other, even though they both lived in Palestine.

Leah is described as a strong, active, large and imposing woman who dressed in the style of Orthodox women.[10]

We do not know the exact date of Faitlovitch's *aliyyah*, but it is important to note that his immigration seemed to be more of a haphazard, temporary event, a stage in his continual wandering, rather than a considered option or a definitive choice.

He had had property registered in his name in Palestine since 1927[11] and had spent several years in Tel Aviv, mixing with the *yishuv* and with important figures of the time, such as Yosef Klausner (Amos Oz's uncle), Ch. Bialik, Y. Ben Zvi, M. Dizengoff, and various members of the Italian Jewish community (Rabbi D. Prato, Professor E. Bonaventura, B. Ascoli, Castelbolognesi, A. Pacifici) and the Ethiopian community, such as *Ras* Kasa Hailé (a member of the Ethiopian aristocracy, loyal to the Negus, who was exiled in Jerusalem after the Italian conquest of Ethiopia), or the Empress Menem, whom he welcomed to Jerusalem with her entourage in 1933. During that visit, Faitlovitch was also decorated with the order of 'Poland Restored' from the Polish General Consulate in Tel Aviv.[12]

At the time of his wedding, Faitlovitch was living mainly on the rental income he received from his properties in Palestine,[13] which was barely enough to support a new family.

A few months after the wedding, after spending a short time with his wife at his brother Haim's house in London, Faitlovitch left for a long period in the US,[14] hoping to land a professorship in Semitic studies or Ethiopian studies, or perhaps a Guggenheim fellowship. He left England on 18 September 1937, and would spend more than a year in the United States, re-establishing contacts with old friends and supporters. His purpose was twofold: to resume his fundraising efforts for the Falashas, who were now under Italian occupation, and to find an opportunity for himself and his wife to settle in the US. He was successful in achieving his first goal, but he never found the job he had hoped for, and he returned to Palestine feeling embittered.[15] He left New York on 4 January 1939 and returned to Tel Aviv just a few months later,[16] after having wandered through France, Switzerland and Italy, just Europe was on the brink of war. Faitlovitch's had intended to stay in Palestine just a short time before heading abroad again, but the outbreak of war prevented him from leaving Palestine. Faitlovitch described the life of the *yishuv* in 1939 as 'really tragic'. At one point, he even advised an Italian Jew, who was intending to leave Italy due to the promulgation of the racial laws, against coming to Palestine,[17] thinking that the situation would get even worse. During those months, he made several attempts to leave the country to go to the United States or at least to Cochin in southern India. At a time when Europe was committing the worst barbaric acts in its history, India must have represented an oasis of peace and a possible 'elsewhere'.[18] In the summer of 1940, he prepared to leave for India and the Far East, with the intention of proceeding on to the United States. In a curious exchange of correspondence with Abraham Barak Salem, a well-known representative of the *meshuhrarim* Jews in Cochin ('Freedmen', the emancipated Jews of Cochin), the community he belonged to, who struggled against the discrimination by the *paradesi* (known as the white Jews of Cochin),[19] Faitlovitch expressed his wish to visit him: 'Will that season [summer] of the year be suitable for visiting your country? What places would you advise me to tour in order to get some insight into Indian life and especially into our fellow Jews there?'[20] In the eyes of a European Jew in 1940, India must have seemed an idyllic place:

> I hope that your country is not and will never be affected by the accursed anti-Jewish agitation, and may Providence grant that Indian Jewry, especially those of you in Cochin and Bnei-Israel, will be a constructive, beneficial and salutary progressive element in the spiritual and moral development of your compatriots.[21]

However, Faitlovitch never made it to India. Instead, he went to Ethiopia in 1942, having been appointed by the Negus to the post of Inspector- General of the Ethiopian Ministry of Education, thanks to Taamrat's intervention. He made a final attempt to find a job in the US after the war (in 1948, and again with his wife in 1950). When he returned to Israel for good at the end of the summer of 1950, he was 69 years old.

Thus, Faitlovitch's path seems similar to the one followed by most diaspora Jews – a wandering linked to a network of international connections – as opposed to the Zionist path of the early twentieth century. Faitlovitch's Zionism seems to have been tinged with ambiguity and contradiction. On the one hand, there was Tel Aviv, the place of return from his travels and on the other, a continual search for an 'elsewhere', be it Ethiopia, the United States or India. This search was more in keeping with his spirit as a wanderer and romantic adventurer. Until the creation of the State of Israel, he appeared to be undecided about his own future, although he had no trouble convincing others to join in the reunification of the 'dispersed of Israel'.

PROSELYTISM COMMITTEES FROM 1940 TO 1950

In the 1940s and early 1950s, Faitlovitch worked to form numerous committees and movements in Eretz Yisrael, interpreting the events of the age as a sign of the arrival of a Messianic era. These movements were created and supported by influential, high-ranking people: Zionists active in the creation of the State of Israel, such as President Yitzhak Ben Zvi; Zionists belonging to Chovevei Tziyyon, such as Nahum Slouschz; revisionist Zionists like Shalom Ben Chorin (Fritz Rosenthal); and *chalutzim* such as Israel Ben Zeev. Slouschz[22] in particular worked closely with Faitlovitch in Tel Aviv in the 1940s and 1950s, and together they founded committees and projects to promote the reunification of Jews and would-be Jews scattered around the world. Their work continued until Slouschz, who was eight years older than Faitlovitch, was left with the task of giving his friend's funeral oration.[23]

They felt that Judaism would also appeal to other peoples, especially in Asia and Africa, if only it were known to them. After centuries of silence, the invitations of the prophets Isaiah, Jeremiah, Zephaniah, Ezekiel, and Zachariah could finally be proclaimed, thereby illuminating these peoples with the light of Judaism. The creation of the State, which was seen as a fulfilment of the messianic promises, acted as a catalyst for these movements.

But not everyone agreed.

There was opposition to universalism and to the committees, not only from the press and the public, but also from the rabbinate, which supported neither these positions nor the policy of proselytism.

The plan to send a Jewish conversion mission to Japan in 1954, which was warmly supported by Ben Zvi and Faitlovitch, was strongly opposed by Rabbi Herzog.

Japan had interested Faitlovitch as a potential country for missionary work since the 1920s, when he began to collect newspaper cuttings about Jews and conversions to Judaism in Japan.[24] In 1954, one year before his death, he and Rabbi Herzog were invited to Japan to create a centre for Jewish Studies with a missionary outreach programme. During an official discussion in the presence of the president of the State of Israel, Ben Zvi, Faitlovitch reasserted, for Herzog's benefit, his belief in the Talmudic concept according to which the people of Israel had been dispersed among nations in order to spread Judaism. This was contested by Herzog, who quoted a text often used by opponents of conversion: '*kashim gerim le-Yisrael ke-sapahat*' (proselytes are like impetigo for the people of Israel).[25] The discussion between Rabbi Herzog and Faitlovitch shows that conversion was still a hotly contested issue in Israel in the 1950s.

MOSAIC LAW FOR ONE WORLD: DAVID HOROWITZ AND JACQUES FAITLOVITCH

The correspondence[26] between Faitlovitch and Mosaic Law for One World, a missionary movement founded in New York in 1944 by David Horowitz and Eliezer Schindler for the purpose of spreading Judaism throughout the world, provides an excellent understanding of this group and of the debates that were raging in Palestine in the 1940s on the themes of the *nidhei Yisrael* and proselytism. Faitlovitch had met Eliezer Schindler, a contributor to *Der Ruf*, at Bex Les Bains (Switzerland) in 1937, at the home of Moritz Asher.[27] Schindler, a writer and poet, had been on the Austrian front during the First World War after which he had travelled and worked in Russia, where he took an interest in the Subotniki group of converts.[28] Horowitz had an Orthodox Jewish background and was married to a convert. His missionary work began in California, which was chosen for the great variety of sects present there.[29] Initially he had few successes, but he eventually expanded into other areas of the United States, where he began to win converts (including an entire village in Michigan).[30] The movement also managed to establish links with Jewish groups in Israel (in particular with the 'Canaanite' movement), and with figures such as Dolla Ben Yehudah Witman, the daughter of Eliezer Ben Yehuda, and Shalom Ben Chorin, the editor of *Yediot Hadashot.* Ben Chorin, a revisionist Zionist and contributor to the journal *Der Ruf*,[31] who had immigrated to Palestine from Germany in 1934/5, became a frequent visitor to Faitlovich's house, especially during the last years of his life.[32] The *United Israel Bulletin*, the organ of the movement, was founded by Horowitz. The above-mentioned correspondence reveals the work they had in common, in which the greatest difficulty lay in breaking through 'the veil of darkness that hovers over a Hellenistic-Roman-influenced world Jewry and world Christianity'.[33] Horowitz informed Faitlovitch that he was sending him materials on the movement while he awaited news of the work being done among the Falashas. Faitlovitch replied promptly,[34] saying that he had been unaware of Horowitz's movement, but that he congratulated him on the undertaking and was in complete agreement with the general idea.[35] Faitlovitch even went so far as to use Horowitz's words:

> our *raison d'être* is justified only by fulfilling this task that Judaism has, as preordained, of evolving into a universal, catholic religious conviction of all nations, as you rightly state in your paper and as every pious Jew recites in his prayers three time a day ... ' they shall all accept the yoke of thy kingdom.[36]

Faitlovitch freely expressed his thoughts on the subjects of conversion and Jewish universalism, and on the mission that Judaism had to fulfil in preparation for the messianic period. Horowitz replied, thanking Faitlovitch for his encouragement and telling him that he had published part of his declaration in the association's bulletin. In particular, he had quoted Faitlovitch's comments on 'the necessity of promoting Jewish religious knowledge among gentiles, a duty inherently incumbent upon every one of us'.[37] Horowitz contacted the American Pro-Falasha Committee of New York and added the Falasha issue to his organization's agenda for the unification of the whole of Israel. He also added a specific reference to the missionary action under way at that particular moment in history, i.e. after the catastrophe of the *Shoah*:

> No doubt you recognize that we are living in historical times that call for realistic and brave men and women to face the realities confronting the world, and we Jews have the greatest of all duties to fulfil, namely, to make good our messengership to all peoples in the world. Let us, even we few in this decisive generation, try to make good the shortcomings and mistakes of our fathers in the past 2000 years, *let us embark upon our truly biblically appointed tasks before a groping world of people – Jew and Non-Jew*.[38]

Horowitz encouraged Faitlovitch to contact Shalom Ben Chorin, who had shown an interest in opening a centre for the movement in Palestine.

Faitlovitch's interest in Horowitz's movement is evident from the fact that when he arrived in New York on 7 January 1948 for his campaign to raise funds and draw the attention of American Jewry to the Beta Israel, he was met at dockside by David Horowitz himself.[39] Faitlovitch spent many evenings with Horowitz or with members of his association during his stay in the United States, which turned out to be longer than expected because of the abrupt change in the situation in the Near East after the proclamation of the State of Israel. In particular, the difficulty of obtaining visas and other documents, the outbreak of Arab rioting, and the difficulty in finding a ship that would sail directly to Israel without stopping in Alexandria forced Faitlovitch to remain in the United States until 29 June 1948.[40]

Even if Mosaic Law for One World, 'an international movement to disseminate the Decalogue both within and beyond the confines of Jewry', gained little support from either rabbis or Jewish laymen, according to J. Rosenbloom,[41] 'apparently because of the kind of Judaism advocated' nevertheless, Horowitz succeeded in circulating his message among the Black Judaizing movements in Harlem.[42]

THE SOCIETY FOR CONVERTS IN ISRAEL AND IN THE WORLD

We have no precise date for the foundation of the more explicitly missionary association known as Agudah le-ma'an gere tzedek bi-Yisrael u-va-olam (Society for Converts in Israel and in the World), which had its headquarters in Faitlovitch's large house on Vitkin Street in Tel Aviv. His home was used for meetings and cultural activities, and served as the headquarters for many of the associations and committees established between 1948 and 1955. It is likely, however, that the society was formed after Faitlovitch's return from the United States. In his large library, the *gerim* gave talks,[43] as did other members of the association, on the problems associated with conversion[44]. One of the members of the conversion movement in Israel was Israel Ben Zeev (Wolfenson),[45] who had known Faitlovitch since 1906, when he was a student at the Hilfsverein school (Lemel) in Jerusalem, where he had seen Faitlovitch enter the classroom as a hero, accompanied by two young Ethiopians.[46]

Ben Zeev came from an old *yishuv* family; his forebears had immigrated as members of the Hazon Tziyyon group in 1809. In the 1920s, he was a professor of Arabic literature at the University of Cairo. Later, he worked hard to foster links between Arab and Jewish intellectuals in the Palestine of the British Mandate and to forge a better understanding of their respective cultures. He represented a certain cosmopolitan Mediterranean culture,[47] and he continually sought ways to foster the coexistence of different worlds. He served as the head of the Arab schools in Israel and as a professor at Bar Ilan University. Although he did not agree with Faitlovitch regarding the policy for a 'Judaization' of the Beta Israel[48] along the model of European Judaism, Ben Zeev joined the committees set up by Faitlovitch in the 1940s and 1950s, as he shared his 'missionary' spirit. He also wrote a commemorative introduction to the Hebrew translation of Faitlovitch's book *Meine Zweite Reise zu den Falashas*.[49] Ben Zeev (then known as Wolfenson) helped Taamrat and Tadesse to survive in Egypt in the 1930s.

The missionary association was preceded some years earlier by the Vaad le-ma'an nidhei Yisrael (Committee for the Lost of Israel), founded by Faitlovitch in 1942 – along with Yitzhak Ben Zvi and Nahum Slouschz (who served as its president)[50] – shortly before he returned to Ethiopia after an absence of almost eight years. In order to raise funds for the school in Addis Ababa and for hiring teachers, he addressed the Jews in Palestine in a bulletin of the Committee (1943), in which he reminded them that it was a

> duty for every man in Israel to give generous help to fulfil the words of the prophecy in the vision of the prophet Zephaniah: 'For then will I turn to the people a pure language, that they may all call upon the name of the Lord, to serve him with one consent / From beyond the rivers of Ethiopia my suppliants, even the daughter of my dispersed shall bring mine offerings' (Zeph. 3, 9–10).[51]

The Committee tried to involve the rabbinate, especially Rabbis Herzog and Uziel, who had demanded thorough investigations to verify the Jewishness of the Beta Israel, about which they had doubts. The rabbis cautioned that the *giyyur* procedure would have to be performed before they could commit themselves to religious education among the Beta Israel. As noted earlier, the rabbinate was not in favour of the *giyyur* and had contrasting opinions as to the proper attitude to adopt with regard to the Falashas.

The Committee later became an association called Agudah le-ma'an nidhei Yisrael, which was very active in the early 1950s and worked alongside the Agudah le-ma'an gere tzedek be-Yisrael u-va-olam. The association, too, was headed by Faitlovitch, and its secretary was Wurmbrandt.[52] A close link with Brit Ivrit Olamit was guaranteed, as the president of the Brit, Ben Zvi, and its director, Alexander Rosenfeld, were both members.[53] The Jewish Agency and the Education Department of Ha-Histadrut Ha-Tziyyonit ha-Olamit were also represented.

Brit Ivrit Olamit played an extremely important role in reviving the work on behalf of the *nidhei Yisrael* and the Beta Israel. With funding from the Jewish Agency, Rosenfeld visited Ethiopia as a representative of that organization in October–November 1951,[54] in the hope that the Falashas would disseminate the knowledge and the culture of the *Torah*.[55]

The agenda of the Agudah le-ma'an nidhei Yisrael referred explicitly to the question of the Jewish tribes that had been separated from the rest of the Jewish people by the events of history, and the need to reunite them in the new Jewish State:

> in the early days of our history, several tribes separated from the great Golah of 'Beith Israel'. They wandered as far as India, China, Abyssinia, and even reached the American Continent, thus becoming estranged tribes ... Now with the establishment of the Jewish State, it is our noble duty to bring those alienated brethren back to us. For this very aim this Association was established.[56]

Among the aims of the association were to provide cultural, religious and educational assistance to the 'lost tribes' of the diaspora and to assist them in their emigration to Israel.

In 1952, the members of the group that had formed the association (Faitlovitch, Slouschz, Wurmbrand, Rosenfeld, and Ben Zeev) published various articles in the Brit Ivrit Olamit journal *Ha-am ve-ha-sefer* on the Beta Israel, the *anusim* and the *gerim* of San Nicandro. Faitlovitch, in particular, drew attention to the need to expand the frontiers of Judaism, and to the responsibility of the generation that had seen the birth of Israel to recover the 'Lost of Israel'.[57]

THE SOCIETY FOR THE KNOWLEDGE OF JUDAISM AND THE SPREADING OF *TORAH*

The Brit ha-ne'emanim/Agudah le-yeda ha-yahadut u-le-hafatzat toratah (the Alliance of the Faithful/Society for the Knowledge of Judaism and the Spreading of *Torah*), the last organization to be created by Faitlovitch, was registered in 1952,[58] but it was the culmination of a project conceived some 20 years earlier with Birnbaum and the group connected with the journal *Der Ruf*. This group primarily consisted of A. Pacifici[59] and Ben Chorin;[60] other participants included M. Asher and E. Schindler. In the correspondence between Birnbaum and Faitlovitch[61] concerning the creation of the Society for Promoting Knowledge of Judaism, its aim was said to be 'to restore the broken contact with the Falashas and with other remnants of Jewry in all distant countries, to revive and strengthen Judaism among them and to ameliorate their social and economic conditions', and to work 'for the preservation and promotion of Judaism and to inculcate it in those who feel drawn towards the house of Israel'. For the first time, there was a mention of the possibility of creating a missionary institute in Palestine with students from Abyssinia and other countries 'in order that they may be prepared for the knowledge they would acquire in service of the preservation and promotion of judaism [*sic*] … to serve as messengers'.[62] This was not just a project aimed at the preservation of Judaism, but one that promoted active proselytizing by missionaries[63] trained specifically for this purpose. The Brit ha-ne'emanim was influenced by the apprehensions of the period in the wake of the *Shoah* and the founding of the State of Israel. The association proposed to widen the sphere of activity of the previous associations, while retaining the central aim of saving the *nidhei Yisrael*. It opened up new horizons for the expansion and consolidation of Judaism, following a more precise and well-organized scheme. Its agenda, which was quite concrete and more detailed than previous plans, called for the creation of an institute for training capable young people as Jewish missionaries. Some of them, according to a memo in Hebrew, had already been trained and were ready to leave immediately; they would begin by addressing the groups most favourably disposed towards Judaism in various parts of the world.[64] A pamphlet in English, which is more detailed than the above document, lists the goals of the association:

> we will carry the word of God to Jew and non-Jew alike. This is a task which is ours. We have neglected it though not completely abandoned it. It was not altogether a voluntary act on our part that wc failed to carry out our mission. Forces and conditions not within our control compelled the Jews to remain inactive in a field of endeavour full of promise. First the Romans, then the Christian Church forced us to abandon this field of endeavour for God … We had lost the zeal of the missionary. Anyone familiar with the history of Judaism knows quite well that in all its glorious moments it knew quite well how to exploit every opportunity to assert its convictions that its destiny is to serve as an eternal light, a beacon unto the nations … We are fully convinced that the time has come to raise the banner of Judaism not only in the presence of the nations but also among the nations … Obviously we have no intention of imitating the methods and practices of other religious systems. But we do want to publicize Judaism and its

> teachings ...While hospitable to proselytes we shall exert no pressure in efforts to persuade any one to embrace our faith ... Our effort will be confined to education.[65]

The training institute was to be established in Jerusalem. The association itself, organized in a pyramid structure, had a six-level hierarchy, beginning with the rank of 'brother' (Hebrew: *ach*) and rising to the highest rank of 'father' (Hebrew: *av*), to use the terminology taken from the Church.[66]

A document from the Department for Education and Religious Culture in the diaspora,[67] explicitly defined the term *nidhei Yisrael* and listed the groups to be included and excluded. For example, neither the Karaites nor the Samaritans could be included as they were considered 'independent Jewish religious sects'.[68] However, the Yemenite Jews who, although isolated, had managed to preserve the correct reading of the *Torah* and the ancient *midrashim,* were included. It divided the map of the 'lost of Israel' into continents. In Africa, it mentioned the Falashas and the Bahutzi of the Sahara desert, who had been studied by Slouschz(and who were given this name by the Jews of Djerba because of the fact that they 'sleep outside'). This document gave considerable attention to the Falashas, whom it defined as the most important tribe of the *nidhei Yisrael*, and it mentioned the ongoing discussion about their origins. The Falashas, like the Benei Yisrael in India, the black Jews in Cochin and the Indian Jews in Mexico, were considered to be a population that had become detached from the rest of Judaism for geographical reasons and had integrated a certain number of *gerim*. In its conclusions, the document reasserted that the return of the 'lost' should not be considered an ethnic question (*geza*) but a spiritual and religious one, in keeping with the biblical dictate of 'the people that were gathered out of the nations' (Ezekiel 38,12). The document concluded by affirming the goals of the Brit ha-ne'emanim, and describing the role that Jewish volunteers were to play in bringing the *anusim* and the *nidhei Yisrael* back to Judaism thanks to a *mission yehudi* (Jewish mission) modelled on the Christian missions. The activities of the Church Missionary Society, which Faitlovitch observed first-hand during his trips to Ethiopia, probably influenced his programme and his vision of how to increase world Jewry. In his published works, Faitlovitch compared the *shevet Yisrael* (tribe of Israel) in India to that of the Falashas,[69] pointing out that both groups had been able to preserve their faith in the Jewish religion and, despite adversity, to remain faithful to it while awaiting the Messiah. Faitlovitch's contention that the Falashas, having fought for centuries to defend their Jewishness, should unquestionably be considered Jews, was accepted by the most important figures in the movements of the 1940s and 1950s, including Ben Zeev[70] and Slouschz.[71]

The main purpose of the various associations founded in Eretz Yisrael was to re-establish contact, first with the Beta Israel and then with other groups. Even the Society for Promoting Knowledge of Judaism, which was decidedly 'missionary' in its outlook, had as its primary goal 'to restore the connection of the Falashas with Israel, which has been broken for so many centuries, to revivify and strengthen Judaism among them ... This organization, at the same time, aims to restore (re-establish) the broken contact with remnants of Jewry in all distant countries.'[72] Ethiopian Judaism was often described by Faitlovitch as an *ever meduldal*, a dangling limb, which urgently needed to be reattached to the rest of the Jewish body lest it break away for good. These images alluded to a perceived need for restructuring and reunification within a new messianic-oriented scenario. This was perhaps a necessary utopian phase for those who had seen the disappearance of most of European Jewry and the birth of the Jewish State.

In the 1940s and 1950s, Faitlovitch devoted himself to creating committees and associations that, unlike the pro-Falasha committees he had founded in Europe and the United States, had a wider sphere of activity and were concerned no longer with the Beta Israel alone but with the entire *nidhei Yisrael*. Although support for the Ethiopian Jews remained one of the primary goals of the associations founded in that period and of their promoter, increasing attention was being paid to an active and organized movement of proselytism. In the ideology espoused by Faitlovitch, which had finally found refuge and protection under the aegis of the State, Judaism was to become an increasingly universal religion, to be used to educate peoples like those in Asia and Africa who had no preconceived hostility against the Jews. In support of this view, Faitlovitch argued that 'a body that does not grow is destined to die' and that if the Jews did not wish to fall prey to the accusation that 'we are mean with foreigners and do not wish to let others enjoy the Jewish treasures', then proselytism was the only path to take.[73]

After the Second World War, the idea that Judaism had to expand in order to survive was shared by a number of leading personalities. Notably, in 1949, Leo Baeck, the liberal rabbi of Germany, said:

> Mankind is hungry and thirsts for that which Judaism can say, what Jews full of Judaism can say. Many an example can be remembered. Judaism became, so to speak, attractive to the gentiles and many became proselytes, educated people, high-minded people.

> Should we not begin anew? Should we not send our missionaries to Asia, to East Asia and to other places to the people there waiting for us? We are in need of expansion for our own sake.[74]

The news that a number of non-Jews had converted in southern Italy (San Nicandro), Harlem, Uganda, Japan and elsewhere in Asia, and in Mexico, only strengthened this utopian trend toward a universal Judaism.

In conclusion, in observing what is happening today, it is possible to interpret the action being taken by the North American Conference on Ethiopian Jewry, aimed at converting to Judaism the Falash Muras[75] who have remained in Ethiopia – some of whom (about 19,000 people) the Sharon government has recently given the right to immigrate to Israel[76] under the Law of Return – as a sort of continuation of the 'Jewish missionary' movement launched and sustained by Faitlovitch.

NOTES

1. Letter of 26 January 1938 from Faitlovitch (in New York) to his wife, *Fait. Coll.*, f. 125. He corresponded with his wife in German and with his mother and brothers in Yiddish.
2. Private communication from Faitlovitch's great-nephews in London.
3. A plaque that is still on the front of Faitlovitch's house states that this building is the headquarters of the Yeda-am association, an organization for research into Jewish folklore.
4. She died in 1946.
5. Haim had two children, Charles and Sally.
6. Eliezer also married and had a son (Avraham) and a daughter.
7. Private communication from Faitlovitch's great-nephews in London.
8. Having read Faitlovitch's diaries before knowing the family background, the author initially got the impression that Leah was his wife rather than sister, due to the words and expressions Jacques used to describe the pain he felt at being separated from her.
9. Leah received lavish presents from the Negus. See Taamrat's letter of 3 November 1933, in Trevisan Semi, *L'epistolario*, p. 189.
10. Private communication from J. Faitlovitch's great-nephews.
11. In the early 1920s, Faitlovitch had opened accounts with the Anglo-Palestine Bank and Barclays Bank of Jerusalem, and from 1928 he had regular transactions with Barclays Bank of Tel Aviv. See letter to the Commissioner for Immigration of 26 September 1939, *Fait. Coll.*, f. 131.
12. Various representatives of the Ethiopian court who were present in Palestine also took part in the ceremony. We know the participants thanks to a letter from Taamrat, in which he describes in detail the association between the 'grades' and the honours attributable to the Ethiopians taking part. See letter of 14 March 1933, in Trevisan Semi, *L'epistolario*, pp. 155–6.
13. See letter from New York of 14 December 1937 to his wife, *Fait. Coll.*, f. 125.
14. Jacques left his wife at his brother Haim's house in London. Mara attended English courses, perhaps to prepare for a possible move to the US, but left London early to return to Palestine (she stayed in London from 18 September 1937 to 7 February 1938).
15. Taamrat wrote to him, 'Of course I am sorry that you did not find the support due to you from your friends there for a job, but never mind!' See letter of 18 January 1939, in Trevisan Semi, *L'epistolario*, p. 267.
16. He arrived in Tel Aviv on 21 March 1939.

17. Letter to Rodolfo Levi of 24 July 1939, *Fait. Coll.*, f. 97.
18. Letter to A .B. Salem of 31 August 1939, *Fait. Coll.*, f. 117.
19. See M. Zetlaoui, *Shalom India: Histoire des communautés juives en Inde* (Paris, 2000), pp.197–200.
20. Letter to Salem of 24 December 1939, *Fait. Coll.*, f. 117.
21. Letter to A. B. Salem of 31 August 1939, *Fait. Coll.*, f. 117.
22. See Chapter 1.
23. *Jewish Chronicle*, 21 October 1955.
24. Fait. Coll., f. 82.
25. See Y. Carmel, *Itzhaq Ben Zvi, from the Journal at the President House* (Ramat Gan, 1967), p. 45 (Hebrew).
26. The correspondence between Faitlovitch and Horowitz refers to the summer and autumn of 1947.
27. M. Asher, who had been a great supporter of the pro-Falasha work (see letter of 10 June 1947, *Fait. Coll.*, f. 98), had housed and educated the young Abraham Baruch (one of the Beta Israel young men brought to Europe by Faitlovitch in the 1920s). Asher had also offered to house the son of one of the *gerim* of San Nicandro in 1935/6, *Fait. Coll.*, f. 92. Asher also contributed to *Der Ruf*. For Asher and the converts of San Nicandro, see Chapter 11.
28. He published an article in Birnbaum's journal: 'Bei den Gerim in Russland', *Der Ruf*, 1 (1934) pp. 2–3.
29. For Horowitz, see Sh. Ben Chorin, 'Der Opferaltar von West Olive', *Yediot Hadashot*, 8 October 1950; N. Tirah, 'David Horowitz Converts Americans', *Ma'ariv*, 2 December 1952 (Hebrew); 'Ex-Christians Raise Jewish Altar to God', *New York Times*, 1 October 1950; 'Hundreds of Christians Converted in an American Town', *Ha-aretz*, 9 November 1950; A. Friedman, 'David Horowitz: he teaches "Mosaic Law for One World"', *Examiner*, 22 June 1951. See also J. Rosenbloom, *Conversion to Judaism: From the Biblical Period to the Present* (Cincinnati, 1978), pp. 133–4.
30. For the Jewish missionary movements in the United States, see L. J. Epstein, *The Theory of Welcoming Converts to Judaism* (New York, 1992), pp. 81–96. For the possibility that missionaries existed in Judaism and the debates on this question, see S. Bialoblocki, *Die Beziehungen des Judentums zu Proslyten und Proselytentum* (Berlin, 1939); Sh. Cohen, 'Was Judaism in Antiquity a Missionary Religion?' in M. Mor (ed.), *Jewish Assimilation, Acculturation and Accommodation* (Lanham, 1992), pp. 4–23; L. Feldman, 'Was Judaism a Missionary Religion in Ancient Times?' in Mor (ed.), *Jewish Assimilation*, pp. 24–37; E. Will and C. Orrieux, *'Proselytisme Juif'? Histoire d'une erreur* (Paris, 1992); M. Goodman, *Mission and Conversion* (Oxford, 1994); Rosenbloom, *Conversion*; D. M. Eichhorn (ed.), *Conversion to Judaism: a History and Analysis* (New York, 1965).
31. *Der Ruf*, the journal founded by N. Birnbaum in Rotterdam in 1934 (where he had moved from Berlin after the rise of Hitler) together with A. Pacifici and A. Pallière, continued until 1937, the year of Birnbaum's death. Pallière has been described as 'the most exceptional *ger* of modern history' by A. Shusterman, 'The Last two Centuries' in Eichhorn, *Conversion*, pp. 136–75.
32. See the correspondence between Ben Chorin and Faitlovitch in 1951, *Fait. Coll.*, f. 92.
33. Letter of 5 October 1947 from Horowitz to Faitlovitch, *Fait. Coll.*, f. 100.
34. Letter of 2 September 1947, *Fait. Coll.*, f. 98.
35. 'I completely agree with the general idea of your movement, I congratulate you for the action undertaken and I would much like to know something more about the unfolding activities ... Every detail of how you carry out your missionary work would greatly interest me and I am especially eager to know whether you already have the required trained staff of collaborators, of Jewish and non-Jewish descent.' Ibid.
36. Ibid.
37. Letter of 5 October 1947, *Fait. Coll.*, f. 100.
38. Ibid., underlined in the original.
39. See Faitlovitch's diary for 1948.
40. Ibid. He boarded the *Meridian Victory*, which, he noted, had only 12 passengers!
41. Rosenbloom, *Conversion*, p. 133.
42. See Chapter 12.
43. A talk on the subject 'My Path from Christianity to Judaism' was held by Avraham Zippert, defined in the invitation as *ger tzedek* (document of 16 May 1951, *Fait. Coll.*, f. 92).
44. Goldwasser's talk was on the subject 'Judentum – die Weltanshauung der Zukunft' (docu-

ment of 1 March 1952, *Fait. Coll.*, f. 92.
45. *United Israel Bulletin Newsletter*, December 1956, *Fait. Coll.*, f. 92.
46. See the introduction by Y. Ben Zeev to R. Kashani, *The Falashas* (Jerusalem, 1976), p. 4 (Hebrew). For Faitlovitch's students, see Sh. Weil, 'The life', pp. 40–9.
47. D. Tidhar, *Encyclopedia of the Pioneers in the yishuv* (Tel Aviv, 1947), vol. 1, pp. 378–9.
48. Ben Zeev in Kashani, *The Falashas,* p. 4.
49. Ben Zeev, 'Dr Yaacov Faitlovitch, the Dreamer and the Fighter' in Faitlovitch, *Masa*, pp. 11–24 (Hebrew).
50. The committee was also formed by Rabbi Davide Prato, Leon Recanati, Ya'acov Shapira and Yom Tov Bato, who acted as secretary. On Bato see Chapter 14.
51. CAHJP, P177 (Prato), 1a/5.
52. Faitlovitch had met Wurmbrandt in Tel Aviv in 1948 when, having begun to study Amharic, he asked to become his student. See letter from M. Wurmbrand of 15 December 1948, *Fait. Coll.*, f. 117.
53. For Rosenfeld see Klausner, Tartakower and Ramba (eds), *The Hebrew Wandering Ambassador*.
54. In a letter of 24 September 1951, shortly before his departure, Rosenfeld informed Ben Zvi that Faitlovitch insisted that he also visit the Falasha villages on the Eritrean border, and that he was expecting a reply from Grinberg (Jewish Agency) about an increase in funding to include the trip to Asmara, *CZA*, 116/156.
55. Report sent by Rosenfeld to Rabbi Gold (head of the Department of Education and Religious Culture of the Diaspora of *Ha-Histadrut ha-Tziyyonit*) of 21 November 1951, *CZA*, 116/156.
56. *Fait. Coll.*, f. 82.
57. 'My Lost Brothers facing the Rebirth', *Ha-am ve-ha-sefer* (May, 1952), pp. 24—5.
58. The item was briefly reported in *Ha-tzofeh*, 27 February 1952, *Fait Coll.*, f. 107.
59. Alfonso Pacifici had been linked to Faitlovitch for many years. In particular he had been a guarantor for a Falasha youth educated in Italy, Hizkiahu Finkas. See Trevisan Semi, 'From Wolleqa', pp. 15–39. Pacifici emigrated to Palestine in 1934 (*Der Ruf*, 11, 1934, p. 6).
60. Fritz Rosenthal, emigrated to Palestine in 1934/5 and changed his name to Shalom Ben Chorin. He contributed various articles to *Der Ruf* in 1934–6.
61. The correspondence covers the years 1933–4 when Faitlovitch was in Palestine, *Fait. Coll.*, f. 117.
62. In a letter of 7 November 1933, *Fait. Coll.*, f. 117, Birnbaum asked Faitlovitch for articles 'über die Bedeutung der exötische Judengruppren für die Erhaltung und den Aufstieg des Judentums'.
63. In an accompanying letter of 2 February 1933, *Fait. Coll.*, f. 117, Birnbaum wrote that he preferred the term 'messengers' to 'missionaries' (the term used by Faitlovitch), which is how it appeared in the final version.
64. *Fait. Coll.*, f. 82.
65. *Fait. Coll.*, f. 114 (the document is undated).
66. *Fait. Coll.*, f. 82. A rather detailed document in Hebrew (four pages) outlined all the procedures for the training of the young missionaries in the Institute, the *kenesiat-shelihim* (Church of Missionaries/Messengers) and provided for the establishment of smaller centers in Israel and around the world. The Institute was intended to become the spiritual center for all of Judaism.
67. A ten-page document from the *Histadrut ha-tziyyonit ha-olamit* of 17 May 1952, *Fait. Coll.*, f. 82.
68. In the document *kitot datiyyot (yehudiyyot) atzmayyot*, ibid.
69. My Lost Brothers Facing the Rebirth', *Ha-am we-ha-sefer*, p. 24.
70. See Ben Zeev, *Conversion*, pp. 78–9.
71. See Slouschz, 'The Lost Tribes Affair', *Davar*, 23 February 1952 (Hebrew). In this article, Slouschz compares the Falashas to the Bahutzi and to the *anusim* in Portugal or Meshed, but writes that he does not consider these groups to be *nidhei Yisrael* but Jews in their own right.
72. *Fait. Coll.*, f. 82.
73. Document in Hebrew on the question of conversions, undated, *Fait. Coll.*, f. 114.
74. See the quotation in Rosenbloom, *Conversion*, pp. 134–5.
75. For the Faras (or Falash) Muras, Falasha descendants of today who were converted to Christianity by the Protestants, see D. Friedmann, *Les Enfants de la reine de Saba*, pp. 109, 121; on the Protestant conversions, see E. Trevisan Semi, 'The Conversion of the Beta Israel in Ethiopia: A Reversible "Rite of Passage"', *Modern Jewish Studies*, 1, 1 (2002), pp. 90–103.
76. *Ha-aretz*, 5 March 2003.

14

The Last Missions to Ethiopia and America: Faitlovitch at the Court of the Negus and Conseiller at the Ethiopian Embassy in Egypt

In December 1940, Faitlovitch began preparing to leave for the United States (via Sudan and India), but although he had obtained the necessary permits from the Commissioner for Migration and Statistics of the Government of Palestine,[1] he ended up not going. He may have changed his mind once he received the news that the Negus, backed by the British army, had crossed the Ethiopian border on 20 January 1941. Three months later, the Negus entered Addis; it was the event that Faitlovitch had been waiting for. He considered this the right moment to resume his work among the Falashas. In the early months of 1941, Faitlovitch tried every possible way to join Taamrat in Ethiopia, thinking that he could return to his 'holy work', the regeneration of the Falashas, which he had been forced to abandon several times. However, in the middle of the Second World War, it was not easy to obtain the permits required to go to Ethiopia.

He was helped by the United States government, the American Jewish Committee and Professor Mittwoch (in exile from Germany in London), who tried to get him the necessary permits from the British Embassy in Cairo[2] to allow him go, via Cairo, to the cities of Asmara and Addis Ababa. It was not until one year later (July 1942) that Faitlovitch finally made it to Ethiopia, thanks to the efforts of Taamrat, who had been appointed president of the Board of Education.[3] A few months later, again thanks to Taamrat, Faitlovitch was appointed Inspector-General at the Ministry of Education.

INSPECTOR-GENERAL AT THE MINISTRY OF EDUCATION

Faitlovitch's departure for Ethiopia received great attention in the circles he frequented in Palestine, and a farewell party was organized by Brit Ivrit Olamit.[4] The Vaad le-Ma'an Nidhei Yisrael, in particular N. Slouschz and Y. Ben Zvi, promptly launched a fundraising campaign in Palestine to finance this new phase of the educational project in Ethiopia. The reorganization of the school in Addis Ababa depended on the success of this campaign. New contacts who were willing to back the fundraising campaign had been found among South African Jews, who had come into contact with the Falashas while serving as British soldiers in Ethiopia. According to the Vaad, if sufficiently motivated, the South Africans would create a network of solidarity to help support the educational project launched by Faitlovitch and his friends in Palestine. In 1943, Yom Tov Bato, of the Jewish Board of Deputies of Johannesburg, was quickly appointed secretary of the Vaad le-maan nidhei Israel,[5] and was put in charge of the fundraising campaign in South Africa.[6] However, all hopes in Bato, who was also expected to teach at the future school in Addis, turned out to be misplaced, and he was soon asked to leave the committee. The paucity of the resources scraped together and the improper use of the money once again led to the failure of the operation.

The initial sums of money were raised in Johannesburg and were supposed to have been used to employ two Jewish teachers from Palestine, whom Faitlovitch intended to recruit when he went back to Tel Aviv for *Pesach*.[7] But allegations about the use of this money (and of the additional money received from the American Pro-Falasha Committee), sparked off by Rabbi Davide Prato, poisoned the atmosphere during those months. Rabbi Prato, a member of the Vaad le-maan nidhei Yisrael, accused both Bato and Faitlovitch of using the money improperly. It was true that a lot of it had been spent by Bato to travel from Palestine to South Africa, and that there had been no accounting for the rest of the money, which had been sent to Faitlovitch in Addis.[8] An altercation broke out over the lack of information divulged about the use of the money received, and over the fact that much of it had been spent on the traveling expenses of the very person who was supposed to be bringing in funds. Faitlovitch, too, was accused of misappropriation of funds, which of course was nothing new, and was reminiscent of the arguments that had poisoned the atmosphere of the APFC at the time of Faitlovitch's fifth mission to Ethiopia. Faitlovitch, instead of explaining how the money had been spent, accused Prato of malice: 'we mustn't let ourselves be intimidated by malice and criticism, or be discouraged if someone sees fit to put a spoke in the wheels'.[9] The controversy extended to the teachers that Faitlovitch intended to recruit for Ethiopia.[10] He wanted to reorganize completely the schools in Ethiopia because, in addition to reopening the school in Addis, he wanted to open another one in Gondar. The emperor had promised to give him 'suitable quarters, land and the necessary buildings' in that area.[11] Furthermore, since Faitlovitch was completely unaware of the seriousness of the Jews' situation in Europe, he thought that the emigration to Ethiopia of persecuted European Jews was still feasible in 1943. This was an old plan dating from 1933, which the Negus had assigned to Taamrat, the idea being to bring an elite of Jewish professionals to Ethiopia,[12] to benefit both Ethiopia and the Jews under threat in Europe. However, what may have been possible in 1933 was no longer possible ten years later. It is possible that very little news of what was happening in Europe had reached Ethiopia, as Faitlovitch once asked Bato to send him 'general newspapers or magazines … I am cut off from the world here, I don't receive any newspapers and don't know what is going on in the outside civilized or barbarian world.'[13] In the spring of 1943, when it looked as if the educational project was about to take off, Faitlovitch went to Gondar to meet with 'several scores of Falasha representatives from the neighbouring regions' to discuss the start of the new education programmes.[14] The plan called for schools to be built in the heart of Ethiopia, in the areas inhabited by the Falashas, and it implied a change in the educational policy pursued by Faitlovitch up to that point, which had favoured Addis Ababa, to the detriment of other areas:

> it is essential that the youth should be trained in their own surroundings, in a center of Falasha communities, so as not to alienate them too much from their traditional life and abruptly sever their contact with their people.[15]

These concepts, which echoed what Taamrat and Viterbo had said repeatedly over the previous decade, finally appeared to have been accepted by Faitlovitch. In several of the Falasha settlements, there were to be medical clinics alongside the schools, which would also serve the non-Falasha population,[16] following the model of the Protestant missions' dispensaries.

While the political climate in Ethiopia finally appeared to have improved enough to allow the work on behalf of the Falashas to resume in the areas in which they lived, the rest of the world was a different matter. The events of the war made it impossible for Faitlovitch's expectations to be met. He received no news, and no funding,[17] from the American Pro-Falasha Committee.

Thus, by the end of March 1944, neither of the schools had opened, due to the lack of funds. Bato, after spending some time in Egypt, had returned to Palestine and had given up the idea of working as a teacher in Addis. From Palestine, Slouschz submitted the names of other teachers, criticizing the insufficient level of training of the candidate selected by Faitlovitch (Salomon Ben Jafet). Resentment had grown within the Vaad because of Faitlovitch's refusal to account for the money he had received.[18] Faced with this situation and, in particular, the shortage of funds, Faitlovitch, as a last resort, considered giving up the idea of the school in Addis and opening only the one in Gondar.[19] However, those in Palestine disagreed, and the Brit Ivrit Olamit insisted that Addis school be reopened.[20]

It was probably his conflicts with the Vaad and the Brit in Palestine, in addition to the lack of funding, that persuaded Faitlovitch to leave Ethiopia for good.

A CONSEILLER AT THE ETHIOPIAN EMBASSY IN EGYPT

In July 1944, Faitlovitch left Addis to accept an appointment as a Conseiller at the Ethiopian Embassy in Cairo.[21] During the months he spent there, he worked to improve Ethiopia's diplomatic and commercial relations with Egypt and the Middle East, including the import–export business.[22] He also strove, in particular, to initiate diplomatic relations with Greece and Yugoslavia[23] and cultural ties with Egypt.[24] But he did not last long in this new role. While on the one hand he was making efforts to increase the level of commercial and diplomatic exchange between Ethiopia and the Mediterranean, on the other hand he did not seem to have a feel for the rhythms of diplomacy and court bureaucracy. His correspondence with Deputy Foreign Minister Aklilou Habtawold degenerated into an exchange of accusations and insults.[25] This was a very trying period for Faitlovitch. It was while he was in Cairo that he first learned of the atrocities committed against the Jews in Europe and, in particular, of the loss of many members of his wife's family. In a letter he sent to the treasurer of the APFC, Faitlovitch wrote:

> Mrs Faitlovitch unfortunately lost practically all her relatives, parents, sisters and brothers, captives in the ghetto at Riga and some as deportees in Siberia. Many, many of my own relatives, moreover, perished in the Polish ghettos and the German concentration camps.[26]

Thus the dark atmosphere of the time, in addition to the misunderstandings and disagreements within the Ethiopian Embassy, made Faitlovitch's two years in Cairo extremely difficult.[27] He had not even been there a year when, having become increasingly impatient and restless, he decided to go back to Addis to complain about the situation and confer with the emperor directly. His experience at the Ethiopian Embassy in Cairo came to an end when he resigned from his post.[28]

FAITLOVITCH'S LAST MONTHS IN ETHIOPIA (1946) AND HIS FINAL TRIPS TO AMERICA (1948, 1950)

When he left Cairo, Faitlovitch intended to go to America with his wife in order to resume his propaganda work among the American Jewish communities, relaunch the conversion movements, and find a teaching post that would allow him to devote more time to his scientific work:

> After so many years of absence I shall be only too glad to return to America and arrange matters in such a way that I'll finally be in a position to devote some of my time to scientific studies in my field of endeavour.[29]

After his resignation from the Ethiopian Embassy[30] on 15 June 1946, Jacques and Mara set off for Addis Ababa to conclude some outstanding business;[31] this would be Faitlovitch's last journey to Ethiopia.

During the months he spent in Addis, Faitlovitch was asked to give the emperor an accounting of the living expenses he had incurred while in Cairo. Yet again in his long career as a *schnorrer*, he was accused of wasting money and living in luxury in a hotel. It is true that the Faitlovitches had spent the whole of their first year in Cairo in a hotel, at the expense of the Ethiopian government, and had moved to a furnished apartment only in their second year there.[32] In fact, Faitlovitch spent most of his life in hotels, both on his fundraising campaigns in Europe and during the long periods he spent in New York.

During his last months in Ethiopia, Faitlovitch was bitterly disappointed to see the young people who had been educated in Europe (so that they in turn would teach other young people in Ethiopia) make choices that were radically different from what he had expected. In the new climate of modernization in Ethiopia, these young people had become a valuable elite in their country, and they preferred to take advantage of the education they had received to secure important positions and much better salaries than they would have had as teachers. In a meeting Faitlovitch had in Addis in the summer of 1946 with Roger Sauter, a Swiss Protestant employed as tutor to the Hall family,[33] he revealed his bitterness about the young people's lack of investment in the 'holy work' he had begun almost half a century earlier.[34] Faitlovitch wrote that he could not 'rely for guidance upon my former pupils who, while rising to influence in governmental service, have disqualified themselves from leadership by virtue of a nationalistic assimilation to the public offices we have thrust upon them'.[35] He accused Tadesse Jacob, who had become the director of customs for the Ethiopian government in 1950 but was still involved in the work of coordinating schools on a voluntary basis, of not being committed enough: 'It is regrettable that he has yielded to the temptations of the secular flesh-pots, so that he can give the Falashas but a minimum of attention.'[36] However, Faitlovitch himself had gained from the new political situation in Ethiopia and his remuneration from the Negus, which is probably what enabled him to buy his big new house in Vitkin Street in Tel Aviv immediately after he returned from serving as a *conseiller* at the embassy in Egypt.

In 1947, a year he spent in Palestine waiting to go to the United States, Faitlovitch, on the urging of some kibbutz members, began to consider the possibility of launching a 'Zionization' programme for the Falashas, in order to integrate the Jewish communities of Ethiopia into the *hachsharot* network. A programme of this type had been organized in Europe, in order to train young people for a life in Palestine in anticipation of a possible emigration to Eretz Yisrael. He attempted to put this plan into effect, particularly on a subsequent trip to the US,[37] during which he tried to secure funding for a training centre in Ethiopia that would prepare Falashas for emigration to Israel, and for a camp for a Youth Aliyah organization. Faitlovitch maintained that the enormous tragedy of the disappearance of European Judaism made it a duty to help the Falashas emigrate to Israel: 'With millions of Jews but recently annihilated, we can ill afford to neglect this potential reservoir of Jewish manpower.'[38]

Faitlovitch set sail for the United States on 7 January 1948. He had meetings there with representatives of the movements he intended to work with, including Horowitz, the leader of the conversion movement, Rabbi Matthew, the leader of the black Jews, and members of the American Pro-Falasha Committee. He did not go back to Israel until after the declaration of the State in July, and he arrived in the middle of the bombing of Tel Aviv, amid alarms and sirens. His new house was bombed and had to be repaired. During the summer of 1948, he received a visit in Tel Aviv from the Italian converts of San Nicandro, who had recently immigrated to Israel.[39] It was the crowning glory of his achievements among the *gerim* in Italy in the 1930s.

Faitlovitch stayed in Israel for just a short time; in 1949, he and his wife left to spend another year in the US. It was during this stay that Faitlovitch began to seriously consider the idea of preparing the Falashas (or at least some of them) for emigration to Israel, and to that end he tried encouraged the black Jews of Harlem (through the Union of Ethiopian Hebrew Congregations and Rabbis) to mount a campaign in favour of the Falashas' emigration to Israel.[40] He tried to appeal to the shared sense of identity between the black Jews of Harlem and the Falashas just as the first clear signs of discrimination against the Falashas were beginning to appear in the young State of Israel. False information was circulated about a hereditary disease that affected the Falashas, causing turmoil among the black Jews of Harlem and the organizations that were working for the *aliyyah* of the Ethiopian Jews. This incident will be discussed in greater detail below.

Faitlovitch's arrival in the US, as usual, marked a revival of American pro-Falasha activity. It is no coincidence that during those months, the APFC decided to send Wolf Leslau as its emissary to Ethiopia. Leslau was a scholar who had been a student of the *éthiopisan* Marcel Cohen in Paris and he had already conducted a scientific mission among the Falashas in 1946–47. He was asked to draft a report on the curriculum used in the various schools and on the religious character of the schools that had been founded by Faitlovitch's former students. The APFC and its American supporters were influenced by religious currents and were intent on communicating the Jewish spirit behind the teachings. Thus they told Leslau that they wanted 'to know whether these schools are secular or whether they have positive Jewish religious character'.[41] Faitlovitch was not happy with this decision because he did not trust Leslau, whom he considered too secular and too independent.[42] He would have preferred someone who observed religion more strictly, who was less autonomous, and who took instructions directly from him. Faitlovitch wrote of Leslau:

> to say that such a man as you refer to … could ascertain the spiritual needs of the Falashas is unrealistic when one considers that to the Falashas any person not a devout Jew is taboo. No amount of scholarship (and there are many factual errors in Leslau's first report) will make a casual investigator welcome nor inspire confi-

> dence among the faithful Falashas. That is as true as night follows day.[43]

Faitlovitch wanted to be able to give instructions to someone of his own choosing:

> I would be happy to instruct him in the fundamentals of Falasha habits and customs and languages ... he would go to Addis-Ababa with credentials from me to the proper authorities. Thus fortified, the Falashas would undoubtedly receive him with open arms and entrust their youth to him for Jewish education, as they did to me for many years.[44]

As in the past with Aescoly, Faitlovitch could not stand working with other scholars. This was the side of his personality that had a negative effect on his 'holy work'. As Taamrat said, in reference to Aeskoly's death, it was a pity 'that around those two [Aeskoly and Faitlovitch] there had not reigned that spirit of gentle calm necessary for all work. Who knows how much they would have done for the Falasha cause.'[45] But Faitlovitch's egocentric character precluded collaboration, and every time an opportunity of this kind presented itself, he would oppose it in some way.

The theme of the Falashas' religiosity, within the general context of the progressive secularization of the Jews, had become a *leitmotiv* of the American Pro-Falasha Committee's fundraising campaign in 1950. The religiosity of this lost Jewish tribe in the heart of Africa became a useful piece of propaganda among the most religious Jews,[46] who were reminded that the movement of solidarity with the Falashas had been initiated and developed by practising Jews and should remain under their control: 'The fate of the Falashas rests upon the support of traditionally minded Jews rather than the other type.'[47] These views, which were shared by the Mizrahi movement in Israel, should have been addressed by the Israeli government when the mass *aliyyah* of Ethiopian Jews later arrived in Israel. In reality the core education of the Ethiopian youth was considered a task to be left to the network of religious schools, as it had been when most of the oriental youth came from Arab countries, beginning in the 1950s.

The information circulated by the Jewish press[48] (and later denied by the *aliyyah* department of the Jewish Agency for Palestine), which maintained that it would be impossible to let the Falashas emigrate to Israel because of 'an inherited and infectious disease', provoked an immediate reaction from Taamrat, then the cultural *attaché* at the Ethiopian Legation in Paris. It also made Faitlovitch highly indignant, particularly since it was groundless no medical mission had ever visited Ethiopia.[49] This information, which revealed Israel's unwillingness to accept the Falasha immigration, had been spread by Jacob Vainstein, and sent by the Jewish Agency's Immigration Department to Addis Ababa in November 1949. However, in his report he had written not about hereditary illnesses that might prevent the *aliyyah* but about the fact that there were priorities to respect – meaning that Yemeni Jews, North African Jews, and Jews from Eastern Europe and Iraq should have priority.[50] However, the authorities categorically denied that there was any question of discrimination based on skin colour in their decision ('There is utterly no discrimination based on colour').[51]

Word of Israel's refusal to receive Falasha immigrants, even in case of emergency or priority, reached the United States just as the APFC was in the midst of a powerful campaign to raise the funds required to send at least six Falasha boys to go to Israel to study.[52] The Jewish Agency's intervention was therefore received with great irritation and indignation by Faitlovitch and the APFC, as it put the breaks on the fundraising effort. Faitlovitch was also disappointed in his search for a teaching post in a department of Semitics.[53] No doors were opened to him and he was forced to return to Israel.

THE LAST YEARS OF FAITLOVITCH'S LIFE IN TEL AVIV

The last years of Faitlovitch's life were devoted to establishing a programme for the spread of Judaism, which he thought could be achieved by creating an actual missionary movement,[54] and to organizing the Falashas' *aliyyah*. He was supported in this endeavour by Y. Ben Zvi and former Minister of Education Sh.Z. Shazar,[55] and also by the Brit Ivrit Olamit and the Jewish Agency. In fact, it was thanks to funding from the Jewish Agency that A. Rosenfeld was sent to Ethiopia to draft a report on the state of the schools and on the possibility of organizing the *aliyyah*. An initial list of 220 people (47 family units) who wanted to leave Ethiopia to fulfil the *aliyyah* was sent to Faitlovitch.[56]

In 1953, Faitlovitch wanted to return to the US, but he had to abandon the idea, probably because his health was becoming increasingly unstable.[57] It may have been at Faitlovitch's suggestion that the APFC sent another emissary to Ethiopia, Henry Shoskes, originally from Bialystock. Shoskes was mistakenly recorded in the APFC's memorandum as 'the fifth white Jew to visit them', after Faitlovitch, Viterbo, Leslau, and Rosenfeld. The American Committee had obviously omitted Josef Halévy, the first European Jew to go to Ethiopia, thereby setting in motion a story that engrossed Western Judaism throughout the twentieth century.[58] On his return to America, Shoskes brought a message from the Falashas for the president of Israel, Ben Zvi, who, as the most important representative of the State, constituted a real hope for an intervention in the fate of the Ethiopian Jews. Ben Zvi was also known for his interest in the 'coloured' Jews in India, Persia, Yemen, etc.[59] Shoskes recommended that two actions be taken: first, the establishment of Jewish schools in the country as 'a bastion against the "shmad disease" [conversion disease] which is now tearing into pieces the remnants of this remarkable tribe'[60] and then the *aliyyah*. The work of the Protestant missionaries had resumed with the arrival of the English missionary E. Payne.[61]

The report must have had some effect because in 1954 a school was opened in Asmara. It was run by Jona Bogale, Rabbi Shemuel Beeri's assistant, who had been sent by the Jewish Agency. Some of the young people educated at the Asmara school went to Israel in January 1955[62] to study for two years at Kefar Batya, a children's religious village founded by a Mizrahi organization, and Faitlovitch was able to invite this microcosm of Ethiopia into his house in Tel Aviv.

By that time, Faitlovitch was nearing the end of his life. His sight had become so bad that he had applied for a visa to go to the United States to be examined by a specialist,[63] but he never had the chance to leave. His heart stopped beating on 15 October 1955.

Thus ended the life of a *chalutz sui generis*, an *ish ma'aseh*, a romantic dreamer, a cultural ambassador, and a bit of a *schnorrer*.

NOTES

1. Document of December 1940, *Fait. Coll.*, f. 124.
2. *GLRO*, ACC/3121/E02/001, Abyssinia 1930–44.
3. Letter from the American Consul, L. C. Pinkerton, to Faitlovitch of 12 December 1941, *Fait. Coll.*, f. 127.
4. The party was organized on 10 June 1942, *Fait. Coll.*, f. 199.
5. See Chapter 13 and *CAHJP*, P 177 (Prato).
6. Letter of 9 October 1942, *Fait. Coll.*, f. 100.
7. Letter of 2 February 1943, *Fait. Coll.*, f. 100.
8. Letter to Slouschz of 30 November 1943, *CAHJP*, P177 (Prato).
9. Letter from Faitlovitch to Slouschz of 23 April 1944, *Fait. Coll.*, f. 99.
10. Letter of 15 March 1943, *Fait. Coll.*, f. 123.
11. Letter of 23 April 1943, *Fait. Coll.*, f. 131.

12 See Taamrat's letters of 29 June 1933, 3 November 33, 22 October 1939 and the introduction in Trevisan Semi, *L'epistolario*, pp. 40–3.
13. Ibid.
14. Letter to E. Solomon (Treasurer of the Pro-Falasha Committee) of 19 November 1945, *Fait. Coll.*, f. 117.
15. Ibid.
16. Ibid.
17. Ibid.
18. Letter of 22 March 1944 from Slouschz to Faitlovitch, *Fait. Coll.*, f. 116.
19. See letter from Taamrat of 9 March 1942, in Trevisan Semi, *L'epistolario*, p. 319 and letter of 23 April 1944, *Fait. Coll.*, f. 99. He was thinking of accepting the offer of help promised by Fabian Hendel, a trader in Mogadishu who had established a commercial network between Ethiopia, Somalia, and Palestine.
20. *Fait. Coll.*, f. 117.
21. Letter of 2 August 1944 to Haile Selassie, *Fait. Coll.*, f. 123. The emperor paid him a fee of 200 lire.
22. Letter of 5 September 1944 to the Ethiopian Ministry of Foreign Affairs, *Fait. Coll.*, f. 123.
23. Letter to Haile Selassie of 19 November 1944, *Fait. Coll.*, f. 123.
24. He tried to persuade the emperor to donate objects of cultural and cultic interest to the Coptic Museum of Egypt. Letter of 2 October 1945, *Fait. Coll.*, f. 123.
25. *Fait. Coll.*, f. 123, Letters of 9 January 1945, 31 January 1945, 15 February 1945, 14 March 1945, 31 July 1945, *Fait. Coll.*, f. 123.
26. Letter of 19 November 1945 to Solomon, *Fait Coll.*, f. 117.
27. Letter of 14 March 1946, *Fait. Coll.*, f. 127.
28. Letters of 31 July 1945, 5 August 1945, 12 August 1945, 10 September 1945, 8 October 1945, 18 November 1945, *Fait. Coll.*, f. 123.
29. Ibid.
30. Letter of 14 March 1946, *Fait. Coll.*, f. 127.
31. *Fait. Coll.*, f. 124.
32. Letter of 24 July 1946, *Fait. Coll.*, f. 123. Faitlovitch had to supply receipts from his hotels and from the landlord of his apartment, specifically stating that meals were not included in the prices. Letter of 12 September 1946, *Fait. Coll.*, f. 123.
33. The descendents of Moritz Hall, a Polish Jew who went to Ethiopia in the second half of the nineteenth century and was later converted to Protestantism by the Church Mission to the Jews. The Hall family acted as intermediaries between Ethiopia and the German government.
34. R. Sauter's personal communication and letter of 12 October 1946 from Sauter to Faitlovitch, *Fait. Coll.*, f. 100; and letter of 10 December 1946 from Faitlovitch to Sauter; and of 24 December 1946 from Sauter to Faitlovitch, *Fait. Coll.*, f. 117.
35. *Fait. Coll.*, f. 142.
36. Letter of 6 March 1950 to W. Leslau staying in Addis, *Fait. Coll.*, f. 142.
37. Letter of 5 April 1949 from Kramer, chairman of the Pro-Falasha Committee, *Fait.Coll.*, f. 142.
38. Letter of 3 May 1950 to the *APFC*, Joint, Joint Abyss, 1933–54.
39. Diary, 29 July 1948 and 1 August 1948.
40. See the first issue of *African Israelite*, *Fait. Coll.*, f. 142.
41. Letter of D. de Sola Pool of 19 December 1949, *Fait. Coll.*, f. 142.
42. *Fait. Coll.*, f. 142.
43. Letter of 26 February 1950 from Faitlovitch to Ch. Kramer, *Fait. Coll.*, f. 142.
44. Ibid.
45. See letter of 20 January 1949, in Trevisan Semi, *L'epistolario*, p. 332.
46. Letter from L. Jung to leaders of the *APFC* of 27 February 1950, *Fait. Coll.*, f. 142.
47. Letter from *APFC* to Faitlovitch of 1 May 1950, *Fait. Coll.*, f. 142.
48. An article in Yiddish published in a Jewish Telegraphic Agency dispatch in 1950, *Fait. Coll.*, f. 115.
49. Document of 2 May 1950, *Fait. Coll.*, f. 115. Faitlovitch also wrote an article on *Herut*, 29 December 1950 and another one on *Ha-Boqer*, 29 December supporting their right to unification.
50. Letter of 3 May 1950 from *APFC* to E. Warburg, *Joint*, Joint Abyss, 1933–1954.
51. Letter from I. L. Kenen to E. Gomberg 1 May 1950, *Fait. Coll.*, f. 142.

52. Letter of 1 May 1950, *Fait. Coll.*, f. 142.
53. Letter from M. Kaplan to A. A. Neuman of 12 January 1950, *Fait. Coll.*, f. 142.
54. See Chapter 13.
55. Notification of 1 February 1951, *Fait. Coll.*, f. 142.
56. Letter of 14 January 1951 from N. Ben Menahem (the Jewish Agency) to Faitlovitch, *Fait. Coll.*, f. 115.
57. Letter of 23 December 1952, *Fait. Coll.*, f. 199.
58. Memorandum of Ch. Kramer and H. Shoskes, *APFC* of 7 December 1953 and Minutes of the Committee on Cultural-Religious affairs of the Joint 8 December 1953, *Joint*, Joint Abyss, 1933–54.
59. Ibid.
60. Ibid.
61. For the revival of missionary activity in this period see Trevisan Semi, 'The conversion' 6. Letter of 9 October 1942, *Fait. Coll.*, f. 100.
62 . *Fait. Coll.*, f. 99. Letter from M. Y. Gavriahu (Jewish Agency) to Faitlovitch of 20 January 1955, *Fait. Coll.*, f. 99.
63. Letter of 30 August 1954, *Fait. Coll.*, f. 199.

15

Conclusion

The intent of this work has been to illustrate the journey of an individual whose life spanned the history of the last century, leaving his mark not only on the fortunes of the Beta Israel population, but on the history of Israel. The impact of this prophetic, messianic visionary – a Jew of Polish origin and a product of the Jewish melting pot in post-Dreyfus Paris – on an era that saw the destruction of much of European Jewry and its great cultural centres, as well as the birth of the Jewish State, was a determining factor in the inception of processes that are still under way in Israel. Jacques Faitlovitch and the groups associated with him were a seminal influence on the ideas and issues that have defined the history of Israel.

The image of Faitlovitch that has emerged thus far from papers on the Beta Israel is ambiguous and contradictory. He is sometimes portrayed as a crusading Orthodox Jew, the saviour of a Jewish population that had been targeted by Protestant organizations and was in danger of being swallowed up by the conversion effort. At other times he is depicted as a Western Jew convinced of the superiority of Ashkenazi Judaism, who worked for the regeneration of Jewish communities in the East based on the theories of French and Western Judaism. Another image is that of the Zionist Jew who planned for the *aliyyah* of an African population, a goal eventually attained with their mass immigration to Israel. A contrasting impression tends to belie the importance of Faitlovitch's activities in Ethiopia and his actual impact on the Falashas' religion and culture. According to this view, his influence was limited to the tiny elite of young men educated in Europe and Palestine at the beginning of the twentieth century and to the few young people who were able to attend the school in Addis. Clearly, each of these aspects contributes to the portrait of Faitlovitch painted in this book.

However, I would like to emphasize the importance of Faitlovitch's presence, whether among the Beta Israel or among Western Jews. He played a role in the creation of an imagined community whose links with world Jewry were established through the network of young men he placed in Western Jewish institutions and through the *tomare* he wrote in Amharic, which were kept as precious relics by the families that possessed them. In these *tomare*, the notion of the larger Jewish family to which Falashas belonged was central. But the fantasies about 'the Jews of Africa' that prevailed in Jewish communities thanks to Faitlovitch fostered the Orientalist viewpoint among Western Jews, who played a role in regenerating and revivifying 'their own blacks' after trying to negate the Falasha identity, which they regarded as based on an 'African lethargy' that they saw as the cause of their 'backwardness'.

This book attempts to shed some light on the complex figure of Faitlovitch, and, at the same time, to bring his persona into relief against the backdrop of ideas with which he interacted, examining the influence that each exerted on the other. These complex interactions gave shape to a story that was different from the one imagined and sought after by Faitlovitch and by the groups that became involved in his plans. The overall impact of Faitlovitch's 'holy work' on the processes under way in the environments in which he operated certainly had repercussions, especially at the mythical and symbolic level, whose scope was far greater than might be expected from the small number of players involved.

The theme of Judaism as a universal religion based on the words of the prophets, which is central to an understanding of Faitlovitch's activity, must be considered in conjunction with the influence exerted on him by religious Zionism. In the mind of Faitlovitch and the pan-Hebrew and pan-Jewish movements with which he identified himself, Eretz Yisrael was a vast, far-reaching entity. Its borders were more biblical–messianic than real, encompassing both the 'historical' Jews and the mythical lost tribes – the *nidhei Yisrael* – as well as new populations in Asia and Africa that would be converted by Jewish missionaries. This was the grand plan that Faitlovitch tried to implement through the solidarity and philanthropic networks of the Jewish Diaspora in both Europe and America, particularly those linked to traditional religious circles. In fact, from the time of his first journey, which was financed thanks to support from Rabbi Zadoc Kahn, Faitlovitch found his main source of backing in rabbinical circles. This is evident in the support he received from Zvi Margulies, the Rabbi of Florence, during the organization of the first Pro-Falasha committee, from the German rabbis at the time of the formation of the Pro-Falasha Committee in Frankfurt, and from various Orthodox, conservative,and reform Jewish leaders in the United States. His young Falashas stayed in the homes or institutions of rabbis in various European countries. Moreover, it was the more traditional European organization, the Hilfsverein, that offered its hand to Faitlovitch, while the Alliance, the more secular and less observant French Jewish group, was restrained by its own ideological ambiguities. The Mizrahi movement was involved in the various stages of Faitlovitch's plans, right up to the end of his life, when it financed the journey of a group of young people to the village of Kefar Batya, run by religious Mizrahi Zionists.

The individual choices made by Faitlovitch and by the groups that supported him, although they may seem coincidental or fortuitous, gave rise to the policies generally implemented by the State of Israel. A close look at Faitlovitch's activities provides a glimpse into the embryonic stages of strategies of great importance.

The decision to educate the young Beta Israel within the Mizrahi-run educational network foreshadowed the educational policy choices of the new State, where the education of young people from large communities in Asia and Africa was entrusted to the network of schools run by traditional religious groups linked to Mizrahi Zionism, in order to assure what this political movement considered the correct interpretation of Judaism.

From Faitlovitch's first expeditions among the Beta Israel to the recent immigration to Israel of the Benei Menashe,[1] and from the first committees for the *nidhei Yisrael* during the *yishuv* period to the founding of the Amishav organization in Israel in 1975,[2] there is continuity. The birth of Zionism, which provided fertile ground for messianic views and was interpreted as a universal event of cosmic importance that would lead to the redemption of all humanity, triggered forces that were determined to expand the concept of Judaism from an ethnic religion to a universal one, guaranteed by the existence of a nation-state. The victories of the Six Day War and the Greater Israel Movement provided the lifeblood for these trends, which had existed since the beginning of the twentieth century and which Faitlovitch's cohorts, Sh. Ben Chorin, N. Birnbaum, and A. Pacifici, writing in the journal *Der Ruf*, had predicted.

The confrontation with the Church Missionary Society led to the creation of an actual Jewish missionary movement. Its early activities were dictated by rivalry and by the need to demonstrate to Christian circles the existence of Jewish pride (an expression Faitlovitch frequently used to solicit funds for the counter-mission), and later evolved into initiatives that conformed to the Christian model. The counter-mission in Ethiopia became just such an imitation of the Protestant missions. The translation, printing, and distribution of the Gospel in

Amharic was initially undertaken by the Christian missionaries, and it had a strong effect of converting people, who then joined the Christian world. But the translation of Faitlovitch's letters into Amharic also had a very strong impact among the Falashas, creating imaginary links with the Jewish world. Christian missionaries accused Faitlovitch of distributing money to people in order to convince them not to abandon their religion. However, this was an old technique that they themselves had practised before the Jewish counter-mission existed. Faitlovitch, like the missionary Martin Flad, took his relatives with him so that they could help him with his educational work in Ethiopia. In the end, Faitlovitch practised conversion among the Falasha Christians, but he also 'converted' Falashas who were not Christians, by means of immersion rituals. This increased fervour for conversion led to the creation of an actual missionary movement that aimed to convert the populations of Asia and Africa. Faitlovitch's presence among the Italian *gerim* of San Nicandro and the blacks of Harlem, and his projected journey to Japan, were all part of the same plan. The Sharon government's recent decision to accept the Faras Muras, the Falashas converted by the Protestant missions in Ethiopia, can be considered a continuation of the process that began earlier.

Among Orthodox Christians in Ethiopia, a child could be given a Christian name that would become child's last name, and Faitlovitch adopted this custom. Beginning with the very first mission, he introduced the practice of changing the Ethiopian fathers' names of the young boys he brought to Europe into a Jewish name, just as the Christians did. It is worth noting that the significance of this practice is larger than a simple name change, as it involves the question of identity. When the Jewish State introduced the practice of changing the names of Jews arriving from Arabic countries, which sound too Arabic to European Jewish ears, it was not attempting to imitate the practice that Faitlovitch had introduced earlier. However, the policy revealed that it had similar attitudes, tainted by Eurocentrism and Orientalism.

But this is only the outline of the life and work of Jacques Faitlovitch. Faitlovitch's personality undoubtedly influenced the processes discussed here. For example, there is no doubt that the nature of his relationships with his *protégés*, which were characterized by paternalism, authoritarianism, and despotism, fostered their dependence on him. The first victim of this situation was Taamrat Emmanuel, his favourite, despite the latter's attempts at resistance and opposition. The private lives of these young people, who found themselves uprooted from their own country and culture and faced with the difficult, complex challenge of asserting their identity against an inflexible 'master', were certainly upset. However, it is equally certain that those who managed to survive were able to glean enough advantages from their situation to become the first elite in Haile Selassie's Ethiopia, a country then moving towards modernization, and to see their children become the elite of the *aliyyah* in Israel.

Faitlovitch was an itinerant Jew of the twentieth century, and in many ways a *schnorrer*. However, while there may be an element of truth to the accusations that he squandered the money he raised for his 'holy work' among the Falashas of Ethiopia by treating himself to expensive hotels and cruises, it is also true that it was only his presence in Europe and in America, and his evocative speeches about faraway 'heroic tribes of our brethren' in Africa and the victory of Jewish pride, that succeeded in impassioning American Jews and ensuring the raising of funds.

NOTES

1. For the Benei Menashe see Sh. Weil, 'Double Conversion among the "Children of Menasseh"' in G. Pfeffer and D. Behera (eds), *Contemporary Society: Tribal Studies* (Professor Satya Narayana Ratha Felicitation Volumes), Vol. 1, *Structure and Progress* (New Delhi, n.d.), pp. 84 ff.; and Parfitt and Trevisan Semi, *Judaising Movements*, pp. 17–38.
2. Amishav (in Hebrew 'my people is coming back') is an organization devoted to the ingathering of the dispersed remnants of Israel, see ibid.

Glossary[1]

ach: brother
aleka: sir, leader (a)
aliyyah: Jewish immigration to Israel
am gadol: a great people
anusim: Marranos, Jews compelled to convert
av: father
avi ha-falashim: father of the Falashas
balambaras: a military rank (a)
bar mitzvah: 'son of the commandment', a Jewish boy who has reached the age of religious responsibility
Beta Israel: 'House of Israel', a term used by Falashas to refer to themselves (a)
buda: sorcery (a)
chalutz/im: pioneer/s
Chevrat nidhei Yisrael: Association of the Dispersed of Israel
Cheshvan: second month of the Jewish calendar (October–November)
chillul ha-shem: profanation of the Lord
chovev Tziyyon/chovevei Tziyyon: lover/s of Zion
debtera: a learned man who often assisted priests (a)
Eretz Yisrael: the Land of Israel
frendji: foreigners (a)
ge'ez: 'Ethiopic', the religious and literary language of Beta Israel and Christians (a)
ger gerim: convert's
geza: race
giyyur: conversion
goel: redeemer, saviour, Messiah
halakot: code of the Jewish law
hachsharot: groups training for a life in Palestine
haskalah: the Enlightenment
hatafat dam: bloodshed
hatafat dam berit: circumcision
hatafat musar: sermon

Ha-tiqvah: 'The hope', Israeli national hymn
ish ma'aseh: practical and devout man
kahen: priest (a)
kantiba: title of the mayor of Gondar (a)
kiddush ha-shem: martyrdom, praiseworthy work
kippot: skull-caps
knesset: Israeli Parliament
maskil: 'cultured' man, the first degree of Rabbinical instruction
mesguid: Beta Israel house of prayer (a)
mezuzah: small case attached to a doorpost of the home
mizrahim: Jews who come from Arabic countries
mohel: the man who performs circumcisions
moshav: partially collective Jewish settlement
Negus: emperor (a)
nidhei Yisrael: dispersed of Israel, lost tribes, tribes of Israel
olim: Jewish immigrants to Israel
Pesach: Passover
Purim: Feast of Esther
qes: priest (a)
qevurah: burial
qinah: dirge
ras: head
rehov: street
rosh chodesh: the first day of the Jewish month
rotzeach: murderer
seder: Passover night service
schnorrer: beggar
sefer Torah: the book of the Bible
shabbat: Jewish Sabbath
sheloshim: thirty days after death
shevet Yisrael: tribe of Israel
Shoah: holocaust
shochet: ritual butcher
siddurim: prayer books
tallit/tallitot: ritual prayer mantle/s
Talmud: written interpretation of the Bible
Talmude Torah: religious Jewish schools
tevet: the fourth month of the Jewish calendar (December–January)
tefillin: phylacteries
temqat: ritual immersion as performed in Ethiopia (a)
tevilah: ritual immersion

Tishri: name of the first month of the Jewish calendar (September–October)
tomare: letters (a)
Torah: the Pentateuch, used to refer to all the Bible
yeshivah: talmudic academy
yishuv: Jewish settlement in Palestine

NOTE

1. Most of the words are in Hebrew; when a word in Amharic appears, it is marked (a).

List of Associations

Agudah le-maan gere tzedek bi-Yisrael u-va-olam: Society for Converts in Israel and in the World, founded in Tel Aviv by Faitlovitch and active in 1950s.

Alliance Israélite Universelle (AIU): organization founded in 1860 with headquarters in Paris to defend Jewish civil and religious liberties.

American Jewish Committee: organization founded in 1906 'to prevent the infraction of the civil and religious rights of Jews in any part of the world'.

American Pro-Falasha Committee (APFC): organization founded in New York in July 1922 by C. Adler, the vice-president of the American Jewish Congress. Harry Schneiderman was named secretary *pro tem* and Rabbi Ephraim Frisch president.

Bet B'nai Abraham: movement led by Josias Ford, a black Jew of Harlem in the 1920s.

Brit ha-neemanin/ Agudah le-yeda ha-yahadut u-le-hafatzat toratah: The Alliance of the Faithful/ Society for the Knowledge of Judaism and the Spreading of *Torah*, the last founded by Faitlovitch in Tel Aviv, in 1952.

Brit Ivrit Olamit: the World Organization for the spreading of Hebrew Language and Culture. Attempts to organize an association for the promotion of Hebrew Language were made during the Sixth Zionist Congress (1903) and at the Hague conference in 1907 (by J.Klausner, H. N. Bialik, and M. Ussishkin) but only after the establishment of the State of Israel the First Hebrew Congress (1950).

Chevrat nidhei Yisrael: Association of the Dispersed of Israel, founded by Faitlovitch.

Commandament Keepers (of the Royal Order of Ethiopian Hebrews): movement let by Rabbi Matthew (a black Jew of Harlem) starting from the 1920s.

Ha-Histadrut ha-tziyyonit ha-olamit: Worldl Zionist Organization.

Hatzaad Harishon: 'The First Step', a movement created by Hailu Moshe Paris and Jacob Gladstone in New York that lasted until 1972.

Hilfsverein des Deutschen Juden (Hilfsverein): German Jewish association founded in Berlin in 1901 to assist Jews in Eastern Europe and Oriental countries that continued to exist until 1941. The organization maintained a network of schools in Palestine and the Balkan countries from 1903 to 1918.

Italian Pro-Falasha Committee: association founded in 1907 in Florence by Rabbi Zvi Margulies that lasted until 1914.

Jewish Agency: the Jewish Authority in Palestine during the British Mandate, a public body recognized for the purpose of advising and cooperating with the British administration of Palestine which acted as the spokesman for the interests of the Jewish population. After the establishment of the State of Israel in 1948 it continued as an international non-governmental body coordinating all Jewish overseas efforts in Israel.

Joint (American Jewish Joint Distribution Committee): American Jewry's overseas relief and rehabilitation agency created in 1914 in New York.

Mosaic Law for One World: organization for conversion led by David Horowitz founded in New York in 1944 to propagate Judaism throughout the world.

Union of Italian Jewish Communities: official association representative of all the Jews in Italy. This organ was created in 1930 by the fascist government.

Vaad le-maan nidhei Yisrael: Committee for the Dispersed of Israel, founded by Faitlovitch, Slouschz, and Ben Zvi in 1942 in Tel Aviv, which later on became the association Agudah le-maan nidhei Yisrael.

Bibliography

ARCHIVAL SOURCES AND ABBREVIATIONS

Arch. AIU Italie ID4: Alliance Israélite Universelle, Paris.
CAHJP: Central Archives for the History of the Jewish People, Hebrew University of Jerusalem, P3–471, A 116/156, P 177.
CMJ Bodleian Library, Oxford: Church Missionary for the Jews, box 13.
CMJ: Church Missionary for the Jews, St. Albans.
CZA: Central Zionist Archives, A 116/156.
Fait. Coll.: Sourasky Central Library of the University of Tel Aviv.
Faitlovitch's diaries: years 1904–05, 1908–09, 1911, 1913–15, 1920–39, 1948–50 in Sourasky Central Library of the University of Tel Aviv.
Genazim: Makhon genazim, Tel Aviv, 109–46621/46622.
GLRO: Greater London Record Office/s Board of Deputies British Jews– ACC/3121/E02/001 Abyssinia 1930–1944.
Joint: Archives of the Joint/New York/Joint Abyss, 1919–21, 1921–32, 1933–54.
JTS: Archives of the Jewish Theological Seminary, New York, Marx 80–29, Marx 80–17, Adler 26.
Kressel: Kressel Archives, Yarnton Manor, Oxford.
LBD: London Board of Deputies.
Schomburg: Schomburg Centre for Research in Black Culture, New York, SCM 97–9.
Viterbo private archives.

PERIODICALS

American Jewish Year Book, 1901–02, 1907–08, 1920–01.
Bulletin mensuel de l'Alliance Israélite Universelle, 1909.
Bulletin de l'AIU, 1909.
Der Ruf, 1934–06.
Ha-am ve-ha-sefer (Hebrew), 1941, 1952.

Il corriere israelitico, 1906, 1908, 1909.
Il vessillo israelitico, 1912, 1914.
Israel, 1955, 1964.
La rivista israelitica, 1907, 1909.
La settimana israelitica, 1913.
London Society Reports, 1906–08.
Paix et droit, 1924.

SELECTED PUBLISHED BOOKS AND ARTICLES

Admor, H., 'Le testament de Jacques Faitlovitch' in D. Friedmann (ed.), *Les Juifs éthiopiens: de Joseph Halévy à nos joures, un siècle de rencontres et vingt-cinq années d'emigration massive* (Paris 2007).

Aescoly, A. Z., 'The Falashas: a bibliography', *Qiriat sefer*, 12 (1935–36), 13 (1936–37) (Hebrew).

——, *Recueil de textes falachas* (Paris, 1951).

Ahi Efraim, Y., 'A Journey to the Falashas', in Y. Eisenberg (ed.), *The Duty to be a Messenger* (Tel Aviv, 1985) (Hebrew).

Anderson, B., *Imagined Communities: Reflections on the Origin and Spread of Nationalism* (London, 1983).

Andreatta, M. 'Outlines of a first bibliographical survey of Joseph Halévy's works' in D. Friedmann (ed.), *Les Juifs éthiopiens* (Paris, 2007).

Bahru, Zweide, *The History of Modern Ethiopia 1855–1974* (London, Athens and Addis Ababa, 1991).

Benbassa, E. '*L'Alliance Israélite Universelle* et l'élection de Haim Nahum au grand rabbinat de l'Empire Ottoman (1908–1909)', *Ninth World Congress of Jewish Studies*, Vol. 3 (Jerusalem, 1986).

——, *Un grand rabbin sépharade en politique 1892–1923* (Paris, 1990).

Ben Dor, Sh., 'The journey towards Eretz Israel: the story of Abba Mahari', *Peamim*, 33 (1987) (Hebrew).

Ben Jochannan, Y., *We the Black Jews* (Baltimore, MD, 1983).

Ben Zeev, I. (Wolfenson), *Conversion to Judaism: Present-Day Problems in the Light of History* (Jerusalem, 1961) (Hebrew).

Berger, G., *Black Jews in America: A Documentary with Commentary* (New York, 1978).

Berkovitz, J. R. *The Shaping of Jewish Identity in Nineteenth-Century France* (Detroit, IL, 1989).

Boykin, J. H., *Black Jews: A Study in Minority Experience* (Miami, 1996).

Brotz, H., *The Black Jews of Harlem: Negro Nationalism and the Dilemmas of Negro Leadership* (New York, 1964).

Carmel, Y., *Itzhaq Ben Zvi: From the Journal at the President House* (Ramat Gan, 1967) (Hebrew).

Cassin, E., *San Nicandro: The Story of a Religious Phenomenon* (London, 1959).

——, *San Nicandro: histoire d'une confession, avec une postface de l'auteur* (Paris, 1993).

Cividalli, G., 'Ritorno a San Nicandro', *La Rassegna mensile di Israel*, 39, 4 (1973).

Clark, E., *The Small Sects in America* (New York, 1937).

Cohen, I., *Mirrors* (Ramat Gan, 1968) (Hebrew).

Cohen, Ph. A., 'Ethnicité et solidarité chez les Juifs de France au XIXe siècle', *Pardès*, 3 (1986).

Cohen, Sh., 'Was Judaism in antiquity a missionary religion?', in M. Mor (ed.), *Jewish Assimilation, Acculturation and Accommodation* (Lanham, MD, 1992).

Del Canuto, F., 'Come si giunse alla missione in Etiopia presso i Falascia', in F. Del Canuto (ed.), *Israel. Un decennio 1974–1984. Saggi sull'ebraismo italiano* (Rome, 1984).

Dorman, J. S., 'Hatzaad Harishon: Integration, Black Power and Black Jews in New York, 1964–1972' (Palo Alto, CA: BA thesis, 1996).

Ehrman, A., 'The commandement keepers: a Negro "Jewish" cult in America Today', *Judaism: A Quarterly Journal*, 8, 3 (1959).

Eichhorn, D. M., (ed.), *Conversion to Judaism: A History and Analysis* (New York, 1965).

Epstein, L. J., *The Theory of Welcoming Converts to Judaism* (New York, 1992).

Faitlovitch, J., *Quer durch Abessinien* (Berlin, 1910).

——, 'The Presumed Traditions of the Falashas', *Tarbitz*, 7, 3–4 (1936) (Hebrew).

——, *Journey to the Falashas* (Tel Aviv, 1959) (Hebrew).

Feldman, L., 'Was Judaism a missionary religion in ancient times?' in M. Mor (ed.) *Jewish Assimilation, Acculturation and Accommodation* (Lanham, MD, 1992).

Friedmann, D., *Les enfants de la reine de Saba* (Paris, 1994).

Gavriahu, H., 'For the *nidhei Israel*', in Y. Klausner, A. Tartakower, and A. Ramba (eds), *The Hebrew Wandering Ambassador: dr. Alexander Rosenfeld* (Tel Aviv, 1957) (Hebrew).

Gerber, I. J., *The Heritage Seekers: American Blacks in Search of Jewish Identity* (New York, 1977).

Godbey, A. H., *The Lost Tribes, A Myth: Suggestions Towards Rewriting Hebrew History* (Durham, NC, 1930).

Goglia, L. and. Grassi F. *Il colonialismo italiano da Adua all'impero* (Rome-Bari, 1981).

Goodman, M., *Mission and Conversion* (Oxford, 1994).

Grinfeld, Y. 'Jews in Addis Ababa: beginning of the Jewish community until Italian occupation', *Sixth International Conference in Ethiopian Studies* (Tel Aviv, 14–17 April 1980).

——, 'Taamrat Emmanuel – Forerunner of the Revival of Ethiopian Jewry', *Peamim*, 22 (1985), pp. 67–8 (Hebrew).

——, 'Jacques Faitlovitch: "Father" of the Falashas', in Y. Avner, N. Berger, and K. Kaufman Shelemay (eds), *The Jews of Ethiopia: a People in Transition* (Tel Aviv, 1986).

——, 'The Hebrew school in Addis Ababa at the Beginning of the Italian Occupation (1937–37)', *Dor le-dor*, 5 (1992) (Hebrew).

Guandalini, C., 'Gete Yirmiahu and Beta Israel's regeneration: a difficult path', in T. Parfitt and E. Trevisan Semi (eds), *Jews of Ethiopia: the Birth of an Elite* (London-New York, 2005).

Gurock, J. S., *When Harlem was Jewish 1870–1930* (New York, 1979).

Halévy, J., 'Travels in Abyssinia', in A. L. Loewy (ed.), *Miscellany of Hebrew Literature*, vol. 2, ser. 2 (London, 1877).

Haramati, Sh., *Three who Preceded Ben Yehudah: Sephardi-Oriental Forerunners in the National Revival* (Jerusalem, 1978) (Hebrew).

Harris, J. E., *African-American Reactions to War in Ethiopia 1936–1941* (Baton Rouge and London, 1994).

Herskowitz, M. J., *The Myth of the Negro Past* (New York, 1942).

Hobsbawm, E. and Ranger T. (eds), *The Invention of Tradition* (Cambridge, 1990).

Howe, S. *Afrocentrism: Mythical Pasts and Imagined Homes* (London and NewYork, 1998).

Kaplan, S., *Les Falachas* (Belgium, 1990).

——, *The Beta Israel (Falasha) in Ethiopia. From Earliest Times to the Twentieth Century* (New York and London, 1992).

——, 'The invention of Ethiopian Jews: three models', *Cahiers d'études africaines*, 132, 33–4 (1993).

——, 'Can the Ethiopian change his skin? The Beta Israel (Ethiopian Jews) and racial discourse', *African Affairs*, 98 (1999).

——, 'Black and white, blue and white and beyond the pale: Ethiopian Jews and the discourse of colour in Israel', *Jewish Culture and History*, 5, 1 (2002).

Kaplan, S. and Ben Dor, Sh. *Ethiopian Jewry: An Annotated Bibliography* (Jerusalem, 1988).

Kashani, R., *The Falashas* (Jerusalem, 1976) (Hebrew).

Kepel, G., *À l'Ouest d'Allah* (Paris, 1994).
Kessler, D., *The Falashas, The Forgotten Jews of Ethiopia* (London, 1982).
King, K. J., 'Some notes on Arnold J. Ford and the New World black attitudes to Ethiopia', *Journal of Ethiopian Studies*, 10, 1 (1972).
Klausner, Y., A. Tartakower, and A. Ramba (eds), *The Wandering Ambassador: Dr. Alexander Rosenfeld* (Tel Aviv, 1957) (Hebrew).
Landes, R., 'Negro Jews in Harlem', *Jewish Journal of Sociology*, 9, 2 (1967).
Lapide, P. E., *Les Compagnons de San Nicandro ou retour aux sources* (Paris, 1961).
Lincoln, C. E., *The Black Muslims in America* (Westport, CT, 1973).
Lifschitz, D., 'A school for Jewish children in Addis Ababa', *Ofaqim* (May 1932) (Hebrew).
——, 'Un sacrifice chez les Falachas, juifs abyssins', *La terre et la vie*, 9 (1939).
Malciom, J. V., *How the Hebrews Became Jews* (New York, 1978).
——, *The African Origins of Modern Judaism* (Trenton, NJ and Asmara, 1996).
Marcus, H. G., *A History of Ethiopia* (Berkeley, CA, Los Angeles and London, 1994).
Margulies, Z., 'Per la storia del movimento Pro-Falasha', *Rivista Israelitica*, 6 (1909).
Messing, S., *The Story of the Falashas: 'Black Jews' of Ethiopia* (Brooklyn, MD, 1982).
Miniati, M., 'Joseph Halévy: un outsider dans la ville', in D. Friedmann (ed) , Les Juifs éthiopiens: de Joseph Halévy à nos jours, un siècle de rencontres et vingt-cinq années d' emigration massive (Paris, 2006).
Osofsky, G., *Harlem: the Making of a Ghetto* (New York and Evanston, NJ, 1968) (1st edn, 1963).
Parfitt, T. *The Road to Redemption: The Jews of the Yemen 1900–1950* (Leiden, 1996).
——, 'The Rabbi Nahoum's anthropological mission to Ethiopia', in T. Parfitt and E. Trevisan Semi, *The Beta Israel in Ethiopia and Israel* (London, 1999).
Patai, R., 'The Ritual Approach to Hebrew-African Culture Contact', *Jewish Sociological Studies*, 24 (1962).
Porton, G. G., *The Stranger Within Your Gates: Converts and Conversion in Rabbinic Literature* (Chicago and London, 1994).
Quirin, J., *The Evolution of the Ethiopian Jews: A History of the Beta Israel (Falasha) to 1920* (Philadelphia, 1991).

Ravitzky, A., 'Radicalisme religieux et messianisme politique en Israël', *Pardès*, 24 (1998).

Rodrigue, A., *De l'instruction à l'émancipation. Les Enseignants de l'Alliance Israélite Universelle et les Juifs d'Orient 1860–1939* (Paris, 1989).

——, *Images of Sephardi and Eastern Jewries. The Teachers of the Alliance Israélite Universelle, 1860–1939* (Seattle, WA and London, 1993).

Rosenbloom, J. R., *Conversion to Judaism: From the Biblical Period to the Present* (Cincinnati, 1978).

Sagi, A., and Zohar Z.; '*Giyyur*, identité juive et modernisation', in F. Heymann and Storper Perez D. (eds), *Le corps du texte: pour une anthropologie des textes de la tradition juive* (Paris, 1997).

Santamaria, U., 'Black Jews: the religious challenge or politics versus religion', *Archives Européennes de Sociologie*, 28, 2 (1987).

Salomon, H., and Kaplan S., *Ethiopian Jewry: An Annotated Bibliography 1988–1997* (Jerusalem: Ben Zvi Institute, 1998).

Scott, W. R., *The Sons of Sheba's Race: African-Americans and the Italo-Ethiopian War (1935–1941)* (Bloomington Indianopolis, 1993).

Shavit, Y., *The New Hebrew Nation: A Study in Israel Heresy and Fantasy* (London, 1987).

——, '"French spirit" and "French culture" in the Jewish yishuv in Eretz Israel (1982–1914)', *Katedra*, 62 (1991) (Hebrew).

Sherman, A., 'Appendix: the Black Jews of America', *Le Monde religieux: L'Afrique païenne et juive* (Lezay, 1956–57).

Shusterman, A., 'The Last Two Centuries', in D. M. Eichhorn (ed.), *Conversion to Judaism: A History and Analysis* (New York, 1965).

Stein, L., *The Hope Fulfilled: The Rise of Modern Israel* (Westport, CT, 2003).

Summerfield, D., *From Falashas to Ethiopian Jews* (London, 2003).

Szajkowski, Z., 'Conflicts in the *Alliance Israélite Universelle* and the founding of the Anglo-Jewish Association, the Vienna Alliance, and the *Hilfsverein*', *Jewish Social Studies*, 19 (1957).

Tidhar, D., *Encyclopedia of the Pioneers in the Jewish Settlement*, Vol. 1 (Tel Aviv, 1947) (Hebrew).

Trevisan Semi, E., *Allo specchio dei Falascià: ebrei et etnologi durante il colonialismo fascista* (Florence, 1987).

——, 'Continuity in the educational projects of Faitlovitch in the light of his correspondence', *Peamim*, 58 (1994) (Hebrew).

——, 'The Dainelli and Viterbo missions among the Falashas (1936–37)', in S. Kaplan, T. Parfitt, and E. Trevisan Semi (eds), *Between Africa and Zion: Proceedings of the First International Congress of the Society for the Study of Ethiopian Jewry* (Jerusalem, 1995).

——, 'Faitlovitch, Margulies and the Alliance: which educational policy for the Ethiopian Jewry', in A. Crown (ed.), *Noblesse Oblige: Scholarship and Community* (London and Portland, OR, 1998).

Trevisan Semi, E., 'Universalisme juif et prosélytisme: l'action de Jacques Faitlovitch, "père" des Beta Israel (Falashas)', *Revue de L'histoire des religions*, 216, 2 (1999).

——, 'From Wolleqa to Florence: the tragic story of Faitlovitch's pupil Hizkiahu Finkas', in T. Parfitt and E. Trevisan Semi (eds), *The Beta Israel in Ethiopia and Israel: Studies on the Ethiopian Jews* (London, 1999).

——, *L'epistolario di Taamrat Emmanuel: un intellettuale ebreo d'Etiopia nella prima metà del XX secolo* (Torino, 2000) (Italian/French).

——, 'Ethiopian Jews in Europe: Taamrat Emmanuel in Italy and Makonnen Levi in England', in T. Parfitt and E. Trevisan Semi (eds),*Jews of Ethiopia: the Birth of an Elite* (London-New York, 2005).

——, 'The conversion of the Beta Israel in Ethiopia: a reversible "rite of passage"', *Modern Jewish Studies*, 1, 1 (2002).

Viterbo, L., 'La nomina del rabbino Margulies: un excursus nella Firenze ebraica di fine Ottocento', *La Rassegna mensile di Israel*, 60, 3 (1993).

——,'Cronache dal passato fiorentino: la difficile successione del Rabbino Margulies (1920–1926)', *La Rassegna mensile di Israel*, 60, 3 (1994).

Waitzkin, H., 'Black Judaism in New York', *Harvard Journal of Negro Affairs*, 1, 3 (1967).

Waldman, M., *Beyond the Rivers of Ethiopia: The Jews of Ethiopia and the Jewish People* (Jerusalem, 1989) (Hebrew).

Weil, Sh., 'An Elegy in Amharic on Dr. Jacques Faitlovitch', *Peamim*, 33 (1987) (Hebrew).

——, 'The Life and Death of Solomon Isaac', in T. Parfitt and E. Trevisan Semi (eds) *The Beta Israel in Ethiopia and Israel: Studies on the Ethiopian Jews* (London, 1999).

——, *Bibliography on Ethiopian Jewry (1998–2001)* (Paris, 2001).

——, 'Abraham Adgeh: the perfect English gentleman', in T. Parfitt and E. Trevisan Semi (eds), *Jews of Ethiopia: the Birth of an Elite* (London, New York 2005).

Weill, G., 'Le Discours idéologique de l'*Alliance Israélite Universelle*. Emancipation et humanisme au XIXe siècle', *Les Nouveaux Cahiers*, 52 (1978).

Wild, J., *The Lost Ten Tribes and 1882* (London and Ontario, 1879).

Will, E., and C. Orrieux, *'Prosélytisme juif'? Histoire d'une erreur* (Paris, 1992).

Wolf, E., 'Negro "Jews": A Social Study', *Jewish Social Service Quarterly*, 9 (1933).

Zetlaoui, M., *Shalom India: Histoire des communautés juives en Inde* (Paris, 2000).

Index

References to Jacques Faitlovitch throughout the index will be abbreviated to JF. Direct entries to him will be in chronological order.